W9-BLZ-515

CIA SpyMaster

CIA SpyMaster

Clarence Ashley

Foreword by Leonard McCoy

PELICAN PUBLISHING COMPANY
Gretna 2011

First printing, August 2004
First Polish edition, March 2011
Second printing, June 2011

Library of Congress Cataloging-in-Publication Data

Ashley, Clarence.
CIA spymaster / Clarence Ashley ; foreword by Leonard McCoy.
p. cm.
Includes bibliographical references and index.
ISBN 978-1-58980-234-6 (hardcover : alk. paper)
1. Kisevalter, George G., d. 1997. 2. Intelligence officers—United States—Biography. 3. United States. Central Intelligence Agency—Officials and employees—Biography. 4. Espionage, American. 5. Espionage, Soviet. 6. Cold War. I. Title.

JK468.I6A882 2004
327.1273'0092—dc22

2004007473

Printed in the United States of America

Published by Pelican Publishing Company, Inc.
1000 Burmaster Street, Gretna, Louisiana 70053

For George's old buddies in the clandestine operations group, who went unheralded, who did not get medals, and yet who continued on in their service, rewarded only by the self-satisfaction that they received from knowing that they had done something worthwhile.

Contents

Part IV: The Reluctant Warrior

Foreword

George Kisevalter's story is part of the epic struggle during the last century to determine which set of governing principles would prevail in civilized societies. The world from which he came, Tsarist Russia, was dying. But even as he left it for America in 1915, a new one was forming, one with new leaders determined to wrench Russia out of its feudal traditions, relieve the oppression inflicted for centuries on the majority of its rural population, and set it on a path of industrialization and economic growth befitting its potential. Any such objective, with the great obstacles and uncharted course its champions faced, however, was obliterated by the cunning and vicious assault led against the nascent Russian democracy by a coterie of Marxist theorists. The civil war that their actions provoked then raged on in George's background. One after another, his friends and relatives were swept up into the war or driven out of Russia and into a drifting population that journeyed to all corners of the globe, often only to spend a generation and then move on.

While its origins may be different, the violent end to Tsarist rule in Russia had remarkable similarity to the changes precipitated in America by its own Civil War. The Russian serfs and the American slaves had occupied similar positions in their respective societies, and their liberation was a crucial theme in the two civil wars. In Russia, however, liberation was only a slogan, a rhetorical theme, mobilizing the serfs to help subjugate those elements that opposed the seizure of power by Marxist theorists. The nobility of Russia, of course, were natural enemies of those about to launch an irrational social experiment across a region whose area was one-sixth of the land mass of the entire world. As with the slave-holding families of the old South, the Russian upper classes contributed to the circumstances of their downfalls, but the consequences of the years of violence that then descended upon the two societies were diametrically opposite. Whereas America erased the blot of slavery that overshadowed the nation's developing grandeur, Soviet Russia brought forth tyranny that was to generate wave after wave of callous and brutal exploitation of its people for the benefit of its unprincipled leadership, the so-called "Nomenklatura."

The ensuing problems in U.S.-Soviet relations during the 1920s and 1930s abruptly seemed irrelevant, however, when both nations were drawn into World War II as allies in the fight with Germany. At that time, George became an integral and unique part of the U.S. effort to supply massive amounts of war materiel to the USSR. The period of direct contact between the national military teams formed in this common goal nonetheless demonstrated a lack of Soviet gratitude as well as a high degree of Soviet suspicion of Americans and American motives. The war was hardly won when the U.S. began to discover overwhelming evidence of hostile espionage activity conducted against the U.S. by its ally, the Soviet Union.

The postwar conflict between the U.S. and Soviet societies threatened more than once to involve the world in a new conflagration that could mean the end of the human race. Nevertheless, awareness of its involvement in this mortal conflict by a trusting, idealistic, even naïve America was slow in coming. Some Americans, like many in other countries, were deceived by Soviet propaganda into collaborating in the oppression of the Russian people as well as the people of Eastern Europe and Asia. Even when defectors came to the U.S. out of the Soviet regime and revealed some of its tyranny, listeners too often doubted the news' validity as well as the motives of the messengers, or erroneously minimized the damage that Soviet espionage and propaganda were then inflicting upon America.

Fully appreciating the conflict between these two nations was the preoccupation of the adult life of George and is the basis of the debt that we all owe him. The profession in which he become a giant was first abolished in the United States as the war ended, then was reestablished as Soviet political intentions in Eastern Europe—and Soviet espionage against the U.S.—became apparent. The newly formed Central Intelligence Agency then began to assemble information from all sources to help us to understand the Soviet leadership, their intentions, their plans, and their capabilities. Draconian controls on Soviet society made this task practically impossible, while Soviet threats and hostile actions, particularly in Berlin, intensified. A nuclear confrontation between the two countries seemed ineluctably closer with each crisis. The requirement for accurate and detailed information on Soviet intentions grew ever more urgent. At precisely this point, George took his place in the Plato's cave shadows of Cold War history.

In 1953 the United States still knew very little about the Soviet regime and its plans. Early that year, a Soviet Military Intelligence officer in the Soviet Southern Group of Forces occupying Austria volunteered to provide the U.S. with significant information. George took his Russian heritage, his extensive knowledge of Russian history, as well as his masterful fluency in the Russian language to Vienna and met the officer. The interview provided our first in-depth knowledge of Soviet military capabilities. More importantly, it began to give us insight into the Soviet mentality as it viewed the western world—and particularly the United States. The American government consequently began to develop some confidence that it could evaluate Soviet intentions, and that it had a reliable glimpse into Soviet capabilities. The CIA then realized that George was the only individual capable of efficiently working with this agent. George followed the officer to Germany in 1956 and maintained the flow of invaluable information until the man's ultimate return to Moscow in 1958.

Perhaps George's most vital contribution to our national security came in 1961, when a Soviet Military Intelligence officer senior to George's former contact provided information of staggering value. Again, the CIA reaffirmed its belief that only George was the appropriate conduit for the stream of information this man was to provide. The Secret Intelligence Service of the United Kingdom concluded the same. This Soviet officer had access to the highest levels of the Soviet government and over the next two years, the intelligence information that accrued from this liaison significantly elevated our level of confidence in dealing with the USSR. This increased understanding of Soviet thinking may well have drawn us back from the very brink of nuclear war on at least two occasions: the Berlin crisis during the autumn of 1961 and the Cuban missile crises in October of 1962. George's remarkable knowledge of Russian history and language and, above all, his immutable love and understanding of his fellow man, Russian or otherwise, provided much of the intelligence on which our national policies were based until the collapse of the USSR. Thus, it is reasonable to conclude that George played an important part in ensuring our very existence.

LEONARD MCCOY
Retired senior CIA officer and longtime professional
associate and friend of George Kisevalter

Prologue

On April 26, 1999, the Central Intelligence Agency, with unusual fanfare, named its headquarters facility in McLean, Virginia "The George Bush Center for Intelligence." The Honorable George Bush, former president of the United States, who directed the Agency from January 1976 to January 1977, was in attendance for the festivities that extended throughout much of the beautiful spring day. Later that afternoon, in a subdued ceremony with a limited number of attendees present, another dedication took place in one of the small suites of the former headquarters building. There, the George Bush Chair for Leadership was presented to its first recipient, Allen D. Smith. Concomitant with that award was the dedication of the Kisevalter Center for Advanced Studies, to be led by Mr. Smith. CIA director George C. Tenet chaired the proceedings and, in his speech of dedication, recalled some of George G. Kisevalter's traits of character, personality, and ability. He then introduced former president Bush, who spoke some kind words to the memory of George Kisevalter, as did Jack G. Downing, deputy director for Plans at the CIA, the clandestine operations group. Finally, Mr. Smith rose, applauded George's career, and spoke fondly of him. Other than the naming of the headquarters complex for President Bush, no other facility at the Agency had ever been named for an individual.

Who was George G. Kisevalter? Certainly, I would not presume to write the definitive story of the man, but I can describe those facets of him that I came to know by simply listening to him and to others who knew him before I did. My association with George did not come about until 1973 after both of us had left the Agency. His departure was in conformance with the Agency requirement of mandatory retirement at age sixty; mine was related to my desire simply to do other things after almost six years there. He labored in the world termed "Human Intelligence," managing spies. I worked first as an intelligence analyst, trying to piece together the mosaic of Soviet missile systems, and later as a systems analyst helping to develop computer models that could facilitate evaluations of major collection programs. Our paths did not cross. Although some of his contributions were legendary, I had never heard much of his activities except for the Oleg V. Penkovsky case, and I had never heard of George Kisevalter, himself. While the principal reason for this lack of awareness was the considerable amount of compartmentalization of the highly classified information involved, a routine requirement for security purposes, it was also due to limited interest on my part, at the time.

Years later, we were in each other's presence for long periods of time, while working in our real-estate practice, and George began to share with me some of the anecdotes of his fascinating life. I then began to appreciate his life and work. By that time, his intelligence exploits were mostly declassified and, in some instances, known by the general public. He went further back, telling me of the simple trials experienced by an only child growing up in a world that, although privileged, was in constant turmoil and change. He included accounts of experiences with famous people and told how he had profited from the advantages that were presented to him. With a remarkable attention to detail, he described complicated relationships among the numerous players in these narratives and their multiple agendas. He had an adroit memory from which he could recall the most remote facts of history as well as the incredible minutiae of complex scientific discoveries. He was fluent in four languages and competent in at least four others. He could recall just which Swedish princess had married which Spanish prince and which English count had wed which Hungarian lady, for multiple generations. He could recite the railroad gauges of virtually all of the train systems in the world, and he could explain agricultural phenomena as well as any professional agronomist. He indeed was a storehouse of facts and knowledge, most of which were extremely interesting.

For his work with Soviet intelligence officer Lt. Col. Pyotr Popov in the 1950s, George was awarded the Distinguished Intelligence Medal, the highest award one can obtain at the CIA without giving one's life. For his work with another Soviet intelligence officer, Col. Oleg Penkovsky, George received a Certificate of Merit with Distinction. Less than two months before his death in October of 1997, George was selected as one of fifty "unique contributors" in the fifty-year history of the CIA and was presented with the newly established Trailblazers Award. He alone was recognized with this award for his work as a case officer (spymaster). He was the first case officer promoted to supergrade rank (GS-16), a status reserved almost exclusively for managers of major programs involving many personnel. Even today, it is quite rare for non-managerial personnel—the collectors of information, the sorters of data, the analysts, the case officers, the writers of reports—to be awarded such a rank.

After much prompting on my part, in October of 1991 George allowed me to record some of the stories of his life. At that time our only reason for doing this was to provide a record for his daughter, Eva, so that she would know something of her family. He was one of the few known, living, direct descendants of what had been an extensive, prominent Russian family. After recording about eight hours of mostly family history, we made rough, unedited transcripts of the conversations and filed them away.

In October of 1997, less than a month before he died, George agreed to let me piece together a rudimentary biography. We made about ten additional hours of tapes. Although some of the more recent tapes were difficult to understand because of his health, most of them guided me to a number of intriguing avenues. Following his death, I took these clues and pursued the full stories from his friends and associates. Many were eager to help. Fortunately for me, George documented his life as no one I have ever known. I collected boxes of personal materials from his daughter and commenced digging in. There are hundreds of photos, years of records (e.g., grammar school report cards from the 1920s, and financial logs of 1932), extensive correspondence (some recent, some over eighty years old and written in Russian), and other artifacts of his life. Some materials were trivial (World War II gasoline ration stamps). Some, such as old passports, which indicated when and where he had traveled, were important to me. Some—a bundle of old letters—describe a family's struggle with vast historical changes. This incredible clutter provided a timeline of George's life.

With this as the basic framework, I recalled the many wonderful stories that he had told me over the years and inserted them into their proper places in the sequence. The tapes and the details later supplied by those who knew George augmented his earlier accounts. Through this process I have tried to convey a good portion of his life. In many cases, then, the anecdotes are a synthesis of conversations with George. None of the conversations is completely verbatim, but they all are accurate representations of talks that we actually had. I have also transposed parts of some conversations in order to present an understandable chronology of events, but I tried to retain the original flavor of George's storytelling ability.

Many of George's operational activities at the CIA have been written about. *CIA SpyMaster* addresses these, as well as other operations, in a more personal way than heretofore provided. In addition, it presents a reasonably complete life history of the man in the form of his own intriguing stories, and it attempts to capture a bit of George's incredible spirit. He was a fascinating individual, and the lessons of his life are worthwhile for all to consider. He spent his life among the wealthy, the famous, and the powerful, yet he had great humility. He had great advantages in life but never let these experiences affect him in any but a positive way. His life was full of sadness, but he had a wonderful sense of humor and a positive outlook. He was one of the most capable of men, with abilities that bordered on genius, but he was extremely modest. But it is equally true that George was not perfect. He was human, and I have tried to convey, accurately, his shortcomings as well as his strengths, as best I could.

George could have been successful in many walks of life. Since he elected to dwell in the world of intelligence, however, the reader might recognize that these pages provide an intimate keyhole through which one might peek into the fascinating modus operandi of a classic CIA case officer. No doubt the reader will conclude that these experiences are described quite differently from those observed in most fictional accounts of espionage. Perhaps, as I have, he or she will find them to be every bit as dramatic and exciting, and a little more inspirational than those conjured-up fantasies. More importantly, all of these tales are true.

Each of our lives can be defined by a series of little stories. These are the stories of a man who witnessed momentous events in the world during his lifetime. Among them were two world wars, the Korean War, the Cold War, the Great Depression, and three separate collapses of the governments of Russia, the land of his origin. He was a part of those events, and his experiences were a classic example of how one may use his time and talents to create a useful life, one story at a time. He was a friend of mine as well as that of so many who knew him. I believe that his stories are both interesting and instructive. I would like to share them with you.

Acknowledgments

While preparing this book, I approached many of George's former associates for help. Almost everyone wished to contribute—a testament, I think, to his ability to make and keep good friends. Their help is deeply appreciated.

Malia Natirbov, a fellow Russian expatriate as well as a close personal friend since childhood, provided critically important descriptions of the world in which George grew up and contributed a vital part of the "Turkish Rondo" chapter. Mrs. Wayne Allen, a niece by marriage and a business partner of George, added humor and spice to the alfalfa story.

Three of George's old army buddies, Michael Gavrisheff, David Chavchavadze, and Otis E. Hays, Jr., George's boss in wartime Alaska, made the "Olive Drab" tale complete.

Dick Kovich's close personal association with George over many years enabled him to supply many intimate vignettes that help to illustrate George's unique character. Dick's descriptions and technical expertise regarding the Pacific Ocean operations for the CIA chapter as well as other information for the Nosenko episode were most beneficial.

Ted Poling, a longtime professional partner to George and a close personal friend to him from their first meeting in the early 1950s until George's death, provided critical insight into the Popov operation as well as general guidance throughout my effort with this work.

Leonard McCoy's patient advice, encouragement, and corrections helped me begin and complete the project. He also provided essential facts for the Penkovsky, Nosenko, and Cherepanov operations. Paul Garbler's contributions to the CIA chapter and the chapters on the Penkovsky and Cherepanov affairs were equally vital.

I especially wish to acknowledge the help of Harold T. ("Shergie") Shergold of the British Secret Intelligence Service, without whose counsel I could never have accurately completed the chapter on Penkovsky. His willingness to host a special meeting with Michael Stokes, his partner in the Penkovsky operation, so that the three of us could discuss the episode in detail, was particularly beneficial.

Yuri Nosenko, former KGB officer and now grateful American citizen, offered much of his time and unique understanding of events for the Popov, Penkovsky, Cherepanov, and Nosenko episodes. Numerous other publications have presented the Nosenko story, but this version is corroborated by him.

First Lt. Christian Teutsch, presidential firing party platoon leader of the Old Guard, provided demonstrations and explanations of the intricate maneuvers of the military burial details at Arlington National Cemetery.

The manuscript benefited considerably from a reading by George H. McLoone, Ph.D. His patient suggestions on style are much appreciated. For her suggestions, additional thanks go to my cousin, Laura S. Ashley, Ph.D.

Brig. Gen. Robert C. Cassibry, U.S.A. Ret., and his wife, Patricia; the Reverend William F. Myers; Judge Clifford R. Oviatt, deceased, and his wife, Diana; Eleanor J. Riles, Ph.D.; as well as James C. Roberts, president, Radio America, all made significant contributions to the writing.

Many more of George's friends were extremely helpful; a number of them are recognized in the notes. Some prefer not to be named. I thank all of them, as well as those mentioned above, for their help in making this work possible. Any errors remaining in the text are mine.

The CIA's Publications Review Board has reviewed the manuscript for this book to assist the author in eliminating classified information, and poses no security objection to its publication.

However, this review should not be construed as an official release of information, confirmation of its accuracy, or an endorsement of the author's views.

CIA SpyMaster

PART I

The Good Soldier

CHAPTER 1

The Old Guard

With a bit of nervous apprehension, all parties sat down. The uneasiness would last only momentarily because George soon created, as he had with Pyotr Popov, a warm relationship with Oleg Penkovsky. They all knew this to be a vital element in the proper handling of the prospect. They recognized that defectors want to be taken into the family of their employer and that George could accomplish this better than anyone else could. It was obvious to all that George should be the leader of the discussions; consequently, the team left it pretty well up to him to run the meetings.

Speaking in Russian, George began, "You know, Penkovsky, what do we speak, what language? How's your English?" Penkovsky, responding in Russian, forthrightly replied, "My English stinks. Let's speak Russian."

Harold Shergold and Michael Stokes from British intelligence spoke some Russian. American Joe Bulik's Russian was rusty, so George translated everything, back and forth. George asked Penkovsky to be plain and distinct. He asked his fellow case officers to be very quiet while he listened to the Soviet colonel. He would translate and explain as necessary. He especially wanted the team to get very accurate recordings, so he said, "Penkovsky, what we have to say is very important. We would like to tape it. We ask your permission. Do you want us to?" (They had been doing it anyway.) Penkovsky replied, "I insist upon it." "Great," responded George. Now the case officers could use the good Dutch electronics for their recordings. It was bulky and could not readily be secreted like the diminutive CIA recorders they currently were using. Now they could record with true fidelity.

George continued, "Penkovsky, this material which we are anxious to get from you, and which you are almost killing yourself trying to get to us, what is it all about?" Penkovsky paused, leaned forward, and began to speak.

George Kisevalter, who had successfully shepherded in Popov, the first great Agency coup, would now marshal in Penkovsky, the man who wished to become the greatest spy in history. Who was George Kisevalter and how can one account for his unique ability to relate to these Cold War Soviet military officers? Although I cannot provide the definitive statement on George, I can describe that part of the elephant that I felt. This is that narrative. It begins on one brilliant morning in early November of 1997. I am suddenly conscious of the bright sun, unchecked by even a single cloud anywhere in northern Virginia that day. It beams down on the burial escort assembling for a full-honor funeral at Arlington National Cemetery. The light reflecting off the brightly polished brass buckles, insignias, and other accouterments of the forty-four soldiers flashes in my eyes as they begin the trek to their solemn duty. Every man in the escort is in his twenties, stands stiffly erect at six feet and one inch in height, and exudes a sharp military bearing honed by many grueling hours of practice. One hundred burials take place at Arlington Cemetery every week, throughout the year. There is ample opportunity for these men to exercise their craft; perfection is routinely achieved. They are from the U.S. Army's Third Infantry Regiment, the Old Guard, a contingent of proud professionals. The soldiers promptly fall in line behind thirty members of the U.S. Army Band, "Pershing's Own." Together, these formations approach the Old Post Chapel at Fort Myer, just outside the gate to Arlington National Cemetery.

Arriving at the chapel, all halt and snap to the left, facing the chapel entrance. Close by are the company commander, a captain, the chaplain, and a team of eight casket bearers: seven soldiers and one sergeant. Punctually, a hearse rounds the corner, the casket team leader raises his hand in salute, and the escort commander, a lieutenant, ever so deliberately lifts his saber in salute. The hearse halts; the lieutenant and the casket team leader complete their salutes. George Kisevalter will be interred at Arlington, joining his wife, Ferdi, who preceded him eight years before. The most celebrated case officer in the history of the Central Intelligence Agency would no longer be available for the director's special projects.

Suddenly, all present come to a brace. The casket team advances to the hearse and halts. As the captain raises his hand in salute, the band commences "Abide with Me." The casket team steps off and releases the casket lock. The team removes the casket from the hearse and cautiously turn it and themselves toward the chapel. The chaplain approaches the casket, faces about, and leads the team into the chapel. The captain drops his hand and the music stops. The chapel outer doors are closed.

The chapel is almost full, with about two hundred people. George's daughter, Eva, and a dozen of her close associates are here. A busload of people from Vinson Hall has come. There George spent the last eight years of his life, alternately enthralling his new friends with glorious stories of his life and beating their brains out in bridge games. I am reminded that two days after George died, I was walking the corridors of Vinson Hall after meeting there with Eva, and I was following close behind a man and a woman who were deeply engaged in conversation. I could not help but overhear their dialogue. "You won, didn't you?" implored the man. "Yes," replied the lady. "How much?" "Good amount. It was the first time ever that I won." "Who took George's place?" he inquired.

A contingent of retired CIA people is here, a few of the many who served with him forty or more years ago. Dick Kovich, one of George's old CIA buddies, once told me that all of the people in George's group at the Agency were continually concerned about his health because he was always overweight and drank far too much. There was no doubt among many at the Agency that George would not live too long. Accordingly, in every intelligence operation dating back to 1953, an alternate case officer was routinely assigned. Well, he fooled them all. He lived to be eighty-seven while most of the others were going to their graves. Richard Helms, the last CIA director under whom George served, is here. Some of George's friends from the old McLean neighborhood and his real-estate associates are here. Michael Gavrisheff, an old army buddy from WWII, has shown up.

Evoking George's childhood, a sprinkling of Orthodox Russians present will cross themselves three times at the appropriate moments during the service. The officiating chaplain, a young army captain, is Protestant. He leads the two soldiers of the honor guard who wheel the casket into the nave. In the hush, the steel taps on the soldier's shoes strike the ceramic-tile floor of the chapel in unison, like hammers ringing on an anvil.

"I am the resurrection and the life," the chaplain intones. *"He that believeth in me, though he were dead, yet shall he live; and whosoever liveth and believeth in me shall never die."* At the first recognition of the chaplain's voice, the congregation rises. As the procession passes the front pews of the nave, the chaplain mounts the two steps leading to the altar, and the soldiers, guiding their weighty cargo, halt. Simultaneously, the two execute abrupt, disciplined turns and, in unison, step smartly away from one another to opposite sides of the sanctuary. There they each execute another turn and stride the length of the chapel to its rear. The resounding click of their taps on the floor resonates again as they exit. My eyes are focused on the flag-covered, rosewood casket, positioned front and center, just below the altar. It is so close yet so far away. I am trying to review in my mind what I will say. I want to do justice to George's memory. I have memorized my words, and I am determined not to read them. I carry the words in the breast pocket of my jacket just in case.

My thoughts are racing when the chaplain announces that Eva will say a few words. She steps up to the lectern. She is strikingly attractive, a tall, slim, blonde beauty, all decked out in black. She smiles demurely, yet with moisture in each eye. She begins:

"Hi there—I'm Eva—best known to most of you as George's little girl.

"I think I can speak for my father when I say we're both overwhelmed that so many of you are here today to pay tribute to him.

"Because many of you have known my father for at least as long as I have, and because you have had many different experiences with George, you each have your own special and unique memories. However, there is one common thread for all of us who knew him well, myself included, that we all share, and that is that he has beaten each and every one of us at one card game or another. But if you knew him *really* well, there's now a problem that many of us now share; and that is, who's going to do our taxes?

"The only truly unique point of view that I can share with you is that of being the daughter of George Kisevalter. Although my father was blessed with an amazing gift that you all admired greatly, it was no blessing for me, the daughter. He was the man with the remarkable memory; the man who forgot nothing; the father who forgot nothing. Although I did not inherit this remarkable gift, I did inherit the sense of value my father placed on friendship. Maybe it's because we were both only-children. I'm not sure. But I can't tell you how much your friendship meant to him. Some of you I've met only once in my life, and I may have been too young to even recall the meeting. But I know from the warm and enthusiastic way that he spoke of all of you how proud he was of you and how grateful he was to have had your friendship and so am I. I feel so lucky that my father surrounded me with so many interesting, accomplished, and wonderful people. And with the friends I've chosen, I feel that that is the one area where I think I've done as well as my father.

"And it's because of my father's long and productive life that we're all together here today. Again, I'm sure I speak for my father when I say thank you all so much for making him happy and proud.

"Thank you."

She has done well. It had to have been tough for her. She steps down and nods for me to take her place.

I try to convey an appreciation of George's professional life: his engineering and his Agency activities. I explain that he was a good engineer and that engineering was his first love, but I review some of his intelligence accomplishments and tell why he became the backstop for all major clandestine operations during the Cold War. I describe his search for the truth in everything that he did, the high value he placed on personal associations, and his lifetime affection for bears—especially bears: bears in zoos, bear artifacts, bear stories. I even explain how his physical appearance, tall and portly, with small shoulders and wide hips, reminded one of a bear, and many gave him the nickname "Teddy Bear." I speak of his fondness for Eva and Ferdi and how these two affected his life up until the moment he died. And lastly, I relate the way that he gallantly accepted his own death. I descend the steps, take my seat.

The chaplain asks, "Does anyone else wish to say something?" One of George's CIA colleagues rises and declares, "George, there never has been another like you." Others rise and bid George adieu in their own ways. One fellow plaintively evokes something about the "old boys." The chaplain offers a short homily. I never cease to be amazed how preachers can do this at funerals if they had not known the deceased, but he does well. I have the feeling that most of the people here today feel uncomfortable, or at least awkward, just as I do. After all, we are contemplating our own mortality as we observe that of our friend's, a man who seemed bigger than life itself. The chaplain finally issues the invitation, "Let us pray."

Unto God's gracious mercy and protection we commit you. The Lord bless you and keep you. The Lord make his face to shine upon you, and be gracious unto you, The Lord lift up his countenance upon you, and give you peace, both now and evermore. Amen.

The sun bursts through the stained-glass windows mounted on the south wall. The sanctuary is simple yet effective. My thoughts drift back to the days when George and I first got acquainted, the initial impressions that we made upon each other, the struggles we both experienced when we first were getting used to the other during our second careers in the real-estate office, and the stories, especially the stories. It was twenty-four years ago, but it seems even further in the past, in another life and in a place so far away. The first thing that comes to my mind is Mac. Mac and George, George and Mac—they were like brothers in that office, almost twins. Then I recall the story of George's friend, John Lavine, the tale that I call "Swedish Rhapsody." Like most of George's stories, it was interspersed with so many rich asides that one could easily get lost if he did not work to keep track of the main theme. Looking up from my desk one day, I sighed plaintively and contemplated the task before me: how best to market a recently listed piece of commercial land in McLean. Turning my head to gaze out the window and reflecting on which candidates would best be suited to its development, I caught sight of him staring at me. Once more, George interrupted my train of thought.

"I'll tell you a story," he said. "It's about an experience that I had with a good friend of mine, John Lavine, who worked with the Agency. He was with our Technical Systems Division, a fine officer and a splendid electrical technician. He was of Swedish descent and spoke Swedish. He now lives in Minneapolis. I am the godfather of one of his sons. Both of his sons went to West Point. In fact, at the appropriate time, I assisted both of them by writing letters to their congressman, the two then-U.S. senators serving Minnesota, and Hubert Humphrey, who, at the time, was our vice-president. Both boys did very well. One was a national champion parachute jumper for accuracy. He could jump from 3,000 feet up and land on a dime. Brave, brave man. Anyone who jumps from these planes, to me, is a brave man. The two of them are now out of the army. Time has gone by. We're talking fifteen to twenty years ago. Anyway, that is the nature of the relationship.

"John was working for us as chief of our technical services in Berlin while I was there with the Popov operation, an affair with a Soviet defector that consumed more than six years. John kept everything running smoothly from an electrical standpoint while we were there and he was doing a fine job of it all. Eventually, there occurred a long break in the activity with Popov when he left Karlshorst to return to Moscow. An interesting assignment came up during that interval. One day, Bill Harvey, chief of Berlin Base, came to me and said, 'George, we have an important task for you while you're waiting for the next step with Popov. The Agency chief in one of our allied countries would like to see you; he needs some help that maybe you can give to him.'

"I thought that I might need some technical assistance during this sojourn. Moreover, I wanted to do Lavine a favor, so I arranged for him to accompany me on the trip. After I arrived I was introduced to the local security chief. We hit it off quite well, right from the start. He spoke English and that certainly facilitated things because I did not speak his language. Now, I happened to have known, from New York days, a fellow by the name of Henning Christiani. Henning worked with me at Madigan-Hyland Consulting Engineers before the Second World War. While he was with us he managed the design and development of the Cherry Street Bridge in New Haven, Connecticut. He built it on a special assignment. Nice job. Incidentally, the Yale-Dartmouth game is being played right now, this very minute. I've often been to that game and seen Henning's bridge. I was the best man in his wedding. Later, tragically, he was killed in an automobile accident.

"The point of all of this is that Henning was the son of one of the principals of the engineering consultant firm of Christiani and Neilson. They are famous engineers. They built almost everything notable in their part of the world, all kinds of things. They invented a suspension-system bridge with multiple crisscrossing spans. There is a famous stadium in Rio de Janeiro that they built. They designed a bridge between Denmark and Sweden, a railroad, and highway bridge. They built the docks for the ship called *The Normandy* in France. When the Germans invaded their country, Henning's father sabotaged his own firm there in order to prevent any cooperation with the Nazis. I met him, the father, after the son's death. Circumstances. Life. Associations. Right?

"Well, with this relationship to Christiani and Neilson, I was well fixed in that area. So well, that when I went out there, I took my wife, Ferdi. A local official loaned me, or assigned to me, one of his secretaries to squire Ferdi around town, showing her such things as statues and monuments. A car was provided her, this and that, 'wining and dining,' etc. I was working eight hours a day with another secretary, a beautiful girl who was a super linguist. Her specialties were the local language and English; mine, of course, was Russian. We were attempting a penetration of a Soviet intelligence officer there. A high-level Soviet official was attempting to get close to our allies. We were concerned and wanted to help them. So, using a woman as bait, we endeavored to get the Russian compromised. The woman was a government employee of theirs who was willing to sacrifice herself, even to sexual involvement, for purposes of the compromise.

"There, in the safehouse where this was to go on, we set up a microphone and a transmitter. It was a highly elaborate package and was activated all of the time. The transmission was directed to an LP, a listening post. That is where we would be, along with our recorders. I had nothing to do with setting up this attempted penetration. I was only an instrument in this thing, there to translate into English, in real time, what was going on. That is, I was to translate everything that I heard in the Russian language. Understand that the principal language used in this operation was Russian. The secretary was translating some of her native language. All of this was to be done with the blessing of CIA, the local government, and everything else.

"My technician friend, John, got together with the hometown technicians and he began to help with the technical setup of some of the wiring in the safehouse for the transmission to the LP. Everything seemed to be going well in this cooperative effort. The technical end of the operation was set.

"As I mentioned, he has this Swedish background, whatever that means. Anyway, with the local technicians' broken English and John's presumed ability to speak a bit of the languages in that region, it appeared that communication would not be a problem for us. Without anyone's awareness, however, something became lost in the translation during the setup for the operation. Unknown to us, something of the technical translations between the languages had been terribly misunderstood. So, although everything appeared to be properly synchronized, suddenly, one night at about seven o'clock, news time, our transmission came up from the safehouse and was broadcast on public TV. This carnival was out of this world! The sound was on the TV! All over town. It went on the TV right in the middle of the safehouse action. It was completely devastating. When you realize who the principals were, this was in the category of high treason! A local official and a Russian official being exposed like this on public TV!

"Can you imagine such a misadventure? It may also have been on the radio as well; I don't know. I didn't hear the broadcast. The next day, I innocently was reading my newspaper for the day's news. Lo and behold, there before me I saw an account of the snafu in the paper. I said to myself, 'I am living in fairyland.'

"John, of course, was immediately thrown out of the country. He subsequently was the recipient of a number of missives from headquarters seeking to attach the blame to him. There was no value in having an international argument with one of our allies; so, like a good soldier, he just accepted full responsibility for the gaffe and went off silently. Poor guy. It wasn't his fault. Somehow, something was just lost in the translation.[1]

"This was an international embarrassment. This involved the CIA. It involved the United States. It involved the USSR. It involved a third country. It is a true story. How the hell they officially explained away this blunder, I don't know. I don't speak that language. The baloney to cover this outrageous gaffe really must have been stacked high. Can you imagine this happening? Like lightning striking an outhouse."

When he told stories in the office I could not concentrate on business. I started to exit the premises in order to get some work done. Then I heard Captain McAboy enter the office and it became unnecessary. I knew exactly what would happen. They would play pinochle and I would be free of his interruptions. I returned to my thoughts but heard an occasional comment from the two.

"Deal again, Mac."

"George, I'm tired of losing to you!"

"It's the cards, Mac, just the cards."

"No it isn't. You're reading my mind!"

"Come on, Mac; deal another hand."

"Well, stop looking at me!"

"Looking at you, Mac?"

"Yes, and you're reading my mind. You know just what I'm going to play, every time."

"Come on, Mac; that's ridiculous. Let's play now."

"Well, I'll play one more hand with you, just one more, and then I'm going to do some real estate."

"One more, Mac, one more."

Capt. Lyman R. McAboy, a retired naval aviator, was the leader of our little outfit. We had a commercial real-estate practice in downtown McLean, Virginia, a bedroom community for Washington, D.C., made famous by the presence of the CIA and the Kennedys. We sold an occasional house, but mostly we sold land. We sold building lots in and around McLean and in Great Falls; we sold commercial land in northern Virginia, incurring many agonizing zoning battles; and we sold big tracts of land for development anywhere we could in Virginia. We were a small outfit with just a few agents. Our sales success was somewhat limited when one considers the tremendous growth that took place in the area at that time. We were quite accomplished in at least one respect, however—that of personal relationships. We never once had an argument about money, client designation, or any other competitive aspect of the real-estate operation. There was absolutely no greed or jealousy in the office. During the nineteen years that George and I were together in the firm, no one ever left our office to work for a competing real-estate office. Now, arguments about politics were something else. We were a diverse group with different backgrounds and distinct views.

To understand George, I first had to know Mac, the boss, the only man in my experience to whom George regularly would show deference. George could show respect for many people if he thought that they deserved such treatment, and he was polite with almost everyone, but he had a veiled disdain for authority that was somewhat comical and refreshing. He did not give homage unless he was convinced that the authority was earned. For George, Mac had a position of honor, not just because he was the boss, but because he was a man of great character, confident yet kind and gentle. George simply loved him.

I had come to the firm after a career in aerospace and some years at the CIA. There, initially, I was engaged in assessing capabilities of foreign missile systems. Later, I was assigned to a senior staff that planned future intelligence requirements and evaluated collection programs to fulfill these requirements.[2] After six years with the Agency, I left. The atmosphere of the gathering Watergate episode was one impetus. I also saw that my employment at the Agency might be tenuous. The replacement of Richard Helms with James Schlesinger as director of the CIA (with the attendant resignation of all of the other people in my little systems analysis group) meant that I would have to thrash about for another job somewhere in the Agency at a time when people were being asked to take premature retirements because of overstaffing. Finally, the profitable sale of a piece of real estate that I owned contributed to the decision.

The first time I saw George was a beautiful day in April of 1973. As I approached the glazed-glass front door to the real-estate office, I saw him inside. His feet were propped up on the desk and he was asleep. When I opened the rickety old door, George, startled, suddenly awakened and his feet fell to the floor. I thought to myself, how stupid and lazy this man must be.

I soon learned that he was a retired CIA case officer of the DDP, the term for the CIA's clandestine operations group at that time. This knowledge did not endear him to me as I had a negative impression of the DDP. They had contributed little to my department's effort when I was an analyst working on the Soviet ABM problem. Later, when working in the systems analysis group of the CIA, trying to set up methods for evaluating the performance of various collection programs (including the DDP), I found them so secretive and non-cooperative as to be useless in Foreign Missile Intelligence. Most of them were Ivy Leaguers who had studied the soft, liberal-arts subjects in college. They could speak wonderful English, but they could not understand basic mathematics. They were not like the state-university engineers, of which I was one, the people who were supposed to replace them at the Agency. After all, intelligence was now a world of science and technology. I was familiar with rockets, missiles, satellites, computers, and the like. The collection, processing, and analysis of intelligence information were now tasks for technology, not jobs that required the humanities. We had to replace these people with engineers and machines, I believed.

I learned that George had graduated from Dartmouth. This made the picture complete, as far as I was concerned: a former DDP Ivy Leaguer. What bothered me the most, however, was his unkempt appearance. He looked as if he never bothered to prepare himself to leave the house: *Come on clothes, I'm going downtown; if you want to go, hang on.* After I had been with the firm about one year, and felt comfortable doing so, I asked Mac if he would speak to George about his appearance. Mac said he would not. He was not bothered by George's appearance. I was disappointed. I firmly believed that appearance was important.

By 1975 I had borrowed what was to me a lot of money in order to purchase various parcels of land for development. Development became impractical, however, as interest rates for construction projects rocketed over 20 percent. Payments continued to be due and I became seriously concerned with my financial future. Times looked grim. There was an Arab oil embargo and people were lined up at filling stations to buy gasoline. One day, George said to me that the economy was in the first stages of a significant depression and that no matter what I did, things were hopeless. He then volunteered that I was just like a son to him and gave me more advice: I was just thrashing about; I should quit real estate and get myself a real job. Sensing that I resented his advice, he stated, solemnly, that I did not have much respect for him. It was sadly true. My first impressions were strong. *How could anyone be so stupid and so lazy?*

In time, however, I learned to appreciate George's better traits. Even though he was unkempt, he nevertheless was a meticulous record keeper. He exhibited an incredible amount of attention to detail in everything that he did and it did not take me long to learn that George could perform extraordinary mental feats. He could solve virtually any problem related to the amortization tables almost instantly on the back of an envelope. Given the loan amount, the interest rate, and the term, he could determine almost at once and within a dollar just what the monthly payments on the loan would be. He certainly had a great deal of respect for money; his investments in the stock market were monitored hourly and astutely. He also had vast knowledge of corporate America and he used it well to his own advantage. Then, there were those interminable crossword puzzles. Every day, he would routinely dispatch the *Washington Post* crossword puzzle within a matter of about five minutes.

Whenever the phone in the office rang for George, I never knew what type of strange individual might be on the other end of the line. Often, it was somebody from the CIA. It seemed as though he still had some business with them, even though he had experienced mandatory retirement at age sixty. More often it was someone with a very foreign accent. I later learned that these were mostly older people, formerly White Russians, who were calling upon George to help them with the vagaries of life's practical challenges: for instance, doing their income taxes. The people had not yet learned to cope with the new, modern world. George had their trust and understanding. He would help them. Occasionally, a distinguished, older, female voice would be there. This turned out to be Velma, George's former wife, thirteen years his senior and living in D.C. She still depended upon George to get the plumbing fixed, which he did. George seemed to help everybody that he knew. He always seemed to have empathy for those around him. If someone had a problem, he was always quick to suggest an appropriate solution. So, there was an endearing quality to the man. He did not, however, seem to have great compassion for the needy unless he knew them directly; and he had a great deal of mistrust and suspicion of established charities.

He depended upon Mac to give him his daily pinochle "fix." Without that form of mental stimulation, he seemed lost for the day. George would arrive at the office at about nine o'clock, turn on the radio to the yakity-yak twenty-four-hour AM talk station, and await the entrance of Mac. Mac arose each morning at about five o'clock, went automatically to Burke Lake Par-three Golf Course, and played eighteen holes with his regular foursome. He would find his way to the office about midmorning, where George would have the cards shuffled and the score sheets ready. At that time, the radio station would be changed to one broadcasting beautiful mood music, the kind that Mac and I liked. It was part of a daily ritual that had a consistently predictable outcome. After beating Mac's brains out, George would lean back and sigh, Mac would accuse George once more of reading his mind, shouts would follow, and the exercise would be over. Sometimes the game would be followed with political discussions. When these occurred, Mac usually would have to make George tone down his rhetoric for fear of offending the ladies in the office next door. George's language could at times be quite salty but never, ever knowingly in the presence of women.

Early one morning in November of 1988, Mac's daughter, Patty, called and told me that her father had suddenly died. Bam! Just like that. Thankfully, the old boy went very quickly. He couldn't have felt a thing. They would put him down at Arlington National Cemetery. Even though he had been a captain in the navy and had collected many commendations from the Second World War as well as the Korean War, the service would be simple. His wife, Mary, the girl he knew from childhood, the one whom he daily called from the office to say silly, sweet things to before coming home, insisted that it be a simple ceremony. In his will, Mac had requested that "Till We Meet Again," a popular song of World War I vintage, be played at the funeral. Mary could not place the song, but she wanted it played to satisfy Mac's request. I found a copy of it in a music store, and my son Dennis played the piece on the old upright piano at the Fort Myer Old Post Chapel service. He added to it one bar of notes from "Anchors Away." Mary made the connection with "Till We Meet Again" when she heard Dennis play it. Now, every time I hear the song I feel a little melancholy.

George was devastated. He had lost his good friend. He had lost his daily pinochle fix and he feared that he would lose the recreation that the real-estate avocation so vitally provided him. He thus took it upon himself to ensure that we all remained with the enterprise, convincing all of us that it was in our best interest to do so, and he insisted that I assume the leadership of the firm. I was so frustrated with real estate and so saddened by Mac's death that I was about ready to pack it all in and do something else. After all, I was an experienced engineer. I could get a *real* job and move on. George convinced me to continue with the firm, assuring me that he would help in any way necessary. Indeed, he did prove to be quite helpful, both with his advice and his encouragement. Although, by this time, he was not too active with the real estate, he was surprisingly savvy about business. He taught me how to keep the books and how to complete the corporate income-tax returns. He assisted in every way needed. He wanted me to make a success of the enterprise for the sake of all of us, I soon realized, not just for his own recreation.

Then, just as suddenly, George's wife, Ferdi, died. This was in August of 1989. She died of a heart attack, at home, in his arms. At this Arlington Cemetery service, frugal George implored everyone to gather the flowers at the gravesite and take them home. No one could do it, of course.

George then seemed a lost soul. Mercifully, his daughter, Eva, moved back home, bringing with her one of her best friends, Annie Snyder. The girls lived downstairs in the walkout rambler and George lived upstairs. It must have been an absolute madhouse, albeit a loving and entertaining one. Although these two very active and attractive professional young ladies were looking out for the old guy, they had completely different interests and outlooks on life from his.

With Mac gone, George tried to get me to learn all about pinochle. I knew that I had my hands full in just trying to stay solvent, and a daily card game would ruin my chances. Thankfully, Eva took over that duty.

Although George's real-estate activities by then were nominal, he nevertheless continued his daily trek to the office. It was then that he seriously took to telling me his fascinating and illuminating stories—stories about world history, about corporate industry, about agriculture, about his family background in Russia, about his life growing up in New York, and about his experiences at the Agency. He was so full of knowledge, and it all was so very interesting. I began to realize that he was quite an individual, and although at times his visits interfered with my work, the stories were always so intriguing that I never once regretted listening to them.

By this time, George and I had become very good friends. Long gone were my misconceptions that he lacked compassion, industry, and intellect. But I had yet to learn just how wrong I had been on these matters, particularly the last one. He explained the origin of certain words. For instance, he pointed out that there were words in the Finnish language that were similar to some in the Hungarian language because Genghis Khan had brought them to both cultures. He explained that there are few universal-size railroad tracks in the world, that the gauges of almost all of them are different. He recited the gauges. He explained that most of the wheat in the former Soviet Union descended from a strain commonly grown in our own Midwest. This is because there once was blight on the Eastern Hemisphere wheat and the United States sent its best grain seed. He could recite the lineage of most European royalty: counts, viscounts, and discounts included. Eventually, I became as addicted to the stories as he had been to his card games.

Finally, George moved into Vinson Hall, a retirement home mostly for former naval personnel. It is located in McLean and convenient to the office, so he continued to come in often to see me. He even expected to do some real estate through our office with his new associates; but as time went by he gathered some good card-playing buddies at the home and his real-estate interests faded. He was quite happy there, and I later learned that he had made many friends at his new home. Not surprisingly, he had done this in the same manner that he always had in the past: he helped people. He did their taxes, he made financial suggestions to some, and he taught many of them lessons at bridge. On occasion, I visited him at Vinson Hall. I was impressed with the warm, friendly atmosphere of the place and the pleasant surroundings. One of its aspects was quite familiar to me, as it must have been to George. The long, narrow halls of the place, all of which were painted battleship gray, reminded me of the CIA. It was an incredible likeness, except for one thing. At the CIA, the Fine Arts Committee had cleverly and mercifully decided to paint the interior doors in bright colors. If one were walking the long gray walls inside the building, he or she might see a red door, a green one, and a blue one. In addition to giving a bright atmosphere to what otherwise would have been a most drab environment, it provided a quick means of identifying an office.

As the fall of 1997 approached, I became convinced that George's stories should be set to the printed word. I had thought about this for years but now I knew that it had to be done and soon. I could see George failing. I resolved then, somehow, to collect as many of the stories as I could. When I approached him on the subject, he demurred in his permission for me to proceed. A few weeks later, however, he called to tell me that he now agreed to go ahead. There was great excitement in his voice. He told me that his "secret cover" of over forty-five years had been lifted and that he could talk openly. In addition, he was soon to be awarded an unprecedented honor, the designation of one of only fifty unique people in the fifty-year history of the Agency. He was the only individual so honored for his work as a case officer. He was, for the first time I had ever observed, proud of himself. I was very happy for him. We agreed that we would begin to work on his life history shortly after the award was presented. I would start by letting him tell me again, as he had often done before, the stories as he remembered them. Of course, I did not then know that we had less than a month, but once more, I began to listen.

CHAPTER 2

Russian Legacy

The afternoon of 1 October 1997 was a typical early autumn day for northern Virginia: warm, dry, and buggy. Summer had not yet yielded to the incipient fall; only the cherry and the dogwood had begun to surrender their leaves. The foliage of most trees was still quite green. As I meandered up the long walkway from the parking lot to the back entrance of Vinson Hall, I reflected on the well-kept grounds of the retirement home. The fall flowers were beginning to bloom and flying insects were nervously hovering over them, perhaps anticipating their own demise as the cool nights approached. Dozens of squirrels seemed keenly aware of the need to be packing away the acorns spread across the grounds. Some of them scurried across my path when I approached them.

Upon entering the building, I began to contemplate how George and I might begin to retrace his life history. Finally, I decided to just let him talk in the way that he felt best in relating his stories. I could always construct the proper sequence of events later.

I found George in a good state. He was still feeling the glow of satisfaction that had befallen him when he had received the Trailblazers Award. He said that today he would begin with his Russian heritage and background. Next, he would tell me how he got into intelligence work with the army before he joined the CIA, then how he and his buddies first became oriented to this new government agency. I would later augment what he said with other information and perspective from his colleagues.

George's success in dealing with Popov, Penkovsky, Nosenko, and other Soviets clearly was directly related to his mastery of the Russian language as well as his innate ability to empathize with these people intimately and on their levels. His Russian heritage and family history had much to do with these talents as well as his fervid hate of Communism. George treasured the gift of his Russian background and relished expressing his memories of his family's past. His grandfather, Georgi Dmitrievich Kisevalter, was a deputy minister of finance in the governments of Tsars Alexander III and Nicholas II. The family members were hereditary courtiers. They would be classified as intelligentsia, or educated professional people—*dvorian* in Russian, which means noblemen by virtue of social circumstances. Although his father's side of the family had a German genesis, by 1800 the family members had adopted numerous Russian first names in lieu of their Germanic ones.

In about 1870, Grandfather Georgi married a Russian woman of St. Petersburg by the name of Yelizaveta Alexandrovna Stepanovna-Domnina, whose mother's maiden name, Domnina, indicated that she was a person from Domnin. Domnin had been the hometown of Ivan Susanin, a man who had sacrificed his life for Tsar Mikhail. Mikhail, the first Romanov, became tsar in 1613. That year a Polish army invaded Russia and the new tsar went into hiding. Susanin met the invading Polish troops far outside of Moscow for a discussion. He told them that he knew where the newly crowned tsar was hiding and that he wished for them to defeat the tsar's troops. The Poles promised to give Susanin a great reward in return for his help and followed him toward a location where, he maintained, the tsar and the imperial military preparations lay. Such knowledge would make the Polish seizure of the city easily accomplished. He then proceeded to take them into the depths of an almost impenetrable forest. Farther and farther they ventured, as he continued to urge them deeper and deeper into the forest. He kept saying to them, "Come on; it's not much farther." Finally, they understood that this was a ruse. The Poles then killed him, but they also perished in the extreme cold and the deep snows of the Russian winter in a forest that had no roads.

Susanin, of course, became a national hero for sacrificing his life for the tsar. A famous Russian composer, Mikhail Glinka, later wrote an opera based on the heroic tale called *A Life for the Tsar.*[1] It was so musically effective that even the Soviets liked it; however, because of the reference to the hated tsar, they changed its name, calling the opera simply by the man's name, Ivan Susanin.

George's grandmother was the last survivor of Domnin and presumably a descendant of Susanin's. In 1913, the 300th anniversary of the House of Romanov, the Russian historians wanted to have some commemoration of that village and the event, so they brought this to the attention of the court. In response, Nicholas II invited George's grandfather Georgi for a small audience, in which he proposed to perpetuate the name of Domnin. If the family agreed, the grandfather and his sons were to change the name of Kisevalter to Domnin, thus Russifying it completely. The tsar indicated that he would be very happy and proud if they were to consent to this, and he gave Grandfather Georgi a little bag containing 300 gold rubles representing 300 years of Romanov rule. There were, presumably, twenty fifteen-ruble pieces, thus constituting 300 rubles. The grandfather divided them up amongst the family. George's mother had one or two, which were stolen from her New York apartment years later.

The tsar's request was well received by the entire family. There were rumblings of war with Germany, however, so it was decided that "perhaps we should delay making the change until the conclusion of our victorious war against the Germans and their allies, which will transpire very shortly . . . then in great triumph, we will do this." Unfortunately for them, instead of a successful performance by the Russian army against the German front, the Bolshevik Revolution took place. George often enjoyed telling this story of his family and how they almost changed their name to Domnin. In his book, *Mole,* a presumed fictional account of the Popov operation, author William Hood gave the name Gregory Domnin to the character that represents George.

George's father, Georgi Georgievich Kisevalter, the youngest of four brothers, became an engineer. In 1905, war broke out between the Russians and Japanese, and he was appointed inspector of munitions at the Loebensdorf Munitions Factory (Buehle Stahl Werke) on the outskirts of Vienna. There, the Austrian government, under Franz Josef, was manufacturing ammunition for the Russian forces. In Vienna, Georgi met a young lady who taught high-school French. She was Rose, or Rosita, Grillet from the French village of Le Creusot, an industrial community near Dijon. After the termination of the war and a two-year courtship, the two of them were married in Irkutsk, Russia, in 1907. George was born on 4 April 1910, in St. Petersburg.

George was an only child and had the advantages of a wealthy, educated, and influential family. The only home that he remembered in Russia was that of his grandparents in St. Petersburg. There, his grandparents, his parents, two of his father's brothers, his father's two younger sisters, their families, their servants, and George lived in a large, courtly apartment in an elegant neighborhood near the center of town. The apartment's location significantly colored George's life. It was immediately across the street from the zoo near Bolshaya Pushkarskaya Avenue. From his balcony he could view the bears since there was no high wall at the zoo. He became obsessed with these animals.

He acknowledged that he was a real pain in the neck to his nurse because he always wanted to go out, no matter how the weather was, to see the bears. He constantly annoyed her until she took him walking to look at the bears, over and over again. He wanted to see what each bear was doing every day. He knew them all by name and every time he visited he would bring each one something to eat that he had swiped from the kitchen. Whenever they saw him they would perk up, knowing that he would bring a goody of some kind, and then come storming in his direction. This is how the fetish began.

In 1914 Russia went to war against the German-led Central Powers. George's father, a reserve officer in the Corps of Engineers of the Tsar's Army, by dint of his previous munitions experience in processing shells during the Japanese War, was asked to lead a contingent to the United States to obtain weapons. All of the men who came with him were munitions experts. He went with a diplomatic passport, his wife, and George via Irkutsk, Harbin, Puson, Yokohama, Honolulu, and San Francisco to New York City, arriving in January of 1916.

The commission established acceptance teams at facilities in Chester, Pennsylvania, near Philadelphia, to make sure that the munitions were correct and reliable. It was a culling process mostly, but the group also had inspectors who could design and fabricate various types of fuses and new types of armaments, in addition to performing as general inspectors. The munitions then were sent by rail to Seattle, where they were loaded onto ships bound for Vladivostock. Most of the artillery were 76-mm shells. Ultimately, some three million of these were delivered. The need for setting up a testing facility for the shells was immediately realized, so they looked across the Delaware River into New Jersey and found a swampy wasteland that they developed for that purpose. Part of this facility later became what we know of today as Fort Dix, New Jersey, and part of it was set aside for what later became McGuire Air Force Base.

On 11 March 1917 there was a popular uprising in Russia against the imperial government. The next day, food riots evolved into revolt. Key regiments of the army mutinied, and Tsar Nicholas II was forced to abdicate. A provisional government was formed and headed by the Socialist leader, Alexander Kerensky, who, by overwhelming consent, became both prime minister and war minister of the new constitutional democracy.

The United States declared war against the Central Powers on 6 April 1917. Also needing munitions, the U.S. requisitioned from the Russians the factories in Pennsylvania and the testing range in New Jersey. The Russians would now simply purchase the munitions from the U.S. There was a financial settlement made, an interesting ceremony and a parade were held, and George's father carried a Russian flag down Fifth Avenue in New York. That summer, a huge order came in from the provisional government for railroad cars. The senior Kisevalter then took the family to Middletown, Pennsylvania, not far from Harrisburg, where the Standard Steel Corporation had a plant for the manufacture of railroad cars. George's father's group now inspected railroad cars in addition to the munitions. The cars were, of course, made to fit the Russian tracks.

In October of 1917 Lenin returned from exile to Petrograd, and his message of "Peace, Bread and Land" had far more resonance with the masses than did the Kerensky government's appeal to fight a war far away, for a freedom that they did not comprehend. On 7 November (25 October old style, Julian, calendar of Russia) the Bolshevik thugs struck. All armed, they appeared in parliament and forcefully and brutally seized power from the Kerensky administration, stealing the reins of the Russian people's government.

On 3 March 1918, the Bolshevik government signed the Treaty of Brest-Litovsk with the Central Powers. This provided a momentary peace with the Central Powers but it required Russia to give up the Baltic States as well as parts of Poland, the Ukraine, and Finland. Loss of this dominion gave rise to great indignation throughout Russia, and this, coupled with other disenchantment with the Bolshevik Party, by then known as the Communist Party, gave rise to the ensuing Counter Revolution. Fighting erupted between the Bolshevik-Communists, allied with much of the peasantry, and the White Russians, principally supporters of the provisional government and tsarist sympathizers. The fighting raged all over Russia. The Kisevalter contingent in the United States immediately determined that they would support the White Russians, led by Adm. Alexander Kolchak. They continued on as before, but now turning out munitions and railroad cars for the Whites. By then, the group was also procuring munitions from Remington Arms. There were carloads of rifles and ammunition going from Bridgeport, Connecticut, across the U.S. and Pacific and into Russia. Many more of the Russian railroad people came. There were still the two groups: the Munitions Commission and a Commission of Ways and Means of Communication, the formal name for the railroad shop.

As a consequence of their loyalty to the White Army, when the fighting ended in 1921, the White Russian supporters in the United States were *personae non gratae* to the Reds, of course, and stranded in the United States. This ultimately caused the apparent annihilation or the disappearance of all but one member of George's great family in Russia, none of whom would become a faithful Communist. The only family member known by George to have survived the war, the revolution, and the political purges that followed was his first cousin, Alexander Alexandrovich Andreev, the son of his aunt Raisa, his father's older sister, and her husband, George's godfather, Gen. Alexander Alexandrovich Andreev. The general was executed. Aunt Raisa died months later and, presumably, eight of their children, all except for Alexander, were placed in orphanages.

During the years that were to follow, any communication with the Kisevalters in the USSR was rare and guarded. There was no sanctity of mail in the new Red country; the Communists censored everything. One had to be careful in writing anything critical of the regime or the relatives would be punished. Eventually, all communications came to an end as all of the surviving aunts and uncles died off. They clearly were not happy under the Communist regime. The Reds apparently executed many of the family, but there are no official records. Ultimately, the American Kisevalters had no contact with any of them, save Alexander, who, by then, was an Estonian. During that period George made friendships with Russian refugees in the U.S. that he kept throughout his life.

In 1923, George entered Stuyvesant High School, then the most challenging school in New York City. He completed high school in three and a half years. He doubled up twice in English and took extra courses. He received a first prize in mathematics; his score on the New York State Regional Tests, the competitive exams for seniors, was a record 97. He was first in his class in chemistry. He also learned how to use a lathe and to forge steel. He was a member of the chess team, which won the New York City championship. For this he received a medal that he proudly kept all of his life. At sixteen, he played a U.S. Master to a draw, although the man was playing six others at the same time, demonstrating simultaneous chess.

In the fall of 1926, George went up to Dartmouth, where he had friends. They were the main reason he wanted to attend Dartmouth, but he later came to revere the institution. He also made close friendships with others and maintained these associations throughout his life. Some of these people became world famous. George was particularly fond of classmate Nelson Rockefeller, to whom George, on occasion, actually lent a dollar or two and provided transportation for in an old Studebaker car. The Rockefellers were very strict with their children, in their attempt to teach them the value of money as well as core values of life.

George received an award from an alumnus of $100 a year to help with expenses and his father also helped him. In addition, George waited on tables at Dartmouth and had summer jobs in New York City. At the time, tuition was $300 a year.

In October of 1926 the elder Kisevalter took a job with E. D. Ozmand Aircraft Corporation of College Point, Long Island, which manufactured special pontoons for seagoing aircraft. There he met Charles Lindbergh and assisted in the design of customized pontoons for Lindbergh's aircraft. He had patents in his own name for the design of the pontoons on Lindbergh's Lockheed-Vega, used on Far Eastern flights, and his Lockheed-Sirius plane used for European flights. With Lindbergh piloting the aircraft, they tested the pontoons in the East River just before Lindbergh and his bride, the former Anne Morrow, took the plane on a momentous trip to the Far East. Kisevalter also designed the floats for the twelve-passenger plane, the *Condor,* used by the polar explorer, Adm. Richard E. Byrd. During that period, George's family lived in upper Manhattan close to Riverside Drive and the Cloisters. George's father knew many people associated with the federal government, having been a representative of Imperial Russia. He was close to Robert Lansing, the secretary of state under President Wilson and the uncle of John and Allen Dulles. Finally, Lansing suggested to George's father that he become a U.S. citizen and signed his citizenship papers in June of 1931.

Upon graduation from Dartmouth in 1931 George received a master of science degree in civil engineering. The difficulty that followed in obtaining employment during the depth of the depression had a lasting effect on George, but he persevered and always had some kind of work. In March of 1934, George became a naturalized U.S. citizen. Also, like many of his contemporaries, George joined the army reserve that year. He did so partly out of curiosity, partly for the benefit of added income, and partly out of patriotism. Two of his friends, a colonel in charge of one of the reserve units and a Dartmouth man in this unit, convinced George to join them. After passing the requisite examinations, George became a second lieutenant in the 302d Regiment of the Corps of Engineers and a part of the 77th Infantry Division, the Statue of Liberty Division.

At that time, George obtained work with the Parks Commission in New York City. His boss was Robert Moses, commissioner of parks for the City of New York as well as for the State of New York. George would meet with Moses every Saturday morning at the Picture Book Zoo in Central Park and give the big man a status report on all of the many projects under his purview. After gathering data from all of the project supervisors, George would assemble a large map. Buttons, on which were painted the percentage complete of each project, were attached to pins and inserted in the map at their appropriate locations. This duly impressed Mr. Moses, who was to become head of the entire transportation system of New York, New Jersey, and Connecticut. The man was so powerful that he had everyone in New York afraid of him. But he always tried to do what was right for the region and usually he was correct. He would build expressways around and through parts of New York City, ripping up neighborhoods in a cavalier manner, becoming at the same time a pariah of planning and one of the most productive men in the annals of New York. George's connection with Moses was formative. And during these Saturday meetings George would routinely take the opportunity to visit with the bears. He knew every bear in the zoo by name.

George was with the Parks Commission for almost two years. One evening in the spring of '36, at the Dartmouth Club, he met Evan Lyons, who was in charge of building the Taconic Parkway System that went from Poughkeepsie down to New York City. "I'm working for a very large, upcoming company," Lyons told George. "It's going to be the biggest consulting firm of engineers in the city of New York and we're working with Robert Moses. Currently, we're designing the beltway around New York."

George looked at the man in awe. The first leg of the beltway was to be twenty-eight miles long. It would extend from Manhattan, across the Bronx, across the Whitestone Bridge, across Long Island Boulevard, and into Long Island around Queens and Brooklyn. It would extend all the way from Long Island Sound to the Atlantic Ocean, connecting one side of New York to the other. The Triborough Bridge and a few other projects would be involved.

Lyons asked George if he were interested in a job. George's enthusiasm for the prospect of such employment was overwhelming. He started the very next day and savored every moment of the job. He was quite innovative, creating a very primitive computer system by connecting a series of electrically operated Monroe calculators in tandem. This assembly could be accurate up to seven decimal points and saved tremendous amounts of time. He could locate any spot on the map of the city of New York, no matter the quadrant, within one eighth of an inch. If he told the chief engineer in the field to go to a certain location, the man could be totally confident in his position.

That year, through friends, George met Velma Sutton, a fledgling opera singer, a coloratura, and thirteen years his senior. She came from Nebraska and had been graduated from the New England Conservatory of Music. She had studied in France, Italy, and Germany; she had performed in Nebraska, New Orleans, Baltimore, Philadelphia, New York, and even La Scala. They were married on 1 December 1936 in a very simple home wedding in the small town of McCook, Nebraska. His mother accompanied him and his best man was Sen. George Norris of Nebraska, who was a next-door neighbor to the Suttons.[2] The couple then took a modest apartment in Manhattan on Thirty-sixth Street. George continued with Madigan-Hyland Consulting Engineers while Velma continued her work with the Sanitation Department of New York City.

CHAPTER 3

Olive Drab

Quite suddenly, on 11 March 1941, George's father died. Two weeks later George was called to active duty with the mobilization of his reserve unit. Upon being activated, he was made a first lieutenant in the Regular Army, placed with the Corps of Engineers, and ordered to Camp Shelby in Mississippi. It was supposed to be only a six months' mobilization tour, followed by a short period for deactivation of the unit. Large-scale maneuvers were held in Louisiana involving a half a million troops. Three hundred thousand soldiers from the Second Army under General Lear and over two hundred thousand troops from the Third Army under General Krueger competed in war games. For weeks they wrestled back and forth among the bayous of Louisiana, hopping from one mudhole to another.

George's organization, the Forty-second Engineering Regiment, was a general service unit, not a combat unit; it was assigned to the Third Army, a regional command under Gen. Walter Krueger. As the training became more complete, George's commander, Colonel Smith, made George his regimental adjutant, so George had to memorize all of the elaborate adjutant rituals. The other officers encouraged him in the task and some of them laughed at his ordeal, saying, "We went through that hell when we had to do it. You can do it now. Just remember, though, you're speaking for the colonel, you know, so you speak with authority. You are merely paraphrasing whatever orders the colonel issues."

The worst thing about this exercise, from George's standpoint, was his responsibility to purify contaminated drinking water. It was August in the swamps of Louisiana, where one had to chlorinate as well as filter the drinking water in order to disinfect it. This had to be done no matter how distasteful the water became from the use of the purification chemicals. The temperatures were extremely high, with many 110-degree days. Often they had to burn freight cars loaded with red meat that had spoiled.

It was at this juncture that George was called on the carpet for getting a little impertinent in the exercise of his responsibilities. He knew what things were vital to the men's needs, and he was insistent upon getting them. He wrote a letter to the Third Army Headquarters requiring that more supplies be sent to his regiment. They were needed to meet the high standards of water purification for nearly a quarter of a million men in the command. He was responsible, and he was concerned. In reply, he was told to report to the headquarters in New Orleans. He was met by the adjutant, a colonel, who said to George, "Look, as adjutant of your regiment, you naturally want all these things for the command, and you'll get them, but you're going about it in the wrong way. When you want something from me, lieutenant, you don't *require* me to do it. You *request* me to do it. I can require; you request. You got it?" George respectfully replied, "Yes, sir." The colonel said, "Good. In the future, request, don't require. Now, it's a hot day. Let's have a coke, son. Do you have any change?" That was how George met Dwight David Eisenhower. George said that he sensed him to be "a very kind man, a true gentleman . . . he couldn't have been more considerate, and I'll never forget the occasion."

After the maneuvers, the regiment returned to Camp Shelby. Days later, Pearl Harbor was attacked. George sent Velma home to Nebraska to live with her folks for the duration of the war. His mother went up to Stamford, Connecticut, near where the family previously had lived.

By February of 1942, the Forty-second Engineering Regiment was loaded onto several trains and sent by various routes to Fort Lewis, near Tacoma, Washington. George was assigned to Company B, which consisted of about two hundred men. Their destination was Alaska; they would build radar stations, strengthening the Aleutians where attacks by the Japanese were anticipated. The headquarters for B Company was to be at Dutch Harbor on Unalaska Island, primarily a naval base with submarines. With the ice thaws of early March it became possible to navigate in the water, so B Company set out to survey their first radar site, one that would be at 3,000 feet in elevation.

In June of 1942 the Japanese attacked selected targets in the Aleutians with a branch of their naval flotilla while engaged with the U.S. Navy at Midway. Zero fighters as well as bombers were in evidence everywhere on Unalaska the morning that they first came. Various oil storage facilities as well as some submarines were destroyed. The Americans had a few fighters but they couldn't compete with Zeros. Many of the American aircraft were lost. George described them coming down in flames and burning on the ground with the oil facilities. "To see a whole bunch of Zeros flying in formation when you have so little to oppose them is an awesome and a sad sight. Their bombers never broke formation, thoroughly bombing everything for two days before pulling out." At the same time, Japanese troops attacked and then occupied Kiska and Attu at the very end of the Aleutian chain. From that day on, until the United States readied a complete naval task force, along with expeditionary troops to attack and recover them, the Japanese held Attu and Kiska. George and company continued on with their construction. "What else could we do? Thank God the Japanese took a hell of a beating at the battle of Midway."[1]

When the series of radar stations in the Alaskan area was completed, all stations complemented one another. Each kept track of its assigned area, but it also transmitted data to the control center. When all of the station electronics were integrated, the ensemble was capable of reporting all activities in the region. The control center for all of this was back on the mainland, from where aircraft could be deployed.

At Dutch Harbor, George knew a brave naval officer, Howard Gilmore, who came in on the submarine *Growler* that summer, flying a broom tied to the periscope. This meant that the boat had executed a "sweep," sinking a Japanese destroyer. Before the next winter was over, Gilmore was dead.[2]

In February of 1943, George was given a one-month leave, during which time he went to Nebraska. On his way back to the Aleutians he unexpectedly received a change in assignment. He was told to proceed to Fort Richardson, in Anchorage, Alaska, to be the adjutant of a regiment. Along with the assignment came promotion to the rank of captain.

Meanwhile, the fledgling lend-lease program, in which the United

States gave the Soviet Union thousands of aircraft and great amounts of other equipment, was accelerated. As George told me, "Somebody then said, 'Hey, this guy Kisevalter speaks Russian.' You know, people don't look at records very often, but sometimes they do. I was an engineer, so they had previously placed me in the Corps of Engineers. Then, when somebody looked at the records and found out that I could speak Russian, they moved me to Intelligence." He pointed to a book resting on his coffee table, *The Alaska-Siberia Connection,* by Otis E. Hays, Jr., which chronicles the program. George's immediate boss at Fort Richardson was Lieutenant Colonel Hays, the author of the book. The commander of the Alaska Defense Command was Gen. Simon Buckner, Jr.[3]

Buckner promptly asked George to tell him about his experience in the Aleutians. Since the general was responsible for getting the Japanese out of the islands and keeping them out of Alaska altogether, he had an interest in what a participant in the Japanese raid on Unalaska had to say. He, like George, appreciated a good drink, and he invited George to help him finish a bottle of Hennessy. He said to George, "Look, they made me a three-star general and chief of the Alaska Defense Command. They told me that I would have problems with this new upstart branch in our army called the Army Air Corps. They were right. The Army Air Corps thinks that they own the world, but they do not own Alaska or anyplace else. I'm the chief of the Alaska Defense Command, but I have to listen to this bull from old Hap Arnold and others about how they are running the show. I just wish that I could get out of here and have a combat command. I want to fight the Japanese."[4]

George was on Buckner's staff until June of 1943. Then the general sent him to Ladd Field at Fairbanks as the chief of a new organization, the I & I Detachment. This stood for interpreters and interrogators—interpreters of Russian and interrogators of Japanese prisoners of war. The mission would have two other officers and twenty-two enlisted men, all of whom were excellent in Russian. George would be in liaison with the Red Army, living with their regiment and delivering thousands of planes to the Soviets.

Shortly after being given this new assignment, George explored the Northwest Lend-Lease Ferry Route between Edmonton, Canada, and Nome, Alaska. The U.S. Army Air Corps command post at Great Falls, Montana, received the aircraft from the manufacturers and flew them to the transfer point at Ladd Field, almost two thousand miles. George described this transfer at Ladd Field, where he was the Russian Section commander, as the simple action of someone scribbling on a piece of paper words to the effect that "this is now a Soviet airplane instead of an American one." The Soviets flew the aircraft from that point in groups of about twenty. A bomber would lead the way, with its crew doing all of the navigating, while the fighters would follow along visually. There were three additional operational bases in Alaska on the route to Siberia. From Ladd Field the planes flew to Galena, then Moses Point, and then Nome. From Nome they flew over the Bering Strait and across Siberia. There were five stops across Siberia to Krasnoyarsk. The planes then went into battle within a matter of days.

Most of the aircraft delivered were fighters. The Soviets preferred the Air Cobras and an improved version, the King Cobras, made by Bell Aviation.[5] But they mostly wanted to supplement their infantry with flying artillery. They didn't care that much about bombing; they wanted protection for their infantry. The planes were very good aircraft. The Soviets lost very few of them. According to George, the ones that they lost were not lost because of mechanical problems but because of weather, stupidity, or drunkenness. He estimated that, altogether, twelve thousand aircraft were delivered with a price of approximately eleven billion dollars.[6]

George's response to the observation by many that the Soviets never fully paid the U.S. for these materials was: "And what could we say? If the subject were brought up, they could say, 'Well, we paid in blood while you made money on the war.' We did not want that kind of conversation. Their losses were terrific. Their success at Stalingrad, by rolling up a large part of the German Army, saved us countless lives. They lost tremendous manpower, not to mention cities, in the war. It would have been pretty hard to talk finances with them and say, 'Now, you owe us this and that.' We, as Americans, were fortunate that we were, relatively speaking, unscathed by the war."[7]

When George was appointed chief of the I & I Detachment, he had to find Russian speakers in the American army. He remembered that a National Guard regiment from New York City, then stationed in the coastal defenses of Alaska, had a Russian battery and that the battery used to march down Fifth Avenue flying the old imperial flag. George scouted out this regiment and sure enough it was full of Russian speakers suitable for his mission. Lt. Michael Gavrisheff had been at Fort Richardson as well as Ladd Field before George arrived and had spent several months there organizing the unit. Later, when George was transferred back home, Gavrisheff, by then a captain, took over the command. [8]

David Chavchavadze had attended an intelligence school at Camp Ritchie in Maryland. There were Spanish-, French-, German-, and Russian-speaking classes in the school. Most graduates went to England and waited for D-Day. There was very little for the Russian linguists to do. One day, there was a requisition for seven Russian-speaking enlisted men. The requisition, of course, had originated with Captain Kisevalter. George hadn't asked for anybody in particular, just seven enlisted men with good knowledge of Russian. So, the seven men went up to Fort Richardson. After some confusion, they found the G-2 tent and there was George Kisevalter, wondering what had happened to the seven enlisted men that he had requisitioned. When Chavchavadze stated his name, George said, "Oh, I know your parents in New York City." This, of course, made David feel at home.

George spoke fondly of his top sergeant, David Chavchavadze. "Chavchavadze was there; he was only twenty years old then. He was in charge of the Russian interpreters. It was their job to help the Russian mechanics get the planes ready for departure, to check them out and to make sure they were safe to fly. His mother was Grand Duchess Nina of Russia. Whenever he visited England he always slept at Buckingham Palace, because his aunt Xenia, the duchess of Kent, lived there. She was Russian. The Russians and the English were all intermarried, as you know."[9]

In December of 1943 George was officially appointed as the base foreign liaison officer. He then was similar to an ambassador. This status required that he be the principal individual coordinating between the chief of the Russian Ferry Pilot mission, the U.S. Ferry pilots, and the base commander at Ladd. This proved to be a politically sensitive position, since the Air Corps people thought I & I personnel should be reporting to their chain of command, not to that of the G-2, the Intelligence Branch. George could get along with the Soviet military personnel better than with the personnel of the U.S. Army Air Corps. He tried to impress his men with the importance of their job. He said to them, "You realize that you are in a job that expedites combat planes going to fight the Germans in three or four days from the time they are released." He also made it clear that their detachment was not part of the Air Corps. They were there because the commanding general of Alaska, who was in charge of security for the whole of Alaska, had to have his representatives there. Since so many of the Soviets were there, this also was a matter of security.

The planes were very carefully inspected by the Soviet mechanics while the Americans stood by saying, "What the hell? We are giving them the planes. Why are they wasting our time looking them over, right down to the last screw?" Of course, if one of these planes crashed on the way to the front, the Soviets had the name of the mechanic who had accepted the aircraft. In those days, Stalin would then have that man on his way to some suicide battalion and that probably would have been the end of him.

The Soviet and American mechanics could talk with each other through the interpreters. While some in the outfit were up in the control tower translating what the Americans in the tower said to the Soviet pilots during takeoffs, etc., some were stationed in Moses Point and some were in Nome. Moses Point was out in the wilderness, about two-thirds of the way from Fairbanks to Nome and near nothing. Usually two American soldiers just sat there in a Quonset hut using a radio to talk with the pilots as they flew by. The post was there simply for emergency landings. Fortunately, none occurred during the entire duration of the ALSIB operation.[10]

The Soviets brought only a few interpreters and, at first, were suspicious of the U.S. soldiers. George had to get them all fingerprinted and photographed. They did not want to do this for fear that their security was being violated. So, he told them that they would need to be fingerprinted and photographed in order to obtain an ID card and that with the ID card they could buy things in the PX at bargain prices. Suddenly, they were no longer concerned with security. At the PX they bought out all of the officer's pants as well as all of the condoms. They got orange juice for free in the commissary, and they took food and whatever else they could home with them when they departed. One senior officer even managed to ship a disassembled Buick automobile by air transport to the USSR.

One of the first things that George did after he arrived was to have a large map of Europe installed in the liaison office showing the military situation on the German-Soviet front, as reported by daily Moscow broadcasts. The Soviet officers often dropped in to glance at the map. Understandably, they were always anxious to see what was happening at the front. Maybe one of their own hometowns had just been liberated. This map made the liaison office a popular place and stimulated interaction between the Soviets and Americans. George also created some special rules. For instance, mail call was held at night since he didn't want his guys reading letters from home in sight of the Soviet mechanics. It would not be good for morale, as the Soviets received no letters. He did not want to make the visitors more despondent than they already were, realizing that the Soviets were up against a tough war. So those little actions helped make things work out very well, and as a result, they all got along fine. But the dominant motivator for the Soviet personnel was the knowledge that their prompt and continuous delivery of the planes was a vital contribution to the process of winning of the war.

After the Nazi forces began to retreat from Stalingrad in December of 1942, the war turned in favor of the Soviets. By mid-1943 their morale was in an upturn, and they were more complimentary than critical of the Second Front demands when they heard reports of the Allied invasion of Sicily. Then, the Salerno landings and finally the capitulation of Italy made them appreciate more their association with the Americans. This friendliness, inspired by continuous success in the war, was best illustrated by their commander's desire to favor the U.S. Ferry pilots with a monetary gift. Colonel Machin, the chief of the Soviet command in Alaska, called George into his quarters and stated that he wanted to reward the American pilots as well as further encourage their cooperation. He told George that he was going to pay a $300 reward to each pilot who overproduced; that is to say, made extra runs. He was adamant about this.

George said, "Don't do that; just give them a bottle of vodka, write a beautiful little note for their efficiency report so they might get promoted some day, and they'll think you're the greatest guy in the world. If you give them the money, they will just blow it away in the next poker game." Colonel Machin told George, "You're crazy." George said to the colonel, "Try it." The colonel did. He was delighted with the results. So a little psychology and a little knowledge of one's own troops helped to convince the Soviets' chief that the United States could be trusted.

George had problems with Soviet personnel wanting to defect. In one instance, a Soviet major took an officially sanctioned trip to the lower United States. He liked the country, he was good with languages, he learned English fast, and he said to George, "You know, I'd like to stay here, to emigrate to the United States. I come from Odessa and I have never even seen a letter from home. I think my people were all massacred because they are Jewish. I have nothing to go back to."[11] George said to the man, "Look, I'll give you a contact point to make whatever application you wish when the war is over. Or you can go to any U.S. embassy in any country neutral or not controlled by the Soviets and request asylum. Now we are at war; we are allies. We cannot accept your defection. Such a request would only hurt you, and I want to be your friend. So I'm giving you the best advice that I can." The man thanked George. George never told anyone in Alaska about the conversation. He was afraid that if he had, the Ladd Field commander might have heard it and passed it on. If it had come to the attention of the Soviet commander it could have been calamitous. It could have resulted in the death of the man, and it also would have created some very bad relationships in the ALSIB operation.

Since the USSR and Japan were not at war, the aircraft would not be harmed if they were clearly identified as being Soviet. Otherwise, the Japanese might have attacked them, particularly if they were thought to be American. The Soviets used red star decals, pasted on their planes. Once, a delivery failure caused a shortage of the decals. The Soviets were hesitant to schedule a massive flight through Japanese-controlled territory without the red star displayed. George said to them, "I think I can get you flying right away without delay. I'll see what I can do." He went to Fairbanks, found a Texaco facility there, and bought all of the decals available. He came back and said, "'Fly Texaco'—it's a red star on a white background. It can be seen even better than yours can, and you won't be delayed in flight. You're not going to be disloyal and nobody's going to blame you for the difference." He said to me, "I had a picture taken. The picture is in Otis Hayes' book. There it is. *Fly Texaco!*"

Finally, in the spring of 1944, George's orders came through to proceed to Fort Belvoir in Virginia, near Washington, D.C., and a center for engineering forces. He reported to the adjutant at Fort Belvoir, who asked him, "Hey, do you speak Russian? We have an inquiry here; it's from the chief of staff of the army, General Marshall." George observed that the inquiry also mentioned General Bissel, the chief of intelligence for the United States Army, the G-2.

George then saw Colonel Lovell, General Bissel's assistant, who oversaw a unit in the Pentagon called the Soviet Research Section. This section, which ran Camp Ritchie in Maryland, had supplied George with many of his Russian-speaking people in Alaska. The section had been keeping track of everything the Russians had been doing, even though they were allies. Already the U.S. was leery of them and wanted to know what they were up to.

Everybody in the office spoke Russian. Colonel Lovell said, "Well, we can use you. I will confirm your promotion. You'll be a major here; we'll get you released from duty with the Corps of Engineers." So, George switched corps. He already had his insignias for the Intelligence Branch, anyway. Now he was an intelligence officer in the Soviet Research Section and the deputy chief to a Colonel Shimkin, also an excellent analyst. They were in charge of all of the attachés going to the Soviet Union, who provided them with as many of the Soviet military manuals as they could get their hands on. The group was writing a book called *Our Soviet Allied Armed Forces.* Several chapters on Soviet military tactics were assigned to George, who translated the Soviet manuals into English and provided pictures, diagrams of hardware and tactics. Eventually, George was put in charge of the project.

In January of 1945, the war started to collapse around the Germans. U.S. Army general Edwin Sibert, then stationed in Germany, picked up German general Reinhard Gehlen, along with Gehlen's complete staff and a cache of intelligence information documents that were hidden underground in Bavaria, and brought them back to the U.S.[12] Gehlen had been in charge of all intelligence operations against the Soviets. Hitler did not like Gehlen, nor did Gehlen like Hitler. Hitler often threatened him. Gehlen kept telling Hitler the truth, and it was almost always bad news. General Sibert had Gehlen taken to a Fort Hunt, called "the Snake Farm" by some, near Washington, on the Mount Vernon Parkway adjacent to George Washington's former home. The facility was hidden from view; there was only one entrance gate and that was guarded. There were a number of generals there from various countries, including the Soviet Union, Japan, and Germany.[13]

In March of 1946, George was sent to speak with Gehlen and his people at Fort Hunt to compare what they knew with what the U.S. knew about the Soviets. George told the general what his job was and asked, "What is your position? I read where you said that since you lost the war you had one of two choices: to orient yourself toward the

East or to the West. You are here in the West. What we want from you is all of the information that you have on the Soviets, so that we can match it with the information that we have. There is nothing militarily that you are to do. We are not going to fight them or anything like that. We just want intelligence. You are an intelligence officer. Everything is at your disposal. Will you provide us with the information that we want?"

George was selected to do this principally because he could speak excellent German. More importantly, however, he knew how to get along with them. First, the U.S. moved all of these German officers' families to the Western Zone in Germany so that they'd be away from the Soviets. Next, all the high-ranking officers, including General Gehlen, were given a wartime prisoner-of-war paycheck. Each received about twelve thousand dollars or more a year, which furnished a very good income. In addition, George provided them with everything they needed, including cigarettes and chocolates. Then, he made a point to get along with the general personally, as well as with most of the other high-ranking officers, realizing that it didn't require much effort to be pleasant.

Finally, he had a penetration, and the penetration was a clever one. He observed an older German gentleman who was only a captain, which for his age was strange. George asked the gentleman, "Why are you only a captain? You are older than most of these people and certainly as smart as they." The man replied, "I'm a Volga German; I was in the Russian army, under the tsar, during the First World War. I was a colonel." George asked, "Of course, you speak Russian?" The man answered, "Yes." They spoke Russian to one another. During the First World War, the Germans captured the man. Then, after the war, he elected to remain in Germany. He married a German girl, settled down in Heidelberg, and developed a small cheese factory (which the Allies eventually bombed and destroyed). When the Nazis came to power and found out that he spoke Russian, they made him an intelligence officer. They wouldn't promote him except when they needed something of him.

George said to the man, "Well, maybe you can tip me off to certain things that I'm going to be in the dark about, here and there." The man responded, "I'll be happy to." "Well, how about this protocol—why do you do those things?" He said, "Those monkeys in monocles [Germans] do things by habit, whether it's smart or not." So, in the middle of all of these Germans, George could speak Russian with him to get inside information, and they didn't know what the two were talking about. George found answers others couldn't get, and he could do it without hurting anybody.

Gehlen's staff eventually developed their own intelligence service for West Germany. With U.S. help, they established a substantial National German Intelligence Service that was closely allied with and dependent on Uncle Sam; it was called the BND.[14] George later lectured to them in Germany many times. Ultimately, General Gehlen and he became close friends. George left the army before then and had nothing more to do with setting up that organization. He wanted out. He wanted to go back to New York to his old job with Madigan-Hyland Consulting Engineers. He received his discharge from active duty in the army in May of 1946 and returned to Madigan-Hyland. They happily took him back, giving him a big raise consistent with the higher wages after the war. At that time Madigan-Hyland was developing airfields, including Idlewild (JFK) in New York as well as a number in Puerto Rico.

CHAPTER 4

The Central Intelligence Agency

Within months after returning to Madigan-Hyland, George received an interesting letter from Velma's brother, Harold. The brother-in-law wrote, "Come to Nebraska. We can put up some mills for the processing of alfalfa and make a lot of money." Here was an interesting proposition and an opportunity for substantial profits. Alfalfa was needed for all animal feed. Five percent of all cow fodder, chicken feed, and other feed stock in the United States was alfalfa. This was done to ensure that the animal's food contained sufficient vitamin A. Also at that time, children were routinely dosed with cod-liver oil, for the same reason. Eventually, vitamin A from alfalfa could be added to their bread. So alfalfa was a necessary supplement to all feed stock and it had great potential for the human diet. The alfalfa business was a natural.

So, the civil engineer resigned from Madigan-Hyland to try his hand at business, becoming a partner in this family enterprise. George was the general manager; Harold was the financial man. Velma's nephew, Harvey Sutton, and Wayne Allen, the husband of Velma's niece, Lois, were the other partners. George became very fond of his in-laws, and they of him. A friendly kinship continued all of his life. They built mills with family money and U.S. small-business loans. The first was at Willow Island, Nebraska, the population of which was six. It was seven miles from Gothenburg, whose population was about twenty-five hundred. Later, they built one in Scandia, Kansas. Velma's family was located in McCook, about eighty miles from Gothenburg, the headquarters for their operation.

As the enterprise grew to success, the Allens and the Suttons bought small houses in Gothenburg. George and Velma took a suite in the hotel. She had her grand piano moved in, and her daily vocal exercises echoed up and down Gothenburg's Main Street. The two of them often amazed the townspeople by arguing loudly on the streets in French. Later George and Velma bought a cottage on Lake Jeffries, some ten miles south of Willow Island. Here Velma could vocalize to her heart's content in relatively quiet surroundings.

The partnership purchased the alfalfa from farmers and then processed it to its final state. The procedure requires harvesting the alfalfa soon after it matures, immediately dehydrating it, and then keeping it cool until it is ready for mixing into the animal feed. This involves a nonstop, day-and-night operation during harvest season. The alfalfa is placed in huge conveyor troughs that slowly feed the leaves into an enormous rotating stainless-steel barrel, say about thirty feet long and ten feet in diameter. A gas generator creates 1,800-degree-Fahrenheit air that immediately dehydrates the alfalfa. At the end of each cycle, steam exits one opening of the machine and a dry mass of alfalfa exits another. Paddles then move this mass onto a conveyer that takes it into a building. There it is directed through a hammer mill that renders it alternately into a green powder or green, granulated pellets. It is now necessary to keep the finished product as cool as is practical in order to preserve its vitamin A within the carotene.[1]

During the hay season, from April through October, a mist of green alfalfa dust hung over Gothenburg because of its four dehydrating mills. In response, the wives simply bought green sheets and towels. Everyone had an unhealthy-looking pallor, but no one ever caught cold; they were all full of vitamin A.

George had imaginative ideas for the uses of alfalfa. He spoke of them: "I learned a lot about grains. I also know that we could feed the world on green bread, if we wanted to. If animals can eat grass and survive, and if grass can be baled and burned and thrown away, certainly there's more than enough for human consumption. We don't ever have to starve on this planet. Such a thing as *a lack of food* is nonexistent in this world. It is only a lazy man's ignorance. But to compete with huge outfits, like Archer Daniel Midland, is something else. That's another story. A monopoly is a monopoly."

In Nebraska, George and Velma were effectively living apart. Often, she was in McCook and he was in Gothenburg. "We couldn't exactly commute every day," George explained, "and during the winter I couldn't commute for weeks at a time. I was able to take a few trips back East during this period to see my mother. She lived in an apartment in New York City. I would stay with her when I took business trips back East. I was getting sick and tired of being out in the country and with haggling every single day about what a hog was worth. That kind of conversation gets to be boring very fast. They had one paper that everyone read: the *Omaha Bee*. In the wintertime in Nebraska you repair machinery; that's the only productive thing that one can do."

George found a few ways to relieve the monotony. Once the community concert association in Gothenburg scheduled a Russian male chorus that was touring America. George invited them to the cottage. The performers spoke very little English, and only George among the home folks spoke Russian. They were young men and the vodka flowed freely. On another occasion, George tried to play family counselor. There was a small café in Willow Island. One evening, after work, he was enjoying a beer there when a couple got into an argument. The man slapped his wife in the jaw. George rose, picked the fellow up, and tossed him through the wide screen door. At this, the woman began to flay George with her heavy purse, telling him to mind his own business. George also tried his hand at inventing an evaporative cooler for the cottage. He and Harvey installed an automobile radiator in the furnace with a hose dripping water on a cloth screen in front of a fan. When they turned it on, dirt and lint came flying out of every register in the house. After the house and the equipment were all cleaned up, the device worked fine, except that it made the house so humid that the piano keys swelled until they stuck, the doors wouldn't close, and the windows wouldn't open.

Then, since Harvey had been bothered by alley cats raiding the garbage can behind his house, he and George devised the ultimate cat repellent. They took two old wood-stove plates, put gunpowder between them, and connected a fuse to a battery on the ground outside. If the cat were to jump into the can, an electrical connection would be made, blowing the cat out of the can. On the night of its trial, Harvey's wife suddenly went to the hospital to deliver their second child. His mother came over to stay with the two-year-old. The next morning the men went to work; Grandmother took out a big sack of trash and tossed it into the can. Ka-boom! Trash was everywhere, and Grandmother fell over backward. She was not amused.[2]

George eventually found a way to get back East. He received a letter from his childhood friend Malia Natirbov saying, "The next time you come to see your mother, stop by Washington and see me. The CIA could use you; they're recruiting madly." George went to see a recruiting officer and told him of his Russian background. The man was enthusiastic; the CIA wanted him to come right away. George asked Velma, adding, "You know, I'm sick and tired of asking a farmer what his hay is worth and what a hog will be worth tomorrow." She agreed and they were off to Washington. They had altogether about a ten-year project with the alfalfa. George left after five years, while things were still very good. He didn't know it at the time but their days were numbered. The demise of the business took place when modern technology provided a means whereby vitamins could be manufactured synthetically in great concentrations and purity. Moreover, for certain applications, synthetic vitamins were more cost effective, so less alfalfa would be required for vitamin A needs.

On 18 September 1947, the U.S. Congress enacted the National Security Act, which established the National Security Council and the Central Intelligence Agency. In late 1951, George accepted a position as a branch chief in the Soviet Russia Division at the newly organized Agency. His grade was GS-14, which paid about seven thousand dollars per year. His interest in the CIA had been greatly enhanced by the Soviet-sponsored invasion of South Korea in June of 1950. One of his earliest substantive assignments with the Agency would involve operations there. The man who hired him was Peer de Silva. In describing his initial interview with George, Peer stated, "He was a bear of a man who spoke native Russian, as well as other languages, a man of enormous energy and imagination and a man who subsequently would handle some of the Agency's most important work with Soviet intelligence agents." de Silva's admiration for George's ability and the close friendship that developed between the two eventually prompted him to declare George to be "my best friend in or out of the Agency."[3]

Peer assigned George to the important job of branch chief for Soviet operations in the Far East. The region to come under his purview included Alaska, all of Siberia in the USSR, and all of the countries around the horn to Burma, with the exception of China. His branch was charged with developing leads to intelligence about the Soviet Union that came through, or originated in, any of these countries. To that end, George began to hire people and organize the branch.

Dick Kovich considered his first meeting with his new supervisor unforgettable. He had just returned from an assignment in Asia to join the group. Most of them were recent graduates of Yale, Princeton, or Harvard. So, Dick, a Minnesota graduate, was precipitously thrust in among the Ivy Leaguers. Frank Summers, a Yale man, took Dick down to their branch office in the old temporary buildings on the Mall off Constitution Avenue to meet George. They saw him over in a corner lecturing to four or five case officers. Frank turned to Dick and asked, "Don't you think that he is really rather old?" Dick replied, "Yeah, Frank, I guess he is old, but at least he has no gray hair." George was forty-one years old at the time. Right in the middle of the lecture, Frank introduced him to George, who then said in Russian, "Greetings and welcome back from the Orient. I want to sit down and chat with you about activities there." George then went back into his lecture.

When the lecture finally broke up, George and Dick sat down and talked about Dick's case alternately in Russian and in English as George tested Dick's Russian and sized him up. George said that he had heard from Dick's boss, Ed Snow, who said nothing but good things about Dick. The two of them discussed the case of a young agent they had recently dropped into the Soviet Union via parachute. They had dropped him into a marshy area and the man had let it be known that he didn't appreciate their little mistake.

George knew that Dick was of Serbian descent. This would bring them closer together, since they both attended the same church, the Eastern Orthodox. Dick felt that they had clicked.

George's young charges took to calling him "Papa." In many ways, he was sort of a father to them. He was concerned about all of them; he assisted them, gave them advice, and, when necessary, admonished them. Disciplining them, however, was most difficult for him—he simply could not reprimand people. They all got along extremely well. George had a sense of humor, but he was serious about the job and fanatically anti-Communist.

In the meantime, Velma found a lovely home on California Street, "embassy row," right near Massachusetts Avenue and Observatory Circle, where the vice-president's home is now located. The house was made of stone and had three major stories and an elevator. Doctors and diplomats were neighbors and the National Zoo was not far away. George promptly developed a personal relationship with one particular bear at the zoo. Often, he would go down early in the morning carrying bread for the bear. Not surprisingly, the bear would respond to his presence. George's coworkers were very much in awe of the house and became quite enamored with Velma. For some of them, the home became the center of their social life and would continue as such for many years. Likewise, their friendships would be continuous up until her demise. One important thing for George seemed to be "getting to know Velma." George was the type who, after work, would bring home his buddies for drinks. Velma would never know how many were coming. She knew that he loved his job and that he would be coming home with his friends. She would mix the drinks for them, although she did not drink at all. This was the way that he wanted things, so that was the way it was going to be, because she loved him very much.

At the CIA, some of the most important operations under way at that time involved sending agents into Sakhalin, an island formerly a part of Japan that the Soviets had collected after World War II. The Agency design was to put them ashore with PT boats and later retrieve them. Their objective was to find out information relative to Soviet installations and report back. This was dangerous for them, and actually it did not pay big dividends. But the leaders of the new CIA felt compelled to try personal reconnaissance, since flying airplanes over the island had proved to be even more dangerous. The Soviets had already shot down several U.S. aircraft, killing the crewmembers.

That year, the Pentagon made a special request of the CIA that would be fulfilled, in part, by George's branch. The Soviets were constructing an airfield in the southeast region of the Chukotski Peninsula near Providenya Bay. The facility was directly across the Bering Strait from the town of Gambell on St. Lawrence Island and about fifty miles from U.S. soil. From an elevated position, on a clear day one can see the hills of the other. Surely the airfield would serve MIGs, but could it accommodate a bomber large enough to carry an atomic bomb? The airport runway would have to be substantial—thick enough to support the bomb-laden aircraft and long enough for such an aircraft to attain takeoff speed. In addition, it was believed that a pit might be dug at some point on the airfield where a plane could be loaded with the bomb. The loading procedure for the U.S. Air Force was to place the heavy bomb in a hole in the ground, taxi the bomber over the hole, and then, very gingerly, raise the payload up into the aircraft.

The Agency could not parachute in someone to get this information; he would be detected with radar. A PT boat certainly would be observed. So, eventually, they decided to investigate launching someone by submarine. The navy agreed to provide transit. The submarine would approach as close to the shoreline as was practical and surface at night just long enough to launch four agents in a rubber boat powered by a silent motor. The men were to navigate to a landing with the aid of shoreline charts. Upon landing, they were to camouflage the craft, hiding it until the next nightfall. They then would climb the mountains overlooking the airfield and take photographs. At dark, they were to launch the rubber boat and rendezvous with the sub out in the Bering Strait. With the benefit of some special radar-reflecting panels mounted on the boat's sides, the sub crew would easily spot it with its four men.

A lot of time was spent in conference at the Pentagon, coordinating the acquisition of the submarine, rubber boats, silent motor, secure communication preparations, and a host of other details. George and his men actually inflated a rubber boat in their office area and studied such things as where the men would sit and where the equipment would be placed during the voyage. Agent selection was crucial. Four daring men, all of whom were proficient in Russian, were chosen, and extensive training began.

Months later, everyone took his respective position. Dick Kovich was stationed with radio gear on St. Lawrence Island. His main mission was to assist the men if they missed their rendezvous with the sub and had to cross the entire Bering Strait. He could, of course, speak fluent Russian, and he had a great deal of radio experience from the Second World War. The four agents boarded the submarine in Pearl Harbor. Two CIA officers were with them. The captain of the sub was Comdr. Ed Spruance, the son of Adm. Raymond Ames Spruance, commander of the carrier task force that sank four Japanese carriers at Midway during the Second World War.[4] They arrived at the Bering Strait, found the appropriate spot to launch the men, and, on a calm, moonless night, surfaced. The rubber boat was inflated and the men were dispatched to reconnoiter the runway.

The operation did not go as planned. The agents were startled to discover people actively engaged in construction at their intended landing site. Consequently, they did not go ashore and the operation was aborted. There was considerable disappointment on the part of all participants. The naval activity had proceeded successfully, and a worthwhile training exercise had been conducted with no one getting hurt, but the mission was a failure—no useful intelligence information had been gathered. Later, reconnaissance and analysis by others determined that the runway had no loading pit and was not of sufficient dimensions for a bomber large enough to carry an atomic weapon.

Despite this early failure, George's group continued to make plans to expand their activities, hiring others and strengthening the capabilities of the branch. Paul Garbler was one such individual and his first encounter with George was memorable. While he was in South Korea as the assistant naval attaché in Seoul, Paul met two American "tourists" who in fact were working for the CIA. He then left Korea and went directly to Washington for his next assignment. He hadn't been back there more than two weeks when he received a telephone call from one of these fellows. He said that he was in town and wanted to know if Paul would have a drink with him. When they met, the man asked Paul what he thought about the CIA and if he would be willing to consider joining the organization. The man then gave Paul the name of a contact, George Kisevalter, and a time at which to appear. George was a "sort of a hefty guy who had a magnificent pot and big hips, giving him the shape of a bear," Paul recalled. "A cigarette hung out of the corner of his mouth that dropped ashes down to that pot. He was wearing rumpled looking clothing but spoke elegant Russian and talked with sincere humanness." George took Paul up to an office on the second floor. Spoiled food and dirty dishes lay on the hall floor outside of the offices. All dressed up in his spotless navy uniform and accustomed to extreme cleanliness, Paul cringed and asked himself, "What is all of this? What kind of business is this? What kind of people are these?"

George then took the apprehensive naval officer into a small, dim room where a man was crouched down in a corner, pecking away at a typewriter illuminated by a gooseneck lamp. The man didn't even look up until George cleared his throat. "Oh, hi, George," he said. "Hello, Paul. Come on; sit down." For an hour and a half, the mysterious man, Harry Rositzke, went through Paul's whole life, probing and telling him things that he had forgotten all about. The interrogator was quite thorough.[5] Paul and George then left the room and went to another small office. This one was cleaner than a surgical facility. There was nothing on the wall, and the only thing on the desk was a telephone. There wasn't even a wastepaper basket in the room. "What am I getting into?" Paul wondered.

"Ever thought about Alaska?" George asked.

"No."

"How would you like to go to Alaska? You could be our first chief in Alaska."

"I would have to check it out with the family, but it sounds like something that I might like to do."

"There will be a lot of flying involved, back and forth between Fairbanks and Washington. Would you agree to that?"

"Well, I wouldn't join the CIA to fly. If I join the CIA I want to be involved in operations."

"We're doing operations out of Alaska across the Bering Sea into Russia and the Far East, and that's what we want you up there for."

The adventurous sailor went home and told Florence, his wife. She promptly went out and spent a great deal of money on cold-weather gear. About a week later Paul called for George on the phone; that is, he called the number that George had given him. The people on the other end of the line had never heard of George.

"Here I was, completely adrift," Paul remembered. "The only connection that I had with the CIA was George and that telephone number where they had never heard of him! Well, I had been through a navy intelligence course before I had met George, so I went back and saw the chief instructor, who was CIA. I said to him, 'Okay, you guys are whackos; I'm going back to the navy!' The instructor said to me, 'No, no, no; don't do that. There is a guy coming in here next week from Berlin. I know him. Would you like to go to Berlin?' I said, 'Jeez, you know, I'd give my hat and overcoat to go to Berlin.' Well, this fellow came. He accepted me for Berlin and off I went for four years. One day, near the end of my tour in Berlin, I saw this fat guy. I thought that I recognized the fellow; he was just standing there and talking to somebody. I went up to him, I grabbed him by the coat collar, and said, 'You son of a gun, I am going to poke you right in the nose.' He said, 'Whoa, whoa, whoa, don't do that.' You know how George is. He took me out of my anger in a minute. 'You don't understand. I was taken away suddenly. I had no chance to get in touch with you or anybody else. I just had to go.' I didn't believe George at the time, but I later found out that it was true. He had been taken away for the Popov case. So, that is how I met George. The whole Alaska thing depended upon George. It never happened for me." Paul and George were to become good friends and eventually would work together for years on some very significant operations.

George's job required that he travel to the Far East to supervise some of the operations. He did not welcome travel; he had already been separated from Velma too much during their marriage. But in 1952, he traveled extensively. He went to South Korea, Japan, Hong Kong, and other Far East sites, running operations in all locales. During his travels in the Orient, he met Ed Snow, an experienced intelligence officer who spoke very good Russian as well as Japanese. Snow's parents were White Russians. He spent some of his youth in Japan before going to California, where he later was graduated from UCLA. George and Ed were to become good friends and work associates.[6]

As the Korean War continued, George visited some very hazardous areas in torn-up South Korea. The CIA had air and maritime groups there to augment its various operations. Many of these operations were failing, however, for reasons that were not clear. Moreover, several agents and even case officers had been lost. Perhaps the Communists had penetrated the Agency. An analysis of these events and conditions was in order. George spent a month in Seoul reviewing twenty-six operations into North Korea but could not isolate any penetration. Only years later did the Agency learn that a hired foreign assistant had been tipping off the North Koreans and souring many of the Agency plans.

George took along his secretary, Jackie Bush, a young woman from the Agency and an invaluable worker. Having brought her, however, he felt obligated to be her moral supervisor, so to speak. So when all of the wolves asked to buy her drinks and take her out, she could refuse. He had to protect her, but that also meant that he had to buy the drinks.

An army colonel stationed there wanted to take her to a dance in Seoul. She wouldn't go unless George went. George told her, "I don't even dance, for goodness sakes." She persisted, "I won't go unless you go." So, with glares from the colonel, George said, "Okay, I'll go. We'll make this happy for everybody. You take the girl," he told the colonel. "Just give me a pistol and put me in the Jeep. I'll ride shotgun with you."

So they went. She was the most popular of the dancers, being the only woman in a skirt. All the other girls, the nurses, were wearing their uniform pants. Everything was fine until alarms started to ring, many loud sirens everywhere.

Suddenly, all of the nurses ran from the dance hall; a new Chinese attack was under way. The main line of resistance up north had broken. Everyone had to get out of there immediately, crossing a secondary line of resistance that was being formed about a block away. They quickly shot across. Dozens of trucks carrying ammunition came rolling by on their way up the road. Then, moments later, down the hill came a different group of trucks. These were loaded with U.S. casualties. That was why all of the nurses had run to the hospital. There was one and only one bridge that was still standing between their location and the soldiers' position at the front. The trucks had to get the wounded soldiers across, or they would be dead. George winced at the thought of all those poor, hurt soldiers and forgot about the dance business. They got back to headquarters in the Traymore Hotel and climbed up on the roof, where they could see the firing of Chinese artillery on the skyline at one particular UN position that was taking a beating. "The horizon looked like it was on fire," George recalled. "Of all the stupid names, 'Pork Chop Hill.'"[7]

He continued, "Those were the sad days; and we did the best job we could. I was in Seoul, Pusan, and some other locations. All that was left of Seoul in 1952 were hulks of buildings. You could see tradesmen in the street making straight nails out of crooked nails. That was their business. Admonitions posted in our PX read, 'All personnel will fire arms outside, not inside, the building. This is a PX, not a shooting gallery.' We were actually sacrificing drinking money at the bar in order to subsidize orphanages. It was all but impossible to have a drink while thinking of the starving kids. It was that pitiful; it was out of this world."

I said to George, "You lost a case officer. How did that happen?"

"Two. They were young and determined. They boarded a supply plane that served some of our agents behind the lines. Every time they loaded the plane they felt guilty because they were sending somebody else and were not going themselves. 'Ah hell, let's go. What do we have to lose? We'll show these guys we have guts.' And they walked into a trap. They were captured and they stayed in Manchuria for twenty years. This was incidental; it had nothing to do with me, not a thing. I was just a witness; but it was so sad. I knew the activities, but I didn't control them. The resupply of agents over there was under a local jurisdiction. If it were Russian and so on, they would give me a reading of what's what. But if it were North Korean or Chinese I had nothing to say. We all were involved in the same war, but we had different responsibilities.

"We thought that we had reliable agents in the North. We were supplying them with our airplanes. I believe that we were using B-26s. Our people would have gear that they would kick out of the plane in a parachute while flying at low levels. They did other things, as well. They even invented an air-snatch system called *Skyhook* for getting people up from the ground. Anyway, Jack Downey and Dick Fecteau, two case officers working for our chief in Korea, were the ones. They said to each other, 'Heck, we look like chickens. We're dispatching agents and resupplying them; but we are always on the ground. We don't go up in the air. Let's take this trip; it's a milk run. We'll see what the situation is like.' Well, that particular plane was suckered into a trap somewhere that was set up by agents that we thought were on our side.

"These fellows were victimized by the double agents. Then, after they were picked up, the Chinese had some phony trial. I wouldn't call it a trial. It wasn't even a monkey trial, although it was a correct trial by Communist standards. Just because they were fighting against us doesn't mean that the trial was in any way illogical or illegal or improper. It was their trial and Downey and Fecteau were the victims. Those poor guys didn't have a chance.

"As you know, we used cover of all kinds. We used military as well as State Department cover at CIA. Downey and Fecteau were using military cover. Our Eighth Army was in the area; so, ostensibly, they were a part of that, even though they really were working for the CIA, dispatching our agents into China and North Korea. Jack Downey's mother publicly appealed to CIA director Allen Dulles to testify that her son was an American military officer, not an intelligence officer. Asking Allen Dulles? What a move! She literally convicted Jack to a jail sentence. Well, Dick got twenty years and Jack got life. Dick served until 1971 and Jack until 1973. Ironically, Jack was eventually released because his mother became very ill."

George's memories of this incident were incomplete. I later learned that Downey and Fecteau had trained to operate a special apparatus installed in a C-47 airplane that was designed to retrieve agents who had been deposited in enemy territory. The agent would lie on the ground, secured in a special harness. The harness would be attached to long lines hovering in the sky above him that were supported with balloons. The procedure called for the aircraft to swoop low to the ground, where special hooks would grasp the lines and thereby snatch the individual off the ground and up into the air. Downey and Fecteau then could reel him in just as they had in practice. However, for this event, late in November of 1952, they had been doublecrossed. On the fateful evening, the aircraft left a field near Seoul after dark, flew five hours into a remote area of Manchuria, and commenced the low-altitude mission track. As the plane dropped down to the rendezvous point, camouflaged Chinese artillery shot it down. Both American pilots were killed and the two CIA employees were captured. The weapons used to destroy the aircraft were American-made fifty-caliber machine guns supplied the Chinese during World War II.

At the time, Downey was twenty-two and Fecteau was twenty-five. There was no word of them for two years. Then the "show trial" was announced. Only then did their parents know that they were alive. Mrs. Downey appealed to four different presidents, their secretaries of state, various congressmen, the United Nations, and the Catholic Church trying to gain Jack's release.

Shortly after their releases, both were retired from the Agency and went on to successful lives in the civilian world. In June of 1998 they were awarded the Director's Medal for their bravery and loyalty while being incarcerated. On the back of the medals are inscribed the words *Extraordinary Fidelity and Essential Service.*

There were dozens of operations under way in the Far East at that time; not all of them were George's. He was supervising some of them, examining others, checking on some. He went to Hong Kong to do a damage report on a failed operation and to check on Agency resources there. In Hong Kong the CIA had agents, former White Russians working against the Reds. George had one agent who was the wife of an American banker.

I asked him, "How were they penetrating anything worthwhile in the USSR if they were American citizens living in Hong Kong?" He replied, "There was a whole rat line going from China through Hong Kong all the way down to Samar in the Philippines being run by the Communists. The White Russians knew all about them and they were reporting on them to us. We were taking advantage of anything that we could. The details are unimportant today; we are talking almost fifty years ago. The how and where, as well as who was loyal then, is now a moot question. We had penetrations everywhere, against us and for us. We had a lot of trouble with double agents at this time and lost a lot of people. So did everybody else. The whole thing was a complication. But you try to do what you are supposed to do, do what you can.

"A number of humorous things happened. In Hong Kong I made some money exchanges. We used yen for our transportation. Officially, it was 360 to the dollar at that time in Japan and in the United States. It was 400 to the dollar in Hong Kong. When I came back home to make my accounting of what the trip cost, I threw all of this credit on the table. Because of things like that the Agency got more money back than they put out. I didn't engineer it. That's just the way it was, if you follow me. The finance man didn't know what to do with the extra money.

"As soon as I reported back to my office, my next assignment, the one with Popov, was to commence."

The doorbell rang and George yelled, "Come in." A distinguished-looking, elderly lady entered and wryly looked at George as she handed him an envelope that obviously contained a sum of money. "We made a grand slam yesterday, which we shouldn't have," she said to him. "It's not fair for you to win every time, but I love having you as a partner." Noting that George seemed to be tiring, I excused myself. We would continue on another day.

PART II

Popov

CHAPTER 5

The Peasant

By the twilight of 1952, the fledgling CIA was still trying to establish itself among the world's espionage organizations. It needed a significant success. The Cold War was at its height and the Korean War stalemate continued, sometimes with cruel outbursts of hostilities. The U.S. intelligence community did not adequately understand the intelligence apparatus and methods of the Communist nations, particularly those of the Soviet Union. The Agency, however, was about to experience its first notable espionage coup, and George was to play the pivotal role. For six years, he would reel in a wealth of information from an in-place, high-ranking Soviet military intelligence officer and enable the compilation of a significant repository of Soviet military secrets. The information collected would provide the United States with its first insights into the structure of the Soviet Union's intelligence machine and reveal the threat that it posed to the free world. Moreover, the techniques George developed during the case led to an understanding of the people behind that threat—some of them insidious, some merely innocent pawns of their government, and some profoundly tragic. To be sure, the operation succeeded because of precise teamwork on the part of many in the Soviet Bloc Division of the CIA. But George established the beachhead, determined the ground rules of the operation, and delicately assembled the elements of an extraordinary success. He alone had the empathy for his Soviet agent that promoted the cooperation required for success. George simply had the unique ability to personally, and intimately, relate to a fellow human being. As a consequence, Pyotr Semyonovich Popov would trust none other than his father figure and friend, Georgi Georgievich Kisevalter, Jr.

In the early 1950s, the U.S. Army, the CIA, and the intelligence wings of all nations were nosing everywhere in Vienna for everything and everybody. The place was complex and intriguing, with spies everywhere. The 1950s film adaptation of Graham Greene's novel, *The Third Man,* starring Joseph Cotten and Orson Welles, recalls the atmosphere existing in Vienna at the time. All of Austria was still quartered: the French, the British, the Americans, and the Soviets each managed a zone. The city of Vienna, whose boundaries were entirely within the Soviet Zone, was divided into five sectors. Four of these were administered by one of the different allied countries on a somewhat permanent basis. The fifth zone was administered on a rotating basis, one month at a time.

On New Year's day of 1953 an American vice-consul stationed in Vienna was preparing to enter his car parked in the International Sector when he was interrupted by a man who obviously was tense and ill at ease. The man stood about five feet five inches in height, appeared to be about thirty years old, and had an olive complexion and the innocent, trusting look of a cherub. He was neatly dressed and, speaking German haltingly with an accent, asked for the directions to the American Commission for Austria. Notwithstanding the presence of his lady friend, the vice-consul dutifully offered the stranger a ride to the commission. The man demurred, handed the diplomat a letter, and then scurried away on foot.

The letter, dated 28 December 1952, was composed in Cyrillic and read as follows: "I am a Soviet officer. I wish to meet with an American officer with the object of offering certain services. Time: 1800 hours. Date: 1 January 1953. Place: Plankengasse, Vienna I. Failing this meeting, I will be at same place, same time, on succeeding Saturdays." The CIA mission chief thought this might result in something worthwhile. However, he was also leery that the overture might be merely an invitation to a provocation, and he did not deem it to be worth the exposure of any of his regular officers. He therefore decided to use a contract agent, a former Vlasov Army lieutenant, previously obtained through an émigré organization, for the initial meeting on 8 January.[1] Popov was on board.

For this first meeting, Ted Poling and another mission officer surreptitiously surveilled the candidate agent as he approached the tryst with the former Vlasov lieutenant. When they were satisfied that the prospect was clean, that is, not being followed by anyone, they proceeded to the meeting place and hid in a monitoring room before their contract agent and the prospect arrived. A minor oversight, however, almost blew their cover. Ted and his partner had been drinking beer during their stakeout of the rendezvous area, and after the interview got under way, they both needed to empty their bladders. Unfortunately, the bathroom was beyond the interview room from their location in the monitoring room. The interview was taking hours and they had to remain hidden. Eventually, they began to feel as though they were bursting at the seams. Ted looked up at the ceiling lamp, a cheap, giant, basin-shaped fixture. They loosened the lamp bowl, took it down, and relieved themselves in it. By the time the meeting was completed, the fixture was brimfull. Imagination is vital to the success of any enterprise.

At that time, George was on his way back to the States after a tiring trip to the Far East. He figured that he could now enjoy a lengthy spell at home after being away on such a long and difficult tour. When he got to Washington, the chief of operations called him in and said, "Look, everything is fine. You are home, here is your office, here is your desk; but don't unpack. We need you for something else." George stammered, "What is it? What am I going to be asked to do? Where is this?" "I want you to go to Vienna. A Soviet has just showed up," the chief replied. "We have no one else to handle him. The only person there now who can meaningfully react to this situation is a Russian national émigré we have working for us. He was okay for the initial contact but he may scare off any future relationship with the prospect." "Why me?" George persisted. "Because you speak Russian and you are old enough to convince the fellow that everything will be all right. Besides, your papers are already in order and it would take too long to get someone else processed and ready. You have a passport in hand; you are ready right now. All you need is some money and a ticket. Now grab the plane and fly." That is how he went to Vienna. It was a matter of convenient circumstances for the Agency and not so much George's desire. It, however, worked to his everlasting benefit.

When George arrived in Vienna, he was briefed on what had already transpired and what was known of the potential collaborator. That first meeting had gone well, so he was hopeful that he could develop the contact if he reappeared. Luck was with the mission. The Soviet took a chance and came again. George met the adventurous man and reassured him that he himself was for real. They hit it off as soon as they met. The incipient agent immediately sensed a warmth in George that emboldened him. They apprehensively revealed to each other their personal credentials and laughed because they both knew that all of the documents were phony. They decided to tell each other the truth, and this cemented their relationship for some 100 meetings that took place in two different countries over a period of almost six years.

In this particular operation, the CIA was not involved with the British or any other nation; therefore, there were no international sensitivities to be trampled on or otherwise offended. No intelligence organization likes to share its methods and schemes. During most of George's stay there, he was living in the British sector in order to be away from the Americans and avoid any accidental encounter that might jeopardize security. He even had a British car. He knew Agency people there but avoided them like the plague. He couldn't live anywhere near these people; they shouldn't know who he was. He couldn't attend the American social events because there were many unsecured local employees attending these affairs. He was so removed from the Americans there that one time U.S. military personnel, the Counter Intelligence Corps (CIC), arrested him because he appeared strange and suspicious to them. Living like that was very difficult. George had no one to talk with except security people and the defector. This condition of solitude ultimately led to his meeting the lady who would become his second wife and to his divorce from Velma.

The one exception for socializing was poker nights. Occasionally, George would meet for cards with a group of Agency people he knew and trusted. He would sneak in and out of some prescribed location for these events. They played poker in sectors under U.S. control, of course, either the American sector, British sector, or the French sector. In a sense, the defector was the best friend that George had there. He was the one with whom George seemed to have the most contact.[2]

George pretended to be a different American with a different name—an assistant airline pilot shuttling back and forth between Salzburg and Vienna. He might have gotten onto such a plane once, just to look at it, but he never flew any plane. He was given a permanent change of station after being there on a temporary basis for six months.[3] The people at headquarters said, "Let George stay there. Keep his wife out of Vienna. Let him live black.[4] Let him stay away from all of the Americans. He's doing fine. Nobody knows who he is, and the Soviets will never be on to him." So, he lived that way, black, for seven years.

Popov came to the Americans because he had a problem. It was a reasonable problem and George understood it. He needed money to get off the hook. When George helped him with it, Popov saw that George was honest. They then got along. Later Popov shared with George his philosophy of life as well as his knowledge of and experience with the peasant existence. Eventually, he said, "I'm glad I approached the Americans. They are more powerful than the British, and although the British are good people and I like them, my motive is to help my fellow peasants. I can do that better with the Americans. If that helps you too, then good; we both believe that Communism is a negative."

He approached the United States because, to him, it was the most powerful country in the world. He believed that the United States could do something to help the peasants graduate to the general category of people who are human. This disparity of humanity was something that he, as he became older and more educated, began to see more and more sharply. For instance, he once said, "The song, 'The Volga Boatman,' is a misnomer. The song attempts to show that the Russian peasant is fit to do the work of a beast of burden. I want the peasant to be a human being." Therefore, he had his own social-political ambitions.

George's life with Popov was meticulously designed. For example, if Popov and he had a meeting, it would be in some safehouse, lived in by unwitting Americans. The pair used three or four different locations for these safehouses and everything was recorded. Popov never knew it. George had to set up the tapes before each meeting, but he had technicians arrange the equipment so that he could simply press a button and the tapes would roll.

They would always have available some sweetmeats, cakes, sandwiches, and a bottle of vodka to make things comfortable. Before each engagement, George personally went to Cafe Sacher in Vienna, selected certain special delicacies, and carried them up the three or more flights of stairs to that safehouse. George's great attention to detail helped to ensure the success of his many endeavors.

Popov and George would start by visiting socially. They might have a friendly drink for an icebreaker, but they never got drunk.[5] At the end of the meeting, after Popov had left, George would collect all of the bottles and the rest of the garbage, put them in a special bag, and take them all to the city dump. This was done so that no one in the area would see any incriminating evidence, such as the foreign or exotic items, the vodka, or anything else. Doing these things was a part of George's life. When the meetings were over, he would pick up the tapes and garbage and get out of there.

In *Mole,* William Hood's version of the Popov affair, George is the case officer Gregory Domnin. I had read the book but I did not know much about George's personal involvement in the operation, so I asked him to recall those events. George began, "I can tell you all about the way of the man, which in itself is not a philosophy but a truism, that few people, who are not Russians, who are not Slavs, who are not peasants, could understand. I learned from him more about peasants than I could ever have known from any other source. Now I appreciate them more and respect them more as generous, hard-working creatures of God, who are earthy, who love the soil, who love to grow plants from the ground, who love to be diligent, and who love to work very hard. Of course, they are not well educated. Few of them reached any intellectual stature to speak of, either in literacy or any standard of education related to book learning of any kind. I don't think many of them went much beyond what we call elementary school, if that, in the old days. They would be illiterate and they would be ridiculed because of their lack of education. Consequently, they would be willing to say yes to anyone who had a social status higher than their own, which was about everybody. Humility, of course, was their long suit. Like anyone else who would drink too much, debauchery would victimize their behavior and make them look stupid. If they were drunk, they would do things that would be unacceptable, socially, like any other drunk, whether he was a millionaire or a pauper. Unfortunately for them, however, in order to seek escape from their circumstances, they too often were drunk. But to summarize: Popov's own one-sentence definition of a peasant was 'someone to be starved, beaten, ridiculed, exploited, and then used as cannon fodder in war.'

"We gave him a salary. He received only a portion of it. That which we paid him was issued in Austrian shillings or in German marks. He received only as much as he could logically have on his person without attracting undue attention. The rest we kept for him in trust. Actually, there is an account still in existence for him. We owe him a small fortune. He never received 50 percent of his wages for a period of almost seven years. It is all put away, deposited in a fictitious name, in a Washington, D.C., bank. We owe him what is his. It is his money, a salary. It is not a gratuity. We are just custodians of the money he never received.[6] More than that, whatever else he received, he got in kind: a few shirts; socks; soap with which to wash them; toiletries for use when he went out of town; boots, very nicely fur lined, etc. His mother-in-law had a shoe size the same as he, so he didn't even get to keep his. His wife got another pair. I think that he had a girlfriend for whom he bought a raincoat. He usually got things of value to wear. He was always giving things that he earned to somebody else. In short, he gave to anyone in this world whom he liked what he or she didn't have, and he kept nothing for himself. That is the kind of man he was. You cannot call him a mercenary. He was a wonderful man with a heart of gold. He treated me like a brother. I thank God that I knew the man.

"As an example of his orientation, let me tell you of the thing that captured his greatest interest regarding America or Americans. For propaganda purposes, it would be the general custom of Americans abroad in intelligence to have certain magazines or attractive advertisement brochures dealing with American life or American accomplishments lying about in the safehouses. Sometimes these would be the current issues of *Life* or *Time* or something of that sort. In our safehouses we had those, not in a prolific way, but say, numbering to maybe half a dozen. But he would make a beeline for one and one only, *The American Farm Journal.* He wanted to know if American rural people or American farmers really owned tractors. Could things really be like they were displayed in *The American Farm Journal?* What a civilization the Americans had created for themselves! Are there many Russian peasants who have immigrated to the United States? How are they doing? Do they have land? Do they have tractors? Are they prosperous? Are they diligent? Are they worthy of the success they experience? It was an attraction to him for those reasons. Nationalism, language, geography had nothing to do with this. It was only a human attitude, and this incessant curiosity about *The American Farm Journal,* derived from just browsing through it, indicates what kind of thinker he was. The hell with all others: *Time, Life,* and flashy cars, fancy advertising, etc.

"His generosity, as I mentioned before, was far reaching. Once, I smuggled out of Switzerland and gave to him some black-market rubles, what we in the trade refer to as 'red roses.' He thus didn't have to make a money exchange, which could have been dangerous for him. He didn't even have to account for how he got the rubles; he could simply claim that he had sold some old heirloom of gold on the black market. He took the money, went to the home of his sister and his brother, a *kolkhoz* [collective farm], then bought a calf and gave it to them so that they could have milk. We laughingly claimed to have a CIA calf in the Soviet Union.

"His name was Pyotr Semyonovich Popov, that is: Peter, son of Simon, Popov in English. At that time he was a major in the GRU, as opposed to KGB, a military intelligence officer assigned to one of the GRU *rezidenturas* [cover office of an intelligence operation] in Vienna since November of 1951, a very fine, moral person in terms of what was right and what was wrong.[7]

"Popov told me how the peasants revolted and were severely punished before finally being forced, in a very recalcitrant manner and under bayonets, into a collective farm, a *kolkhoz,* formed during the 1930s under Stalin. The story was so simple. They said to the intruders, 'Look, you're soldiers, you have bayonets. You're prodding us. You're also Russians, aren't you?'

"'Yes.'

"'You speak Russian, don't you?'

"'Yes.'

"'It says something on the corner of your rifle—*RKKA*. That means the red flag of workers and peasants. You are workers, we are peasants; we are the ones who put you in power. We are workers and peasants. Red Army, is that right?'

"'Yes.'

'Then why are your bayonets pushing us to force us to a concentration camp?'

"'Shut up. We are sick and tired of listening to your bleating. You peasants made your first mistake when you believed us.'

"That is Communism. So, with this philosophy, he knew which way was up and what was the truth. Moreover, when father repeats to son and mother repeats to daughter the memory, 'We made our first mistake when we believed them,' I can assure you that for the 150 million peasants who lived in the Soviet Union, this small error would not occur again. So, those are the fundamental lessons he had learned.

"Well, enough of the idealism of the man. He was oriented to the rugged outdoors and able. He had native talent. When I say native, I mean like this: he was a crack shot with a rifle; he was a marksman who could compete for his unit and win prizes in all kinds of rivalry from amateur sports to military competition. He also was an avid fisherman, as many Russians are, particularly peasants. He was a very earthy man. For example, instead of going to a resort, to which an officer on leave would be entitled when coming back from rotation on a long tour on overseas assignments, he would make a beeline for his little peasant village *kolkhoz*. There he would shed his high-ranking uniform (being the only officer in the history of the little town) and walk around barefoot, eating cucumbers, fishing in the Volga River and talking to other peasants, as if they were brothers. Being one of them, he was just townfolk.

"Once, to try to make it up to me for having wasted all of his vacation time on these 'indulgences,' he said, 'When I was fishing up and down the Volga, I saw, across the river, an airfield. I made a sketch for you; here it is. So, I didn't waste my time.' Well, that was just fine. But of course, there were a few times over the period of more than six years when he did go to various resorts. After all, during that period he had at least six vacations of thirty days or so. In those places he had conversations with many of the officers of various parts of the USSR who came from many different types of military assignments to these vacations. We picked up a lot information from these conversations, including the location of many potential missile sites as well as assorted nuclear activity. Strange as it may seem, that kind of conversation gets bandied about in whispers much more often than it should be. Most people are blabbermouths by nature.

"His family came from a small peasant village by the name of Kineshma, near a larger town by the name of Ivanov, northeast of Moscow about 125 miles. In olden days the capital of the region was called Tver, which lies to the west of Ivanov. It's an old city, begun in 1180 A.D. as a fort in the western part of what was then called the Suzdal principality. For two centuries Tver was the capital and a longtime rival of Moscow for supremacy in Russia, but the regions were annexed in 1490 under Ivan III. It suffered a great massacre of its citizens in 1570 under Ivan the Terrible. In 1932 Tver was renamed Kalinin in honor of a Soviet hero. It was taken by the Germans in the autumn of 1941 and retaken by the Soviets in December of 1941. The district straddles the Volga River and is on the Moscow-to-Leningrad railroad.

"The story of Popov's older brother has a moral application that might be difficult for some to comprehend. It is a tremendously heartbreaking story with a great deal of significance. It involves the abuse of the uneducated peasants. His father's name, Simon, would never have come to anyone's attention were it not for a group of human circumstances. As a student of irony I know you will relish this. It is absolutely true.

"Theirs was a very submarginal but free peasant village. There were no collective farms at the time; this was after World War I, the Russian Revolution, and the Counterrevolution, just before Stalin's collectivization took place. Pyotr had two brothers and one sister. The sister's name was Lyuba and the oldest brother's name was Alexander. I cannot remember the other brother's name. He had a crippling physical problem, a bad heart; but he also had a little bit of influence in the local village. He was very smart but, like everyone else in the family, uneducated. He could read and write, which really was a big plus for a peasant; so, he was more or less the village bookkeeper, which was a low-paying and hard job. The bookkeeper is not the highest-paid professional in a farm community. The mother had died long before our story begins, but the father was highly respected in the community, even though he was ignorant and uneducated. He also was a popular person in that neighborhood. People would often come by in the evening and, to use an expression of Pyotr's, 'just sit around on the fence and jaw about events of the day.' This was a mark of a little bit of distinction for the father because there wasn't much else in the way of social interaction in the community. The father not only was respected for his earthy wisdom, even though illiterate, but he was highly regarded for his generosity. He often would glance at a neighbor and say, 'Look at that poor man. He has three daughters and only one son. We have three boys; let's help him with his hay.' So, he would balance off mutually needed physical work in this very submarginal area. I know the area; I looked it up in the literature and read about it.

"Now, in those days the district designations were being changed to new names, in order to reflect the change in status from a Tsarist Russia to a Communist Soviet Union. It was originally Ivanovsky. Then, at the time that our story takes place, it was changed to the name of Kalinin District, or Oblast.

"Mikhail Ivanovich Kalinin was the very unattractive, goat-shape-faced man who was, nominally, the leader of the USSR, its first president. His job was politically impotent. He was the titular head of the nation, serving only for ceremonial purposes. Still, his face and the name, Kalinin, were everywhere, even now. Kaliningrad, the new name of the old city of Konigsberg, was named for him. Kalinin was not politically or intellectually, or in any other way, a distinctive man or even important except for this story.

"This history is related to our story by the mere fact that the Popov family was living in a district using the new name Kalinin. The tale takes place during the height of collectivization. This is the period when the peasants were being prodded with bayonets to march off their small, submarginal farms, on which one could hardly eke out a living, and onto some collective farm. When the collective delegation came to the Popov farm, they so infuriated Alexander, the big brother, that a row ensued. Alexander was a giant of a man, very tall and strong. When the commissar leading this delegation began to coax the family to move on and get off the farm, their farm, Alexander became so infuriated that he grabbed the commissar and heaved the man right through their oaken front door. As a consequence, the whole family wound up in the local jug.

"So there they were, sitting on the straw-strewn or otherwise bare ground of a cell, commiserating with one another. Finally, one of them said, 'We have to do something. We are going to be forced to go anyway, and we'll probably be beaten and receive all kinds of other penalties.' So, they began, collectively, with the help of the one crippled son, to write a letter, each one suggesting what the next word of the letter should be. It was a joint effort by a bunch of dumbbells, only one of whom was literate enough to form words. The letter was addressed to Comrade Kalinin, president of the USSR, and sought, without specific remedy, some solution to their plight. Since Kalinin himself had once been a peasant and had advertised himself as a friend of the peasants, they believed that they had reason to hope for success in the endeavor. It read roughly as follows:

"We poor peasants, now living in the district of Kalinin Oblast, named in your honor, are being mercilessly, cruelly, unfairly, and unjustly pushed around. We don't think that you would like this if you knew about it, or permit this type of persecution in a place of your name; so, we are appealing collectively to you as diligent peasants for your help. They are forcing us into this situation. We are not kulaks [tight-fisted, rich peasants]. We are just poor peasants who simply want to work hard and survive. We don't think that you would have peasants treated this way, especially in the district named after you, because you too are an honorable man.

"Miraculously, the letter got to its destination. When Kalinin read it, he thought that he could see political advantage in making a little bit of noise and advertising his action. He ordered restitution made to the family, restitution of a strange nature. So, from Moscow, like lightning striking, in came orders to the local commissar to release the Popovs. That commissar came to the place of their incarceration and addressed the family.

"'We have orders from Moscow to get you out of the jug. Alexander, how would you like to be a commissar?'

"'I won't have anything to do with it.'

"'Well, look, we've got to do something. What do you want?'

"'I want to get out of here with my wife.'

"'Well, let's be practical. You can't just leave this circumstance and take her with you. You have to buy her way out.'

"'So what does it cost?'

"'Well, money is not worth much today—so many 100-kilogram bags of flour, this, that, and the other.'

"'Okay, I'll take it.'

"'You'll take what?'

"'I'll take the freedom for that price. Just you watch.'

"So, he bundled up his sheets, clothing, and all the things that he owned, wrapped them up on his back, and left the area. Where did he go? He went into the woods. Where in the woods did he go? He went to the head of a small lumber plant that belonged to the Lumber Trust and he went to work. He could hew lumber faster and better than anyone else in the area could, being a strong, strong man. The people there instantly considered him to be a great person. They encouraged him:

"'Look, we'll help you throw together a log cabin.'

"'Fine.'

"'You can throw a few potatoes in the ground here. This is Lumber Trust land; it's all right.'

"'How about meat? Can I go out hunting?'

"'You can hunt, too.'

"'Fine, I'll go out hunting. I can hunt for money.'

"'How do you mean?'

"'Well, there are certain animals called martens. They are relatives of sable and similar to mink.'

"Thus, he became a super hunter, and the furs were worth quite a bit of money. Eventually, he began to accumulate some money. He went back with so many 100-kilogram bags of flour, ransomed his wife from the Soviet Union, and took her to the woods. (This was the first pioneer and entrepreneur I heard of in the Soviet Union.) That wasn't enough, however. That was just the beginning. He then came back to the *kolkhoz* where his family lived and where his reputation was sky high among the locals. He got hold of our Pyotr, his brother, and said, 'Petya (which is Russian for Pete), somebody in our family has to be educated. I have just elected you. I know that you are a dope, but you will learn. You never wear real shoes; you wear those soft handwoven things. I am going to buy you some good shoes. I know that they hurt your feet, but you are going to learn how to wear them and you will get used to them. Also, from now on, you are going to go to school, away from the *kolkhoz.*'

"So he put the kid, at thirteen years of age, into grammar school. Pyotr finished grammar school and then went to high school. Four years later, just as he was finishing high school, *bang, bang,* the Germans invaded. Popov and his classmates in their little school in the country immediately formed a regiment and left to defend the town of Tula, a city about 100 miles south of Moscow. He became a second lieutenant in the Quartermaster Corps, not knowing anything else. The Germans attacked. Tula was in a vise. It was surrounded, but the defense held. There was a tremendously cold winter and the Germans almost froze to death. The temperature plummeted to as low as forty degrees below zero. Their tanks wouldn't work as the oil in them froze.

"Popov survived that winter and was promoted to the rank of first lieutenant. His job became that of a supply officer for the Quartermaster Corps, providing *katyusha* (a multi-rocket launcher) rounds for those automatic weapons. The challenge of his work was no big deal. He did get slightly wounded, but he continued on in the war as one of the very few peasant officers in the army.

"Suddenly, in March of 1944, back to headquarters he was summoned. There, someone tapped his shoulder and began to talk with him:

"'Popov, you are now twenty-three years old. We have just won a tremendous victory at Leningrad. Do you know where that is?'

"'Yes. What do you want with me?'

"'Well, the reason that we have you here is that we would like to send you to a very good school, which can advance your career. It is called the Frunze Military Academy.[8] It's the highest military school in the USSR. Do you know about the school?'

"'Yes.'

"'Well, we lost many men at the defenses of Stalingrad, Leningrad, and Moscow. We have lost the majority of our officers, some by attrition, many by death; we have schools with advanced academics and we need people to enroll in these schools.'

"'Why me? I am a peasant.'

"'Exactly; you are politically clean, clean as a hound's tooth. We have nothing against you, politically, and we don't have anybody else for the school. How would you like to go to the Frunze Military Academy?'

"'Fine.'

"Shortly thereafter he acquired a girlfriend. Her family was from the city of Kalinin, but she now was in Moscow, teaching German to intelligence officers there at an intelligence academy. The pair were married later that year and he was able to share with her his private apartment. He was graduated in 1948 and received a diploma from the school. He became a captain, and the commissar came and grabbed him.

"'Popov, come here. Let's go to the general's headquarters in Moscow. Popov, you are a peasant. You are doing well for a peasant. You became an officer; you are now a captain. How would you like to continue on to another academy? A higher academy.'

"'Me?'

"'Yes, you.'

"'Why me?'

"'We don't have enough students who are politically clean like you, a peasant.'

"'Can I keep my apartment? Can my wife stay with me?'

"'Yes, we can arrange that too.'

"So, for an apartment, a place to live in Moscow, he attended the Military Diplomatic Academy, which is the intelligence school for the military. Now, they have to study a language in this academy. He could read and write Russian, but languages were not his forte. He therefore elected to study the Serbo-Croatian language and military intelligence operations toward Yugoslavia. Why? 'Because the people there swear just like the Russian peasants,' he said. 'I can understand their language—*screw this, screw that'*; whatever the equivalents are. So, choosing the language that was easiest for him, he laid down his future. Thus, with this peasant-like logic, his choice of an operational direction gelled. He was graduated, I believe, in the class of June 1951. Since he was to go to Vienna, he also had to learn some

German. That was very difficult for him, but his wife, who was a good linguist, helped him and he was on his way. From Vienna, where they had operations against Yugoslavia, he could cultivate Yugoslavian agents, swearing like Russian peasants, and he could understand some of what was going on. So, that is how he eventually came to Vienna in November of 1951. Incidentally, I later had to help him with some with his German so that he could properly order beer in the restaurants there.

"That was the nature of the man. The matters on which he was reporting to us were whatever rumors he heard from any of his fellow case officers. Remember that he was an intelligence officer and a member of a strategic intelligence residency at a high level. The Vienna residency had many targets among the British, the Americans, and others, as well as targets involving multiple nationalities. He wouldn't know every detail, for he couldn't look into the personal files of every officer; but he did his best. We devised some means with him of forging a special key that would give him access to sealed, classified documents. He would use this to read the documents and make extracts. Afterwards, he would reseal the documents and replace them. This way we could find out who was doing what to whom.

"When we found out something from him, we never took immediate action. To do so would jeopardize him, since the Soviets would realize that a leak had occurred, and possibly could determine where the leak was. It was amazing to what degree we found out things from him. He brought us so much. For instance, when he was on duty at night, he could gain access to the monthly payroll. He copied the whole thing and it contained all kinds of exotic information. We found out who had received special prizes or rewards in money for linguistic accomplishments, who would be next in line for promotion, who did this, who did that, as well as quite a lot of biographic data on every officer involved. These were intelligence officers. So, we made a roster of their organization that displayed just where everyone was assigned, against which country and in which location, as well as their linguistic competence, notably, of course, in handling English.

"He gave us much military information. In some cases we were able to contradict what the Pentagon thought they knew about certain things. For example, there was a particular tank on which he reported. I think it might have been T-10. It was described in detail as a new monster tank. It was not called a 'Joseph Stalin' tank. It was labeled with a numerical designation, with a *T* before the number. Eventually the tanks would be designated T-10, T-54, T-78, etc., for different categories and vintages. This was a radical change from the procedure previously followed (e.g., JS-1, JS-2, JS-3), where everything was Joe Stalin this, Joe Stalin that.

"The Pentagon questioned this report. 'What kind of reporting is that? What is the authority for such a report?' they demanded. His authority was the cutest thing in the world. He told me, 'You know, when I was very much younger and the war was on, my rank was low; I was a lieutenant. I knew a young man who was an up-and-coming officer. He became a colonel and he became very prominent. He became a hero of the Soviet Union and was killed. He had a wife and he had a son. He also had friends. Some of his friends were far more prominent than I. One was the chief of our military intelligence in the Soviet Union, the GRU, who just happened to be my boss at the time.'

"I said, 'So, what happened?' Pyotr went on, 'Well, I was visiting on leave in Moscow, to see the widow of my friend who was killed. She told me that her husband's friend, who was then my boss, the chief of intelligence, had just gotten word of a new assignment of some distinction in the show division of Moscow. That is where they planned for the parades, and it had all of the latest equipment, tanks, etc., which they exhibited in the parades. Also, her son, the son of the deceased war hero, had a job as a commander of a tank platoon; he was the driver of the brand-new T-10 tank.'

"The question was, 'Why did that series have *T* for designation?' They used to be designated as the Joseph V. Stalin series. He said, 'First of all, Stalin died last year. (This was 1954.) People are sick and tired of having everything named after Joseph Stalin. So, they gave it back the dignified name of "tank." Moreover, they gave it a number corresponding to its place in the sequence of technical development. And if he's the driver, he ought to know what the heck he is driving. Also, I spoke to his mother, and I spoke to my boss who is a general who also ought to know a tank from a peanut, and that is the new tank! That is my authority for my statement.'

"The Pentagon had to swallow this one. That story was far too convincing. It was very embarrassing for them, very human. But it shows how the truth in intelligence can sometimes be hard to digest. And you can see how a simple thing like the re-designation of a piece of hardware can have major implications. It reflected some of the growing disdain that the military had for J. V. Stalin, as well as an advance in technology of their weaponry.

"Once, when he went away, I had to wait for him a few months without knowing whether or not he would return. He had been reassigned. I found him on the street and gave him a high sign. He followed me to the safehouse, which was then vacant and wide open. I was able to display all areas in the place in order to demonstrate to him that there were no wires for tape recorders. He thus was reassured that there was no taping of our conversations. He left, comfortable in that knowledge. When he came back for the appointment later, however, it was completely and expertly outfitted for the taping of our session."

The process of George meeting with Popov and charging him to find out things worked out very favorably for the CIA the entire time George was in Vienna. It was a great deal of work for George and it involved many things. In Vienna, sixty-six meetings were held; each lasted anywhere from a half-hour to four hours. A great deal of information was passed. The Agency also acquired a great number of documents and a lot of material that Popov brought with him. George photographed these before Popov returned them to their rightful repository. From headquarters George was getting instructions by cable. "Find this out; find that out; don't let him get into trouble; control him. Don't let him freewheel." Popov wanted to freewheel with the women a little bit. He had a girlfriend. George made sure that he didn't get himself exposed and under criticism by his people, so he did everything he could for Popov. As George stated, "I babysat with him; I even had venereal-disease medications with me for him if he needed them. To make sure that nothing evil happened to him I had to be very, very circumspect."

CHAPTER 6

Ferdi

During this period, while George was meeting with Popov in Vienna, he had little contact with Washington, or even with Americans in Vienna. It was then that George met Ferdi. He was alone. She was a Viennese widow with a small pension. Her husband had disappeared during the war. She had two children by that marriage, Ferdenand and Karl.

About three months after he arrived in Vienna George and Ferdi met through Austrian friends at a garden party in downtown Vienna. Because he spoke German with a Russian accent, Ferdi at first thought George was a Soviet. Accordingly, she told him that she wouldn't have anything to do with him. He countered with the story that he was an American pilot going back and forth between Salzburg and Vienna. He said he was Joe Palmer, a name he invented just for her; no one else knew of it. So, she called him Joe Palmer for two years. The romance began when he took her home from the party and then asked her for a date. They went to the Mess Shop.

Then George had to disappear—not because of her but because of his job with the Russian, Popov. He had to get away from almost all American associations since it was too easy to be spotted. At the time, he was living in the Cottage Hotel in the American sector, which was the center of most American activities. The Agency had leased it and more or less controlled it. The CIA people determined that George had to get out of there. He asked what was available in black housing facilities. They could get him an apartment under a phony name. They would guarantee the rent and they could guarantee the coal. George found an apartment, which was far out of town, in the British Zone—away from the Americans. He had a date with Ferdi and said, "Look, you won't understand this, but I have to move from where I am." She said, "I will help you."

They drove up to the Cottage Hotel and, armful by armful, he dumped all of his clothes, with suitcases half-packed, into his car. He wasn't pretending to travel, so he just dragged the things out piece by piece and filled the car. It was a QP car,[1] a British one, and an official car. It had an Austrian license plate and an Austrian registration under a phony name.

When he completed packing the vehicle, they took off to the new premises. Ferdi helped him set up the apartment, which was half of a huge duplex. The owner occupied the other half. He was a dentist who had a wife and two children and conducted his dental practice there in his house. George had a private entrance into one side of the house. He had a beautiful bathroom, a kitchen, a living room, and a great big bedroom with an anteroom. The dentist was delighted to have George as a tenant because his overhead was very high and he had no coal. George guaranteed the coal and they had an abundance of the fuel. It was American coal; a mountain in Pennsylvania was moved to Austria.

George continued with his story. "You'd die laughing at some of the comical-type activities that went on there. During the course of one hot Sunday, thirteen strangers barged through my door. The lady who did my laundry came in unannounced. Some mailman who had mistaken an address knocked on my door. 'Are you a Burglar?' he inquired. I said, 'Do I look like a burglar?' He goes, 'You live here? Look at your number; look at this letter!' Uh oh, the mail was addressed to a 'Burglar,' a female. A football flies through the open window; kids come in to get it. Anyway, thirteen assorted people, all Austrians, from different walks of life, barge into my living room on that particular Sunday, and I'm still in my bathrobe.[2] So, I was camouflaged, believe you me. I was in deep cover. There was some broken-down garden where I parked my car. I paid five shillings—that's twenty-five cents—a week to keep it off the street. From there I could walk in through the back door to my apartment.

"One night I had Ferdi over to eat. She stayed overnight with me. Well, this starts a romance. After all, we are human. That is what happened. We fell in love, all right? What the hell, she was free; she was a widow. She liked me. She said, 'Well, as long as I'm here, I'll stay if you want me.' So, I said, 'If you'll cook, do this and that, I'll go to work and I'll take care of you. On the weekends, now and then, I have to be away; I have to go to Salzburg.' Which was my way of telling her that's how it was. So she lived with me the rest of the time I was in Vienna. We had fallen in love. I know that it was scandalous, but, you see, I had been alone for a long time, eleven years actually, when you come down to it. There were the five years of the army, including four of war. There were the five years when I was in Gothenburg, Nebraska, running the alfalfa operation. During that time Velma was eighty miles away in McCook taking care of her family and the jewelry store. It wasn't that she did not want to be with me there in Nebraska; she simply felt that she had to take care of her parents. There also was a year of Agency TDY. Velma and I were already, in a sense, breaking up. She was forbidden, for security reasons, to go to Vienna. I was living black and the Agency didn't want her there. She lived in Salzburg. They put her there. I spent most weekends in Salzburg with her and weekdays in Vienna with Ferdi."

George was at least somewhat complicit in the arrangement to keep Velma in Salzburg. He wanted it that way, especially after he began his romance with Ferdi. The American contingent in Vienna cooperated with George, although they were very much concerned with the Ferdi affair. They feared that the operation with Popov, the Agency's foremost intelligence asset at the time, could be jeopardized, particularly since Ferdi was an individual unknown to them. Moreover, Vienna was quite a dangerous place, with kidnappings routine. Perhaps George's safety could be in jeopardy.

George's friend, Dick Kovich, provided additional insight into the situation. He disclosed that when Velma first learned she was to be in Salzburg, she was delighted. The music, history, and atmosphere were things that she so loved. She would be quite at home in the town since it was so steeped in musical history. But she was advised that, for reasons of security, she would be there without George. He would be in Vienna. She did not expect to be so fatefully separated from George while there. In 1953 Kovich made a trip to Germany and took a side trip to Salzburg in order to visit his good friends, Velma and George. He arrived in Salzburg on Thursday. George would not arrive until the next day so Dick had dinner with Velma. She appeared very happy although she was not pleased that she could not be with George all of the time. George arrived on the military train on Friday and Velma prepared a wonderful dinner. She had no idea that George was seeing someone else. Dick knew then about George's liaison with the other woman but said nothing. He resolved not to get himself involved or to take sides because he loved them both. George said nothing to Dick about the awkward situation, but he seemed to sense that Dick knew of it. It was also clear to Dick that George was anxious to get back on the train that Sunday to return to Vienna. He was very much in love with the other woman and he preferred to be with her.

Kovich found the situation so coincidental. George's mother had gone from Le Creusot in France to Vienna to be a schoolteacher. George's father had come all the way from St. Petersburg to Vienna, where he had met his bride. Now George was here, possibly for the first time in his life, and he had fallen in love with this Viennese woman.

George went on: "Velma tended to yap too much on the telephone. She would say things that she shouldn't say. I'd usually speak French to her because it was more comforting to her, in the false sense of security that it suggested. Unbeknown to me, she had a case officer watching out for her welfare. Her phone was tapped and he was reporting on her and on me. When I found out about this, it made me nearly blow my stack. I was madder than hell with them for pulling one like that. It also caused me to get caught in a mousetrap.

"The mousetrap was terrible. Peter Deriabin defected to us in Vienna on Valentine's Day of 1954. He was a Soviet KGB officer, a major.[3] We had the delicate problem of getting him out of Vienna, which was well inside the Soviet Zone, to a safe place in the American Zone. From there he could be flown back to the States. The Soviets would kill him if they could get their hands on him. We couldn't fly him out because the weather had the planes socked in. Even if the weather had been good, we would have been afraid to fly him out for fear that they might shoot down the plane. I knew our chief of technology. We figured out a scheme to get him out of the zone. We engineered a large box with holes drilled through so that he could breathe, and put him inside. We then put the box with him in it on a train going to the American Zone. When we got him out of the box he went immediately to a safehouse in, of all places, Salzburg. So, there the confused guy is, in Salzburg. Naturally, I knew about it."

Ted Poling later explained the events surrounding Peter

Deriabin's defection to the CIA in Vienna. Ted was the first CIA man to debrief him. A day or so before Deriabin defected, a junior Soviet trade-mission official, not an intelligence type, had defected. Ted was debriefing this man when he received a call from his chief, who said, "Drop everything. We have a more important fish on the line."

Ted then ran over to talk with Deriabin. The CIC (Counter Intelligence Corps) had him. Apparently he had simply appeared on their doorstep. After establishing rapport with him, Ted began to determine the reasons Deriabin had defected. First of all, a great cloud was hanging over the KGB following the Lavrenti Pavlovich Beria purges. Secondly, since the trade officer, one of Deriabin's own flock, had left, Deriabin would be held responsible and could face punishment. Finally, Deriabin's marriage had become unpleasant for him. Ted began with a standard list of questions: "Who are you? Why are you here? Do you have any information relative to an imminent Soviet attack?" When Deriabin responded that he was KGB, Ted immediately wanted to know what his position there was and who his American agents were. Then he wanted to know who his British agents were, his French agents, and the ones from other countries. Deriabin replied that he was responsible for the security of the whole Soviet colony in Vienna. His cover was that of a consul. When Ted got to the list of agents of other nationalities, the defector mentioned "Stroitel," which is a Russian word for constructor or builder. Stroitel was the chief engineer of all of the construction projects for the Central Group of Forces in Austria. Poling immediately recognized this agent as one of his own, a Russian émigré from Czechoslovakia who had resumed Soviet citizenship. The Agency's code name for him was "Greatcoat." Ted realized that both of them were "running" the same man. Or Stroitel, a.k.a. Greatcoat, was playing both of them, in order to survive. Ted reflected that he was now face to face with his opposite number in Deriabin, but he continued with his questioning, trying not to tip his hand. Deriabin added that Stroitel had described his American case officer as a man named "Captain Peterson, who had brown hair, brown eyes, glasses, medium build, and wrote with his left hand," all characteristics of Ted Poling, who had been taking copious notes.[4]

Deriabin had come to the CIA at about 6:00 P.M. By 1:00 the next afternoon, the CIA Vienna mission had him initially debriefed and packed into a wooden, casket-shaped crate engineered by George. There were military markings stenciled on the box to make it look like soldier's equipment. Four soldiers from Counter Intelligence Corps carried the crate through the passenger entrance to the train station, put it in a baggage car on the *Mozart,* which was headed for the American Zone, and sat with it, weapons at the ready. Bill Hood and Ted bought tickets and planted themselves in seats up front. They sat there with fingers crossed, hoping against hope that the scheme would be successful. The *Mozart* was a special train and the Soviets were not supposed to interfere in any way with U.S. personnel or their belongings on it. It had diplomatic immunity, but the U.S. had agreed with the Soviets not to use the train for any adverse military or espionage activity. The Soviets did not challenge the American personnel or threaten to open the box. When the train arrived in Linz, within the American Zone, CIC personnel knocked out the back of the crate. Deriabin, after many hours in the dark, was met with a cascade of flashbulbs. This irritated him, but that was the way of the CIC. He pleaded with his masters to allow him to relieve himself before commencing with the standard reception interrogation.[5]

George went on. "Suddenly, the chief confronted me:

"'Are you speaking on the telephone in French with your wife in Salzburg?'

"'Yes. What of it?'

"'Did you tell her that the defector was coming there?'

"'Certainly not! Why?'

"'Did you tell her about the box?'

"'Tell her about the box? No! Why would I do that?'

"Well, everybody was talking about a new movie about World War II, *The Man Who Never Was,* with Clifton Webb. It was very popular at the time. The story was about a dead body delivered to the Germans in a wooden casket. On the body the Allies had placed secret documents to be discovered by the Germans, which presumably would reveal whether the Allies were to invade Sicily or the Balkans and when. The design was to have the Germans believe these phony documents and divert their troops to the wrong region. It worked in the movie.

"I told the chief that I had been talking with Velma about the movie, and that was the whole conversation. Evidently, Velma's case officer had not been able to follow the French too well, and he had gotten the movie story confused with the Deriabin scheme. I said to the chief, 'Besides, the muttonhead who told you this told his own wife, 'Hey, I got an extra wash load for you.' And where does an extra wash load of men's clothing come from but a defector? The case officer was talking to his own wife, an American. She was in Salzburg also like Velma. And she was yapping on the phone to Velma. She told Velma that her wash load of clothing was suddenly doubled. Velma told me this, which meant that there had to be another man. It had nothing to do with me, but that's how the rumor came about that I told Velma about Deriabin. I told the chief this. The other fellow's wife over there was the one who yapped. Nobody got hurt because nobody else knew much about what was going on. So I got off the hook on which I had found myself. I said nothing to Velma about talking to the other case officer's wife. I didn't think that she was a blabbermouth. But she was bored; she had nothing else to do.

"Anyway, we got the guy out. He stayed with Ted Poling. At breakfast, Deriabin repeatedly asked for vodka and Poling repeatedly brought him little glasses of water, as the two words in Russian are similar. Something was lost in the translation.

"That life was very hard—black, in a strange country. And I was pretending to be someone other than myself. Ferdi, of course, did not understand. I did not tell her anything about my real circumstances. I really didn't have to, because she wouldn't understand anyhow. It was too complex for her. We had Russians, Bulgarians, Chinese, Yugoslavs, Germans, Poles, and God knows who else there, all over the place, and they were all spies."

"I was Joe Palmer to Ferdi and George Kisevalter to Velma. For Popov, I had a different name, a phony American name.[6] I cannot now remember every undercover name; I had so many. I used to change them whenever, and I'd then get new documentation. You tend to forget them, you know. But anyway, for more than two years Ferdi did not know my true name. It had to leak out eventually, but I was able keep her in the dark until I left Vienna.

"I was in love. Sometimes, when you are in love, you do things that are stupid. One day, I thought I would be brave and teach her how to drive a car. I had a QP car, phony everything. This was going to be a chore in itself, because she didn't know anything about cars, but I finally taught her a bit after a few bumps. Unfortunately, they had patrols in that town. We called them 'the four guys in the jeep.' One soldier from each of the four sectors would ride together. So, there was some violation while she was at the wheel. These foreign heroes arrested me and they gave me problems. I got out of the situation, but it took some doing. The American gave me the most trouble because I was an American. All of my pleading with him was useless. He said to himself, 'I am going to fix you, you jerk; the American MPs will take care of this.' The British guy said, 'Just a minute here; I have jurisdiction here. What do you people have to do with it? It's my sector.' Naturally, the Frenchman was romantically inclined. He said, 'The lady is driving; that's all right. We're French. We understand these things.' So I spoke Russian, quickly to the Russian. He looked at me. He said, in words to the effect, 'It's nothing.' I said to myself, 'That's fine.' In other words, he's not voting against me. So it was a matter of these four slobs voting. And I won the vote, two to one, with one abstaining. So they let me go.

"Now, when the Soviets controlled their sector, they exercised a lot more authority. They would walk around with machine pistols, and if they didn't like what you said, they would shoot. You didn't argue with them. They were trigger-happy and nuts. Ferdi's sister's husband had this bicycle. He was robbed and killed by a Russian who wanted the bicycle. He was a nice kid, her brother-in-law. I saw him once, then he was dead. The Russian was drunk and he wanted the bicycle, so he just killed the kid. If you didn't give them the Mickey Mouse watch or the bicycle, you would have had it. Those were rough days there. It was too easy for the Soviets. They had too many spies. They had stooges there working for them who would cut somebody's throat for a nickel, whether they were Rumanian, Austrian, or whatever. People were hungry; because of that, they would do lots of things they would not otherwise do.

"Ferdi and her family lived in the French sector, and she had the right to go into the Russian sector. I did not. I stayed away from the Russian sector so there'd be no 'incident.' I crossed the border by accident once, so it was important that I duck and get away from Russian interrogation. I got out before the dummies caught me. I was in a car and they chased me. I got ahead of a train and I bounced over the tracks in front of the train. They couldn't make it quickly enough and had to wait for the train. Then I doubled back, got on the right road, and got the hell out of there. I made sure that I didn't make that mistake again."

The CIA people working with the operation wanted to be able to have contact with Popov when he ultimately would go back to Moscow, but it was extremely dangerous and difficult to get any of their people in place there (actually, all but impossible). Moreover, the U.S. State Department was extremely hesitant about sending CIA people to Moscow. The diplomatic corps did not want an international incident or even a provocation. Nevertheless, due to pressure to utilize this valuable asset, the Agency consensus was that it was absolutely necessary to send someone there and that the individual be under diplomatic cover. Thus, the CIA sent one of its people there, posing as a State Department employee, but without the actual knowledge and consent of the State Department. Unfortunately, the particular man selected for the task was ill prepared for his duty. Frank Levy had just begun the man's training when he, "Little Guy," was dispatched. Frank objected to his going, averring that it was premature to send him. He became the first CIA clandestine services officer ever to be placed in Moscow. When he arrived he tried to set up places for dead drops and brush contacts.[7] When Popov went back to Moscow on a temporary visit George supplied him with the information to check out some of the dead-drop locations that Little Guy had selected. Upon walking by some of these locations, Popov was appalled. He asked George, "Are you trying to get me killed?" The locations were ill conceived, not in safe places that Popov and Little Guy could visit without suspicion or surveillance.

Knowing that the meetings in Vienna could not go on indefinitely, George gave Popov instructions as to how CIA people elsewhere might make contact with him. George gave him a set of gold cufflinks, along with the instruction that someone wearing an identical set would meet him, whenever that might be possible. The cufflinks, designed by Peer de Silva and fashioned after the unmistakable emblem of the United States Military Academy at West Point, Peer's alma mater, consisted of a convex, oval dish, on which was mounted the helmet of the goddess Athena over the scabbard of a sword. Before giving the cufflinks to Popov, de Silva and Ted Poling had asked CIA director Allen Dulles for his approval to present them to Popov as a personal gift from Dulles. Dulles commented that this design was quite familiar and might endanger Popov. Ted felt the same, but he was not about to disagree with Peer in front of the director. Mr. Dulles nevertheless consented. When they left the director's office, Ted told Peer of his own concern. Using two pairs of matching cufflinks was risky, but there were some good reasons for doing so. If George simply had shown a pair of the cufflinks to Popov and told him that his contact would wear these, it was unlikely that Popov would have remembered. Popov needed to see the match between his own and the ones that the contact would be wearing or carrying. Likewise, the contact man had to have the same level of confirmation. Years later, when George retired, the set at the Agency was given to him.

After ten years of occupation by the Allies, the Austrian State Treaty was signed. In the summer of 1955 all of the foreign powers, including the United States, were required to leave Austria. Often before, Popov had remarked on how the CIA had treated him as opposed to the GRU. "The way they [GRU] treat one here in one's work causes much nervous strain. If one does not complete his assignment, he is treated almost as if he were a traitor to his country. . . . From the very beginning . . . you were never concerned about what I would bring, but you always stressed that I should be careful about my own security. . . . For this I am very grateful. In the work of our organization, they are never concerned about how dangerous an assignment may be for someone. They are only interested in squeezing all they can out of a person." On 18 August, Popov was transferred back to Moscow. He and George had their last meeting. George didn't know if he would ever see him again. On this occasion, as he and his Russian friend had a farewell vodka, Popov said to George, "This is what I like about your organization. You can find time to drink and relax. It is an entirely human approach. You have respect and regard for an individual. . . . With us, of course, the individual is nothing, and the government interest is everything." As they departed Austria, George sensed that, in addition to his intimate association with Popov, his love affair with Ferdi was coming to a big halt.

George returned to Washington and headquarters, wondering if the Popov operation would terminate or continue later in some other setting. When he got back, Velma and he determined that they no longer should be married. All in all, they were having no marriage at all. George then went to Reno, Nevada, and obtained a divorce. They separated as amicably as was possible, agreeing that she should keep the house on California Street. He wanted no part of it; it was hers.

George moved in with his good friend Dick Kovich for about a month. Dick enjoyed having him around, although Dick was a bachelor and not home a lot of the time. George was not eager to socialize, so he simply threw himself into this work at the Agency. Dick was very sad that George was leaving Velma. George was terribly embarrassed by the divorce process, but he eventually explained to Dick, "What can one do when one falls in love with someone else?" He added that it is almost impossible for two people to stay together when the romance has gone. Velma had once told Dick that George chased her during their courtship and that she quite reluctantly gave in to his marriage request. She loved him but she realized that she was too old for him and that there would come a day when it would just have to end. Dick believed that the difference in social status could have had a bearing on the matter. Velma had come from a family of some wealth. George, on the other hand, had struggled during the depression. Perhaps, thought Dick, George was bothered that Velma had so many wealthy friends. If so, maybe George realized that he was just not cut out to be married to somebody who was so socially prominent.

CHAPTER 7

Reunited

One method of servicing dead drop in Moscow might be as simple as Little Guy reading some inscription scribbled on a designated telephone booth. Unfortunately Little Guy could not read Russian well enough to effectively do this. When Popov found that he was to be transferred out of Moscow on assignment to Germany, he left a message for Little Guy. He inscribed in chalk a signal at a prescribed contact location. It read, "GDR—Shv 9/55." The intent was to convey that he was being transferred from Moscow to Schwerin in the German Democratic Republic, sometime in September of 1955. The inscription was written in Cyrillic script, however, and Little Guy could not properly decipher its meaning. Of course, even if Little Guy had copied the Cyrillic rendition precisely, it would have been quite a stretch for most to understand what Popov meant.

Shortly thereafter, Little Guy departed Moscow. In his wake was a first-class scandal. Evidently, the KGB had seen the CIA plant coming from the start, because they immediately mounted an operation targeting him. They nicknamed him *Ryzhiy,* "Redhead." Little Guy had the notion that he could seduce women with his good looks. It didn't take the KGB long to take advantage of this. They placed their agent, Valya, an extremely attractive (by many accounts) female, in his path as a maid in the embassy. Valya had a silent camera in her handbag with a timing device that operated the shutter during their sexual tryst. This part of the operation worked very well, as she took photos from wall to wall. Two men from the KGB approached Ryzhiy with the developed pictures. One of them spoke perfect English, as he had been raised in the U.S. He said, "Hey, we know who you are. Look at these. Your career is finished. You might as well work with us now."

Ryzhiy demurred. He did not report this to anyone immediately, as he contemplated just what to do. The men then asked Valya, "What is he up to?" "He's playing Hamlet," she said. "Hamlet?" was the query. "*To be or not to be.* Whether or not to have my second meeting with my tormentors."

They had a second meeting but he never gave them any information. To everyone's surprise and consternation, he then went straight to the ambassador, Chip Bohlen, and told him about his relationship with the CIA and with Valya. Upon hearing that he actually was a CIA employee, the ambassador was quite upset. This, of course, resulted in additional friction between the CIA and the State Department. Little Guy was recalled and fired. He never did meet Popov. He had few defenders but Peer de Silva considered him to have been an excellent army officer and a good friend. He later was killed in an automobile accident near San Francisco.[1]

Popov was able to initiate contact with the CIA on 10 January 1956. From a hotel in Stralsund, East Germany, he sent a note through a British officer. The officer was part of a military mission passing through. He couldn't know who Popov was, but during the contact he had the presence of mind to arrange for Popov to meet with whoever the proper people might be, within a few days. The manner in which the intrepid Popov was able to make the contact is worthy of note. His bold experience is detailed in a report sent by the British officer that is now on file at the CIA.

"On the 10th January, 1956, I was reading in bed in my room in the BALTIC Hotel, STRALSUND, when, at 10:30 P.M., there was a knock on my door and a small, dark man in plain clothes looked in. He apologized, asked if I was English and if he might come in, to which I agreed. He then asked if I would help him, to which I replied that I would be delighted.

"His description was as follows: Age (apparent): 32; Very dark; sallow skin; slightly Jewish in appearance despite fact that he claimed to be pure Russian; hair thinning. Height: approximately 5 ft. 5 ins.; He spoke fluent Russian and German.

"He then explained that he was a Soviet Lt. Col. and stated that he worked at the Intelligence H.Q. in SCHWERIN and that his office was in a building next to the KOMMANDATURA as you look towards the lake. He said that since he had been in SCHWERIN he had seen a number of American Mission cars and that he had been anxious to make contact with American officers, but had not had the opportunity.

"He had come to STRALSUND informally with his chief, a full Colonel of the Soviet Army. He had later told his chief that he was going out for a walk and a drink in the town and, on coming back to the hotel, had noticed a British Mission car. He had asked which rooms the British officer had occupied and had come to see him without the knowledge of his chief."

In accordance with the suggestions of the British officer, within a few days Popov appeared in the hotel café and met two members of the U.S. Military Liaison Mission who routinely visited points in East Germany. These men, with Popov's help, agreed on the next steps of a plan for putting Popov in touch with George. Communicating through the British officer exposed Popov to the British Secret Intelligence Service for the first time, and such exposure was not to the CIA's liking.It turned out to be even riskier than was first realized, because the notorious George Blake, a Soviet mole buried at a very high level within British SIS, easily could have learned about the note. It would have been easy for him to sense Popov's activity, assess it accurately, and report it to his Soviet masters. Evidently, Blake did not get wind of this, so Popov appeared to be safe for the time being.

After his forty days and forty nights in Reno, George went back to headquarters for reorientation. Notwithstanding the fact that the Agency had given Popov information on signal sites and other means of contacting its people, no one had heard from him. They did not know that Popov had been transferred from Moscow to Schwerin, East Germany, in the far north, near Hamburg.[2] Then the cable came from Berlin. "Get Kisevalter over here! We have heard a noise from a guy by the name of Scheinhorst." (Scheinhorst was the cover name for Popov.) They told George that Popov had observed one of the inspection officers of the occupation forces, a Brit, who was legally in East Germany and that Popov had contacted the Brit at Stralsund. The word got to Berlin and to Bill Harvey, the Berlin Base chief. It got to headquarters. "Get Kisevalter over here. His old agent from Vienna has suddenly showed up in Germany and he is trying to re-contact us."

George rushed to Berlin to resume the operation. He had been in the States only a few months. Everyone expected that George was going to be stationed in Berlin for an extended period, so he was given a "Permanent Change of Station" at once. This meant that he would not get a per diem as before.

At any rate, George was back working with Popov and he was going to enjoy the reunion. With Popov's suggestions on how to do it, the CIA people in Germany contacted him. That is a story in itself. Berlin Base sent an old gentleman with instructions to meet Popov at a certain place at a certain time. The man was part of a network of ordinary-looking, "street-type" East Germans who could travel freely throughout East Germany and East Berlin without raising any suspicion. He was a World War I veteran and railroad man. The gentleman as well as Popov wore the cufflinks adorned with the West Point emblem for recognition. This was absolutely necessary because Popov spoke poor German, and the old man was not about to learn any Russian. He was totally unwitting of the actual nature of his activity, or of the danger involved, but he was anxious to help. Ted Poling related that the fellow might have thought that he was working for the kaiser.[3]

Popov met the old gentleman in Rostock, near Schwerin, where neither was known. The old gentleman received a package from Popov and then took the train back to East Berlin. He arrived in the wee hours of the morning and was met by a CIA courier, who then ferried the package into West Berlin and onto Bill Harvey's desk by 7:00 A.M.

Harvey, like George, was quite a heavy drinker, but he could get by with practically no sleep. He could go out drinking at night, get up early the next morning, then play at least nine holes of golf before coming into the office. He would be ready for work at 7:00.[4]

George was always excited before contact meetings. Everyone was on edge. So, George and Ted Poling tied one on that night. They didn't have any responsibility for the meeting. All they had to do was read the "take" when it came in. They were out until about 4:00. The phone rang for them at about 7:00. It was Harvey who woke them up. They then trotted their weary selves in. Bill looked at them, and he was appalled. He chewed them up one side and then down the other. Finally, he said, "George, now you get over here and translate this stuff. Ted, as soon as he starts grinding it out, you go down and run the traces."

Ted and George spent the day with hangovers, translating the notes and tracing down information on any person mentioned in the text, if they knew of him. As fast as they got bits translated, they ferried them up to Harvey so that he could then send OPS Immediate messages (i.e., operations messages requiring immediate attention) back to headquarters about the substance of the information as well as the traces. Both miscreants' heads were pounding. In the afternoon, Bill came down and said, "I apologize for chewing you two out." (He could identify with them.) Then, after pausing a moment, he followed with, "But you deserved it!"

The information from Popov included the code names and brief descriptions of every agent in the Transborder Intelligence Unit, Central Group Forces. Transborder Intelligence is Tactical Intelligence, as opposed to Strategic Intelligence; it is the so-called "battlefield intelligence." These units were reporting on local military activities, but some intelligence agents reported on NATO forces and SHAEF (Supreme Headquarters, Allied Expeditionary Forces), etc., as well as on atomic-warfare dumps, fuel lines, artillery resources, and airfields in Germany, Holland, and Belgium.

For the rest of that year, while George was in Berlin, most of the contact with Popov was through the courier. The CIA intermediary, the old German gentleman, was not likely to be suspected. This worked quite satisfactorily. Personal contact, of course, is much preferred, and Popov managed three trips to West Berlin, where he and George met in a safehouse. These visits were quite dangerous for Popov but he seemed to enjoy helping the CIA and living on the edge.

George continued, "And then there was Ferdi. A month or two after I got to Berlin I sent her clandestine letters, surreptitiously, innocently. I used a friend in Berlin as a dead drop and a friend in Vienna to deliver the letters. Nothing in a letter of a security risk. She knew nothing about me. She didn't know anything about the business, nothing at all. I didn't want to have anything compromised; I didn't want to screw anything up. I thought I'd be a little bit careful here, so I did these secretly. I didn't have permission to do all of these things. I didn't do anything wrong and I didn't want to advertise that I was doing anything wrong. I was concerned about the CIA finding out about this, not the Soviets. You might say that I feared the exposure of stupid correspondence—'What the hell are you doing this for?'—I guess. By this time she knew my name. But she didn't screw anything up. When she replied she mailed as directed. That is all she had to do; and a lady in Berlin gave me the letter.

"Finally, I received an official task from the CIA to go from Berlin to Vienna, taking some documents and other articles. Of course, I ran off secretly and saw Ferdi. That was the time that I told her enough to begin buttoning things up, hoping that she wouldn't drop the ball somewhere. I told her that this was a hazard to me if she were loose with her tongue. Then she understood. That was it. She knew that I worked for the U.S. government, but she didn't know what it was. I mean, we didn't know what it was ourselves. To try to explain to Ferdi would be ridiculous. What in the world is O.S.S.? How could you explain that to her? I suppose that she thought that I was a postman—mailman or something like that. She didn't know or care.

"I was in love. It was spring. Feelings do not evolve from logic. They come and they go, as the case may be. Life is like a game. The Ferris wheel goes around. Why boy A meets girl B, I don't know. That's life, grabbing the brass ring as you go round the merry-go-round. So, shortly after I got to Berlin I asked her to marry me. She said yes. I then politely asked for permission from the Agency to marry Ferdi. I submitted a letter of resignation, as appropriate, in case they did not favor my request. I sent in an official letter to the director of the CIA saying that I had been divorced from Velma and that I was thinking of marrying an Austrian girl. 'Please check her out. Enclosed also is my resignation. Please accept it or give to me permission to marry this girl.' I was at their mercy. That was that. They sent back a reply, 'No, we checked her out. She is clean, legitimate. Go ahead and marry her if you like. We'll accept it. In fact, we'll make her a citizen.'

"I sent a telegram through channels to Vienna and told Ferdi. I then sent her a letter, some money, and a plane ticket. 'Get such and such documents, grab a plane, and come to Berlin. I will meet you. Bells are ringing!' She came up to Berlin; I took her to a safehouse. Three days later, on the 17th of April 1956, we were married. David Chavchavadze was the best man and his wife also was in attendance. He had recently arrived there in Berlin. It was the first that I had seen him since immediately after the war. He's a Russian prince, you know, working for the CIA. His mother, Nina, lived in Newport, Rhode Island. She knew many high-ranking people in the United States.[5]

"The chief's wife came with a bouquet of flowers and we were married. We had a champagne breakfast. Everybody blessed Ferdi and accepted her into our little fraternity. She certainly changed my life, and much for the better. Now Ferdi became aware of my employment—that is, the general nature, but not the details. At that time, Ferdi's two boys were in their early teens, so they stayed with relatives in Vienna. When we left Berlin in 1960, they were in their late teens. They were independent, they had their own jobs, and they had a pension from their dad. The kids never came back to the States to live with us, but Karl later came on visits. Ferdenand, the older, died in 1965 of a tumor."

Soon after George and Ferdi were married, Popov said that he was going on a thirty-day vacation. George told him that was fine and to have a nice time. George then made plans to take Ferdi back to the United States to get her citizenship. The Agency brought them back and in twenty-one days she was an American citizen with a diplomatic passport. She needed the passport to travel as his wife. There is a law in the United States that declares "should a citizen marry a foreign national and this union is in the best interest of the United States," the government will waive any waiting-period requirement for citizenship (e.g., five years, two years, or even ninety days). They then will proceed with the required examination of adequacy—that is, knowledge of the Supreme Court, Constitution, etc.. This must be done in a federal court with a federal judge, but they will grant the citizenship without regard to time requirements, if it is in "the best interest of the United States." So, if one has a sponsor like, for instance, the CIA or the State Department, he or she can do it quite expeditiously. The Agency put in the request for George and Ferdi and it went through immediately.

The couple had taken up residence in Washington, D.C., at Alban Towers Apartments, just across the street from St. Albans School and the National Cathedral. While there, Ferdi studied the Constitution day and night for her examinations. She was trembling as she took the test to become a citizen, but she passed. As George said, "For laughs, to get her passport, she had to raise her right hand and swear this, that, and the other thing, the whole bit. Everybody knows you are a liar, but you have to go through the ritual anyway. I had three passports in three different names. I had to lie each time. She actually didn't lie, but her answers to some questions were just as ridiculous."

CHAPTER 8

Berlin

Ostensibly, George was in Berlin to help with the review of the "tunnel traffic"; this was to be his cover. The tunnel was a CIA project involving an underground intercept of Soviet and East German intelligence communications. From a location on the edge of West Berlin, an 1,800-foot subterranean passage was dug. Nine hundred feet of this was into the East German Sector, where a tap into communication cables was accomplished. It allowed intercepts for a period of eighteen months up until its "discovery" in April of 1956. In actuality, the Soviets knew of the intercept project but kept quiet about this knowledge. To reveal their awareness to the West would jeopardize the cover of George Blake, one of their agents who was placed high in the British Secret Intelligence Service. There were restrictions on the type and quality of information transmitted on these lines, but the restrictions themselves were limited and some good information was transmitted. Otherwise, too many Soviets and East Germans would realize that the tunnel had been compromised and they could not be trusted to keep this knowledge from the West. Similarly, very few people knew of Popov. This operation was kept extremely close, more so even than the tunnel, which the CIA continued to believe, at the time, was a very secure and successful operation.[1]

The tunnel project in Berlin was the exclusive domain of Bill Harvey. He kept it under very strong security wraps. Officially, George had nothing to do with the tunnel or its take, although the CIA people who were not aware of George's contact with Popov believed that he was assigned to the tunnel operation. Since he was there, however, he was available, on an ad hoc basis, to help Bill clarify some peculiar intercepts that were received. One doesn't always get straight talk from a telephone conversation intercept—it's usually garbled. George tried to straighten out some of the intercepts with information that he had obtained from Popov. There were some really tricky circumstances.

In the reference safe in a special room were cards made up for all of the Soviets that the CIA personnel in Berlin were studying. Harvey called this office the "Target Room," and annotated on these cards were abstracts of these individuals. Whenever information that had originated from the tunnel was available about an individual, the card would be annotated with "PSM," meaning "please see me." No details from a tunnel intercept would be on that card, and the individual who wanted the information would have to see Harvey. If he were cleared for tunnel intercept information, Harvey would augment the information that was on the card.[2]

George described the atmosphere as follows: "Harvey's safe was always a mess but he was responsible for the security of its contents. I kept Popov material in there—things like gold hidden in soap bars—which were part of my operational equipment. I had to unearth Harvey's safe for him a few times; I would come to his rescue. One time, some people who were responsible for such things were doing an inventory and had to report the results to headquarters. They couldn't find the gold and said, 'Why did you steal the damned gold, Harvey?' Harvey said, 'I didn't steal any gold. It's in the safe, I think.' 'We didn't see it' was their reply.' 'Oh, yeah?' he said. At this point I yelled, 'Of course you didn't see it, you muttonheads. It's camouflaged in the soap!' Harvey forgot about it. He didn't care.

"I was overwhelmed with work at this time, so the Agency sent in someone to help me. June was an attractive, well-educated lady with graduate degrees. She could speak Polish, excellent Russian, and, most importantly, she could type very well. She came over to Berlin to help me process the take from Popov. Harvey was controlling his operations and we were handling ours. He knew, of course, about the Popov operation and that June and I had this private room. There we processed the tapes. I listened to them three times! I labored over the tapes religiously for at least 5,000 hours. That's an average of about twenty hours a week for five years. We had a binaural system with two microphones, two receivers, two amplifiers, and two sets of speakers. With something like that you can tell from which direction the sound is emanating; you can attenuate the volume of, or cut out, one conversation and emphasize another when you are reducing the data. It's like the situation when you mentally accomplish the same thing, say at a cocktail party, by ignoring one conversation while listening to another.[3]

"The purpose of this exercise was to make the information useful to others. I would dictate to June the proceedings of the meetings with Popov and she would type them. When all of the tapes were transcribed, if I had some time, I would listen to the tape for a second time, just myself, in order to correct any mispronunciations, omissions, or errors that I might have caused by yapping to June when she was typing. This process, then, would bring her up to date.

"The third time was for technical reasons, and very sound ones. I would excerpt from each typed page: (a) the target person, (b) the operation, (c) the technique, and (d) anything of intelligence value. She then would make extra copies, and we would put this information—that is, the names of the individuals and all of the categories associated with them—into notebooks. The notebooks would be annotated numerically progressive, from meeting to meeting to meeting. For five years and eight months they were catalogued: meeting number so and so on such and such date. Every individual was indexed alphabetically by name so that we could trace, at will, any human being mentioned during that period in any one of the meetings that I had with Popov. With this store and wealth of information, I also could transcribe an extra copy of the material, having the finest technical equipment available to man. It was just like movie production equipment. This was equipment bought for use in the tunnel but not needed. Instead of wasting it, I had a couple of units in my room. I could electrically transcribe one tape after another to ship back to headquarters for reference, or for the predilection of the curious muttonheads back home who may or may not listen to them and who may or may not be doing any work. But they had them anyway.

"This was only for Popov. It had nothing to do with the tunnel. Nevertheless, Harvey became curious about some of the tunnel take that was perplexing him, and one day he came down to my office with a query. He said, 'George, you know about the tunnel; I told you. You are sworn to secrecy, right?' 'Sure, of course,' I answered. 'You can help me, George. I need clarification now and then. I think that they are screwing up in London with their translations. We have a whole battery of people there who don't know what the hell they are doing or listening to. Some of this is contradictory. Maybe your book on Popov has reference to some of these names. Please look them up in your records, which you have so scrupulously listed, and see if you can reconcile some of the names, locations, and/or functions. I think there is a major screw-up or at least a minor mistake. Let me know what you can find out.'

"That was where I might get involved, and only in such cases, with the tunnel operation. He was right. Something strange appeared to be happening with some KGB personnel up in Stralsund, a German seaport city directly north of Berlin on the Baltic. We were receiving transmissions of conversations from people there who were not ordinarily expected to be in that area. Shortly thereafter, however, I solved his puzzle. I said, 'Harvey, do you have a sense of humor?' 'I think so,' he answered. 'Are you a hunter?' I asked. 'Yes,' he replied. 'A duck hunter?' 'Yeah,' he said. I finally told him, 'Well, these KGB people are on vacation and they're up at this Stralsund location and they're hunting ducks. It's raining like hell, but it's warm. It's not duck weather. Their allowable leave has expired and they are begging for some more time so that they can bring home some ducks and share them with their buddies. They are telephoning for permission. That is why, although they are KGB, they don't spell out their function. After all, they are on vacation.' He said, 'Jeez, take them off this list and put them where they belong. Let's straighten this out.'

"That was the kind of identification that I did for him from time to time. It was not earthshaking. It wasn't that important, but it helped to eliminate some of the confusing traffic that came with the more useful intercepts. Actually, this type of nonsense came with some repetition. But there are always reasons for the anomalies. There will be an explanation why someone swipes a typewriter from another person's office and tries to camouflage its disappearance. (That particular dialogue also came through on the tunnel tapes, as they were providing an explanation of the act of one of their petty thieves.) Things like that happen in life, and just because an intelligence officer listens to an intercepted conversation and screams, 'I got something,' doesn't mean that it is so important. It may be something as innocuous or irrelevant as the duck hunt. But a guy like Harvey, who is trying to do a job as the base chief, must investigate all intercepts, just to keep things straight. He must see opportunity in every curiosity and investigate it to make sure that nothing of value slips away. So, he came to me and said, 'Does this make any sense?' Sort of like the gold in the soap.

"That was my only involvement with the tunnel. I had nothing to do with what they took or the recording of it. A battery of people did the interpretations for us and the Brits inside a white building in London. I was in the CIA premises in Berlin. Our building was part of a West German army facility; Berlin Base it was called. It was a former German army barracks. We were under U.S. Army cover. It was located near Berlin Dahlem, a local district on Clayallee, a major boulevard. The tunnel was out on the edge of town. I never was there.[4]

"I remember another story about our existence there in Berlin. It's about Sam Wilson. He was not a West Pointer like Peer de Silva but came up through the ranks. I believe they call his kind a 'mustang.' Sam and Peer knew each other but they were not too close, according to Peer. In the army, as you know, they have this date of rank business. I suppose there might have been a certain amount of competitive and professional jealousy. In my days of engineering we didn't have that. We were proud to see a fellow professional do well, better than we perhaps, even become famous; that was good as well. I suppose that the regular army is a different society. Wilson and de Silva both were graduates of a small Russian language institute in Regensburg, Germany. Sam had become fairly fluent in Russian while Peer struggled with the language.

"This was after the war, during the occupation. Anyway, during the course of his career, Wilson was assigned to CIA for a tour. He was a major in the army at that time, 1956. Indirectly, he helped service Popov for me while working for Bill Harvey, running back and forth between Berlin and Frankfurt with encrypted messages. The CIA's European headquarters then were in Frankfurt, where they had the capacity to decipher these messages. They made plenty of mistakes there too. Those were their mistakes and had nothing to do with Sam. He did his duty, running back and forth. In addition, he did many other things for Harvey. He helped me a lot of the time, but mainly he worked for Harvey in the Berlin tunnel operation and in other areas.

"Wilson had a wife who was the nervous type. At the time, she seemed excessively worried about him. I remember her as a very attractive lady, but I can't recall that I knew much about their personal relationship. Often the four of us, the Wilsons and the Kisevalters, went out together and played bingo. We played at a place called the Harnack House, an officer's club for our military forces in Berlin. Ferdi tended to be very lucky. Whether or not they were there, she would win for them as well as for us by hollering, 'Bingo.' She would win nice prizes like expensive silver sets. In those days a dollar was a big thing; a mark was not.

"One night we were playing bingo and Sam was called during a game to go somewhere on an errand for Harvey. He excused himself and took off. Later on, his wife, still sitting at our table, became very upset, almost hysterical. Ferdi was concerned and asked her, 'What's the matter? What's the trouble?' The wife then started complaining. She didn't understand why Sam had to take off like this, and of course there was no way that I could explain operational things to her.

"Eventually, Sam returned and we started home. Sam was driving the QP car that we had borrowed for the evening. Now remember, a Quasi-Personal car is one owned by the station and used *mostly* for operational activities. This one was not assigned to any one individual. As we were bumping along, accidentally the glove compartment of the car popped open and there she saw, laid out in front of her, a glorious array of condoms. She glared at her husband, this, that, and whatever. I tried to explain to her that this was not his car; it was a QP car. It could have been used by anybody, as we shared these vehicles. 'He didn't know what the hell was in it!' Ferdi couldn't explain anything because she didn't understand anything. It was a station-owned car that we had borrowed for the night because he knew that he would have to run an errand for Harvey during the course of the evening. He didn't have any idea what might be in the thing. He was not guilty of anything. She was blaming the unfortunate guy for the wrong reason and he was completely innocent! The poor guy."

Ferdi was there in Berlin all of the time that George was there. She did a lot of work for the Agency. For example, when a Soviet agent came over with a German wife and child, Ferdi would baby-sit the woman and the child in a safehouse. She was obviously a non-American by her appearance and not to be suckered into high prices, etc., so she would bird-dog exotic places for Agency people to rent, using her Germanic background. She did a lot of what might be termed "auxiliary staff work," critical in making things work. It was all goodwill. She didn't get paid. As George said, "I was high ranking enough. We didn't need more money. We were having the time of our lives." At this point, George probably would have paid money to work with the Agency.

Once George and Ferdi gave a cocktail party at their place in Berlin. George was standing in a group talking with Joe Skura, Ben Pepper, and Douglas Stuart, a Marine Corps major. Joe noticed that Ben, who was a graduate of Princeton, was wearing his school tie. Joe remarked to him, "Well, the tiger roars tonight, huh?" Ben said, "Yeah," and laughed it off. Doug then said, "Oh, I also am a Princeton graduate." So Ben and Doug began comparing their scholastic backgrounds. Skura sarcastically remarked, "I wasn't aware that I was in such a presence, an Ivy League congregation." George leaned over and, talking out of the side of his mouth, murmured, "Don't tell anybody, but I also am an Ivy Leaguer." At this, Doug burst out in disbelief, "What! You, George?" George, always slovenly dressed, had a tremendous gut that usually was peppered with cigarette ashes. He looked so silly, hardly like Ivy League material. Doug was completely amazed. George said, "I'll show you something." He then took the group upstairs to his study, and there on the wall, in addition to his master's degree in civil engineering from Dartmouth, were awards and commendations for his work on projects such as the Merrit Parkway in Connecticut. There were framed letters from prominent Dartmouth classmates such as Governor Rockefeller. Doug, Ben, and Joe were duly impressed and amazed.[5]

In March of 1957, Popov sent to George the text of a speech made by Marshal Georgi Zhukov, then the first deputy minister of defense and a genuine hero of the Soviet Union ever since World War II. This speech was delivered to a group of senior Soviet officers stationed in East Germany with Popov in attendance and dealt with strategies for military conflict in Germany. It was extremely interesting to the CIA. Routinely, the CIA people forwarded the text of the speech to the British SIS, where George Blake again had an opportunity to sense that the CIA had a highly placed penetration. Whether or not Blake actually alerted the Soviets to the leak, the KGB did find out that Zhukov's speech had been passed on to the CIA. This prompted them to investigate the source of the leak. Popov would have been on the list of those attending the speech and could have been suspected.

Once, Popov said to George, "You know, I found out a very interesting thing, which is not exactly in my backyard, but I know that you would like to hear of it. It has to do with nuclear submarines." George asked, "What do you know and how do you know it?" Popov then told George his story.

"We have a naval section in East Berlin, and in it we have the chief of the Naval Division of Intelligence, a captain. He is interested in everything to and from the West regarding Bremerhaven and Amsterdam—all of the American traffic that flows in and out, as well as everything British that flows in and out. As I was walking down the hall I overheard him talking to his unit. I am not a part of his particular group, but when I passed his open door, he stopped me and said, 'Come in; sit down. You can be a witness to this.' He was furious, and his speech reflected his anger during the entire meeting with his unit. He continued, 'There is no justice in our system! Can you imagine this happening? I just came back from Moscow, where I heard about this. Here I am a naval captain, I graduated number one in my class, and this idiot, a naval captain who is a dumbbell of the first order, becomes an admiral ahead of me.'

"I replied to the captain, 'Why? How?' The captain continued, 'The dummy had leave. He went from Moscow to Leningrad. He got drunk. He missed his train going back to Moscow, so he was delayed. But as he was in the act of catching the next train, some naval personnel stopped him. They said to him, "Captain, this is fortuitous. We are so glad we found you before you took your train back. We need you here. We are missing a senior member, a naval captain, for a shakedown cruise of a new nuclear submarine that was just floated down the White Sea Canal from Severodvinsk, to be outfitted at Leningrad. We must perform sea trials in the Gulf of Finland. We need you aboard for the shakedown cruise." So, this dumbbell, because he got drunk and missed the train, is detained to go on a shakedown cruise, as the senior officer. As a result of this he launches this sub and gets promoted to admiral. Can you imagine the injustice in this world? What stupidity.' That was his story and I believe it to be true."

George picks up the story: "Naturally, we immediately cabled this information in to Washington. Who is our customer agency to receive this? The U.S. Navy. Unfortunately, the U.S. Navy has some mavericks. One of them was Admiral Rickover, the father of our nuclear submarine force. Well, frequently, he liked to scream his head off, usually for more money to spend on more submarines; so, he rushes to Congress, pounds the table, demands that appropriations immediately be increased, since the Soviets have now launched number so-and-so nuclear submarine.

"On the next day, Rickover's speech was published in the *Star,* Washington's evening newspaper. We explained to the good admiral that this information is classified. We don't like to have this information published in the open press for all to read. Such action tends to compromise its source—our agent, in this case. This could cause a massive search over there to determine from where this information might have been leaked. Such actions just don't do our sources any good. The admiral apparently understood some of this logic but not all of it. So he retracted the story with Congress. The *Star* also printed his retraction on the next day, just to reemphasize the stupidity, I suppose. When we found out in Berlin this had happened, we said, 'We don't need enemies with friends like this. Look what we have: blabbermouths, no matter what rank.' So, we had to live with this. Luckily, the remoteness of our access to the information, requiring the checking out of somebody's remark about an incident in Leningrad, by way of Moscow, that reached a Berlin naval section and was overheard by an army officer, is not that easy to trace. So we don't think that we had a result that was calamitous from that particular faux pas. But it shows you what can happen and often does happen in intelligence."[6]

Happily for the CIA, in June of 1957, Popov was transferred to Karlshorst, Germany, near Berlin. In his new assignment, his stature went up. He was now a lieutenant colonel and on his way to becoming a full colonel. Previously, he had done considerable favors in Vienna for the chief of what they called the "illegals operations" of Soviet Intelligence. When that same chief was transferred to Berlin, he spotted his old friend Popov and had him brought into the headquarters of Eastern European Soviet Intelligence, which is in Karlshorst, an enclave of Berlin. Within what was then called the Karlshorst Compound were almost all of the Soviets operating out of that region. It was the Soviet center for Germany, where their people lived and worked—a city within a city. Popov's new job was very significant. He was part of the Strategic Intelligence Operational Group and was privy to 288 operations that he told George about. The Agency couldn't "roll them all up" (stop these operations) because to do so would reveal that there had been penetrations into the Soviet service. The CIA was very careful in handling this information; it was extremely valuable.

In addition, Popov was the dispatching officer in charge of sending "illegals" abroad. An illegal, in this case, was a Soviet national pretending to have a different nationality. He or she would be provided with complete documentation, from birth certificate and passport to everything necessary to establish apparent residency and citizenship in the target country. After entering that country, the illegal could operate freely without much fear of detection.

One such illegal was a very attractive young lady, a Russian who had all of the documentation she needed to pass as a citizen of Austria. She then went to Constantinople as a modiste. She ran a millinery shop—hats, dresses, etc., for ladies—but she also operated a safehouse there. Because she had the store, she ostensibly had a reason for being in Constantinople, and she also had all of the proper paperwork, the legitimate documentation, of a Turkish resident. The CIA Berlin people knew her real name and essentially everything about her because Popov had dispatched her to Turkey. They knew through him what she was doing, but they did not know all of the details since her operation was in Turkey and not in their Berlin day-to-day interest. They passed on what they knew of her to their people running the Turkish desk. There were also others who went to other countries whom they knew of through Popov.

George continued, "Popov also made us shudder about penetrations of our own. I had once asked Popov, 'Have you ever heard of instances where people would be meeting here in your East Berlin area for operations elsewhere in other countries?' He said, 'Not offhand, but if I hear of such I will let you know.' One day, he said, 'Hey, remember that question you asked me? I found one. You won't like this. This guy Sklavits with the anchor tattoo, he is going to Vienna, for agent operations. He has met with Western intelligence people there. They believe he is working with them but he has come back and reported on them. I found out who some of the people were but not all of them.'

"The proof came the next week. While the chief of that Soviet operation was lecturing his unit, he pointed to Popov and said, 'You listen carefully, Popov. This may one day apply to you.' He continued, 'Sklavits is being reported on by a double agent of ours in the KGB. Sklavits is meeting a guy that he thinks is Western who is really KGB! Always treat your agent like your own brother; don't let on that you realize that he is not playing ball with you, because maybe he is being reported on by our penetration of his service! Do you understand, you dopes? Sometimes you have to keep a stiff upper lip and treat your agent like you really believe him, because you are getting all the poop on him anyway through other penetrations that we have.' 'Yes, sir,' said Popov.

"We knew Sklavits was a Soviet intelligence officer. We thought that he was working with us, but we didn't know all of his activities. I saw a can of worms. Where was the penetration? Who was the Soviet agent who was one of us but was reporting on Sklavits? Into what service: the British, West Germans, or Americans? Not a pleasant thought. So, I asked for leave and went to Frankfurt. I went to Bonn, the headquarters of the German Intelligence. I asked the people at German Intelligence as well as our own liaison staff and found out there was a naval officer in the West German navy who ran an operation called 'Sea Bear.' They inherited the operation from the British, who had another name for it, 'Illustrious.' This navy guy was one of those meeting with Sklavits in Vienna, but we didn't know who else. I looked at this case, 'Illustrious,' and I looked at this case, 'Sea Bear.' I came home and I grabbed my head and I said, 'We are in trouble!' There is a penetration by the Reds. It could be into the British, it could be into the West German Intelligence, or it could be in our outfit in Vienna.

"The penetration, we later found out, was a man named Felfe.[7] He had penetrated the West Germans and was one of their high-ranking intelligence officers. We had to live with this because we could not figure it all out at the time. So that is how we found out, by accidental, incidental information, that we had a serious problem, and that is where life becomes very much on a razor's edge.

"Popov himself didn't know who the penetration was. Sklavits was acting as a double agent but there was a penetration by another intelligence officer of a Western intelligence service. We didn't know which one, whether it was our CIA or somebody else. As for the British, heaven help us, they had their own problems too with those guys Blake and Philby.[8] This is the kind of thing that some thought ultimately did in Popov."

CHAPTER 9

Tradecraft

As the dispatcher of illegals, Popov came to George one day in the fall of 1957 and said, "I have some tough information. It is very sensitive. We've gotten along now for almost five years, old buddy. Nothing evil has happened." "That is right," George replied. "Nothing evil has happened. I don't know what evil should happen."

"I don't know either," Popov stated. "So I'll tell you. I'm not going to keep anything from you. I have this woman, Tropova. She is from Chicago and is now living in Poland. For personal reasons, whatever, she will never go back to Chicago. We have her passport, which we will use for our own purposes. We are sending to New York, as an illegal, a Russian woman by the name of Margarita Tairova, using Tropova's passport, which is a legitimate American passport. We changed the photograph. Otherwise, everything matches: age, size, this, that. She is the wife of an illegal who is operating as our *rezident* [chief of station] of a *rezidentura* in New York, an important one. One of the members of the group is the chief barber on the SS *United States*, a fast liner whose route is from New York to Le Havre, back and forth. His advantage is proximity to seagoing American senators and representatives in the easy chairs of the barbershop of this vessel, getting all of their conversation. At the same time he is acting as courier between New York and Le Havre for this ring. The boss man, the *rezident*, has a store in the garment district of New York he just acquired. It manufactures the loud, colorful Hawaiian-style shirts. The ring started together in England, so they speak English very smoothly. The wife is being sent out for two reasons. One is to supplement his ring, and the other is because she is raising hell in the belief that her husband is unfaithful. She is a hysterical type of woman. She wants to snatch this guy baldheaded if she catches him running around with other women, taking them out, drinking and so forth, which seems to be one of his habits. At any rate, the couple has agreed to this deal. I have to dispatch her. I need your help."

"What do you need?" George asked. Popov went on, "Check out everything. Here it is." He put down the wife's suitcase. George looked at the contents: dresses, underwear, etc. He looked at some panties. They were R. H. Macy. "Good," he said. He looked at a blouse. It was Marshall Fields. "That is fine," he continued. "You said the passport was for a lady who is from, where, Chicago?" "Yes," replied Popov. George explained, "Marshall Fields is a very prominent store in Chicago." He then observed, "Here is a mirror, built into the suitcase. Behind it we seem to have some cash, $20,000. No good. The sum is too large and the denominations are too big. Cut the sum in half. The denominations will stand out like sore thumbs. You'll get caught. Instead of these hundreds use fifties and twenties. Okay?"

After taking off from Tempelhof in Berlin and before arriving at Idlewild in New York, Tairova was going to stop off in Paris at a Soviet safehouse. George said, "Give her some francs, just a few. She will not be surveilled here in Tempelhof or anywhere in Berlin. I will guarantee it. I will make sure she is not surveilled. Don't worry about it. You can drive her up to the airport yourself if you want to." In New York, she was to secretly meet her husband. "And where in New York will they meet?" George asked. "I don't know," replied Popov. 'You tell me. What does this mean?" He then handed George some notes written in Russian, the meaning of which was not clear to him, asking, "Yuncats? Bronkoyer?" George explained, "Yonkers is a town just north of the Bronx in New York City. This is the name of a movie theater there. They are to meet in the back row of the movie house at a certain time. Alternate dates at various specific times are also offered if the first meeting doesn't work out. They will continue attempting to meet until contact is made. Then, he will take her to where he is living." Popov then said, "We're going to gimmick her suitcase with thread. If anybody opens it, she will know that she is being surveilled. She is an intelligence woman; she will know." George said, "Fine. I know what is in it. Don't worry about it. When does she go?" Popov told George. George guaranteed him safe departure for the woman. No problems occurred—no surveillance of any kind, hostile, friendly, or otherwise. She got to Paris. One of the CIA people spotted her coming. He knew the safehouse where she went. She departed for New York; he cabled.

Then they were stuck. Bill Harvey (the one who had the last word on everything) and George had to send a message to CIA director Allen Dulles. They drafted a cable. They ripped it up. They wrote a second one. They ripped it up then wrote a third one. It was so hard to explain the whole story. They had to tell the director that this woman was coming into the United States. Moreover, they knew that, by law, at some point Director Dulles had to tell J. Edgar Hoover, the chief of the FBI, and they were afraid that Hoover would not fully cooperate with their plan to let the woman into New York and monitor her activities.

One of the problems was that Harvey used to work for Hoover, and they hated each other. Hoover finally fired Harvey and Harvey showed up on the doorstep of the CIA, which was glad to have him. The two men continued an interagency fight after that. George did not want that history to interfere with getting this Soviet illegal smoothly into the United States without raising her suspicions. They needed to have Hoover's consent and cooperation for this, so Dulles would have to consult with him. They had to explain things to Dulles so that he could make Hoover understand. This was, in George's mind, like explaining to Dulles how to teach the devil to cross himself. When he received the cable, Dulles told Hoover.

Some of the people at the CIA who knew about the operation wanted to go to Yonkers to case the meeting place. Hoover forbade them to do so, saying, "You will keep your CIA noses away from Yonkers. I'm taking care of the manpower requirements in New York. The security of the U.S. soil is the responsibility of the FBI." Hoover would take care of it. The plane landed at Idlewild. A small platoon of people was there to meet Tairova. Rumor has it that Hoover brought 300 special agents into New York. Of course, they didn't know the city, and that didn't help matters very much; but, just as ordered, they were all under Hoover's control.

Tairova got off the plane. The agents surrounded, watched, and tailed her. She went to a hotel in New York. She went for a walk to check out the big city. The FBI then broke her suitcase to see if in fact the contents were just as George had cabled. Of course, she then detected that she was under surveillance. After all, she was an intelligence woman and she had the suitcase rigged. They knew that she had it all rigged, but it made no difference to them. So, she aborted her scheduled meeting with her husband for security reasons. She did, however, finally make contact with him in Yonkers on an alternate date. He took her to Manhattan and they set up a household. The FBI rented a place to their left and another to their right. They rented a place across the street and other places all up and down the street.

Evidently, the lady didn't mind infidelity as long as she was the one doing it. While her husband was working in his shop she waltzed about town to restaurants and bars, as she tried to appear to her surveillers as a normal resident. If she went out to have a drink in some gin mill with some other guy, however, as soon as she would leave, someone would dash across the counter and grab the glasses—for fingerprints. One can only imagine how this must have looked, especially if it involved a mob of FBI agents.

Then one day Tairova's husband got up and went mechanically to his place of work on Thirty-fourth Street. Likewise, casually swinging a shopping bag, she went strolling among the food stores around her neighborhood, just like a typical housewife. They met somewhere, having acquired different identities. They shot off to Mexico City; from there they went to Havana, then Amsterdam, and then back to the Soviet Union. Neither of them reappeared in the U.S. The barber aboard the SS *United States* conveniently jumped ship in Le Havre. They were gone.

Popov asked George, "Why in the world didn't you just shoot them or something? Now we will have a full-scale investigation. There is a general in the KGB who will be investigating this. The woman is claiming that she walked into a stakeout in New York. She says she was surveilled all of the way from Tempelhof." George said, "Peter, you know that she was not surveilled in Tempelhof. I am telling you the truth." Whereupon Popov replied, "Look, my friend, I believe you, but how can I use your word to tell the KGB general that the woman is a liar and a hysterical fool? I really can't do that, now, can I?"

Popov was so right. The woman was a bit of a hysterical person. But now, there was trouble with a capital *T.* Of course, George was just trying to help Popov improve his performance on the job so that Popov would be entrusted with more and more illegals. In fact, this did happen; he was entrusted with more illegals and he shared information about them with the CIA. Shortly thereafter, however, he went on leave back to Moscow. When he returned he said that, indeed, there was an extensive investigation under way into this episode with Tairova. This sounded ominous. He had been responsible for her well-being.

From January until May of 1958 everything went smoothly with Popov. He was providing a wealth of information. He already had proved to be the best "in place" human source that the CIA had during the Cold War. He was the first intelligence officer, other than defectors who actually came out, from whom the U.S. had ever benefited, and he was well positioned and continually producing information. It was understood that he was never to defect. Even when events and circumstances appeared threatening, defection was almost never mentioned. George made it clear that he could, if he wished, come over to the U.S. at any time and that his family also could come. Both he and Popov knew, however, that getting them all out would be extremely difficult. Yet it never was an issue, because Popov so loved his peasant village. It remained more or less a given that he would continue working with the U.S. from the inside as long as he could, in order to have a chance to better the lot of the Russian peasant. That was his objective in life.

Popov went on leave in May and June. When he returned to Karlshorst, he seemed to be under pressure from the Soviets about his shortcomings. He was also being told that he was not producing enough intelligence. The Agency decided to set him up with a false agent in Berlin in order to give him a higher standing with his superiors in the GRU. This was a dicey thing. First of all, the false agent would be in a dangerous situation. Secondly, the CIA had to give up some amount of legitimate intelligence information. Finally, if the sham were not convincing, then the whole operation could be compromised.

To service Popov in Moscow when he would be recalled from Berlin, the CIA prepared Russell Langelle to replace Little Guy. He was to be stationed there solely to communicate with Popov. Frank Levy and Ted Poling trained Langelle. One day, Frank, Ted, Russell, and the branch secretary, an attractive, statuesque woman, staged a game of "cat and mouse" through the streets of the Anacostia region of southeast Washington, D.C., on foot. The game teaches the fundamentals of surveillance, escape, and evasion. An area of the city unfamiliar to the participants had been selected in order to give the exercise an added degree of realism. Unfortunately, the secretary's activity attracted the attention of the D.C. police. They detained her, believing that she was a streetwalker. Ted and Russell froze, not knowing the best course of action. Frank, however, promptly approached the policemen and indicated that he was her "sugar daddy." This took some of the heat off the secretary, but Frank was arrested for pandering. An inspection of the contents of his wallet and his CIA identification card (which did not actually reveal his employer), as well as Frank's refusal to fully explain what he had been up to, led the police to yet more false conclusions. They assumed him to be an employee of nearby Bolling Air Force Base and to be pursuing a sexual liaison with the young lady, an associate of his, not a streetwalker. Also in Frank's wallet was a photograph of his attractive wife and his three precious little boys. The arresting officer then launched into a most disapproving lecture to Frank about his shameful infidelity. Frank silently endured this painful mortification, his only consolation being the realization that certain sacrifices had to be made in this job.

Langelle, who also was an associate of George, came to Berlin and met Popov later in 1958. He was given diplomatic cover, with the ambassador's knowledge, and dispatched to Moscow. Presumably, if Langelle were apprehended in espionage, he would not to be unduly incarcerated. By this time, things at the U.S. Embassy in Moscow were much different.

Evidently, the charade of a fake agent for Popov in Berlin was not too good. Under the pretense that his superiors needed to discuss the matter of Popov's "agent" personally with him, they summoned him back to Moscow that November. He was not too worried about this issue, but he did not know what was in store for him. In December, his wife closed up their household in Karlshorst and went back to Moscow. Popov never came back to Berlin and George never again saw him.

There has always been considerable speculation as to when Popov first came under suspicion by the KGB for disloyalty. In any event, the actual steps in the process of his ultimate arrest are fairly well known. Using the communication plan previously provided to him by George during their last meeting in Berlin, on Christmas Day in Moscow, Popov signaled to Langelle using a "wrong number" phone call. He wished to meet on 28 December at a children's theater in Moscow. He did not show for the meeting, automatically setting up an alternate rendezvous at the Aragvi Restaurant one week later.

The 4 January 1959 meeting went as planned. In the men's room of the restaurant, Popov passed to Langelle a message that was considered sterling. In it he provided some good intelligence, but he also provided the notice that he had been dismissed from the GRU for disciplinary reasons and was living in Kalinin at his wife's former home. There was the suggestion that several items, either individually or collectively, played a part in his dismissal. Prominent among them was the affair of the illegal, Margarita Tairova, in New York City with the FBI. It may have been a catalyst. Another may have been the suspicion that he leaked the speech made by Marshal Georgi Zhukov in East Germany. Yet another could have been the possible discovery of the false agent provided to him by the CIA in Berlin. Finally, even another may have been Popov's association with a female Austrian agent, "Mili," whom he purportedly used in Vienna. She cast her allegiance to the Austrians while Popov continued to communicate with her. Popov's message to Langelle also said that he was in the Reserves anticipating an assignment and that he wished to talk with Grossman (George). Langelle passed to him a brief message, suggesting that he write to George at a specified address in Berlin and explain what had happened to him.

Popov signaled for a second brush contact to be on 21 January at a familiar bus stop. As a backup to this rendezvous, a letter was mailed to Popov's Kalinin address. This would ensure that Popov had the information deemed necessary for further communication if the meeting did not go as planned, say if he were transferred away from Moscow prior to the brush contact. The meeting proceeded, however, and Langelle passed to Popov a message containing the locations and details for some future meetings, some technical instructions regarding communications, and the advice that he destroy some older materials of their trade.

Throughout much of 1959, Popov had additional brush contacts with Langelle in Moscow, and they passed each other information. Agency operators sensed that Popov no longer was able to provide quality information, but they did not know, exactly, his status. First of all, his messages contained very low-grade intelligence. This was so unlike him. More significantly, the letters were written in a conventional, front-to-back fashion in the notebook that he used. In the past, Popov had always written from the back to the front. This was a dead giveaway that something was wrong and CIA operatives caught it immediately. Also, Popov did not number his messages as he routinely had in the past. He provided these flags although he was under extreme duress, because, as the Agency people later learned, he was living in a jail cell.

Ultimately, it was confirmed that the KGB had, in fact, observed all of these contacts since the one on 21 January. The Seventh Directorate of the KGB, the one devoted to surveillance, had astonishing capabilities. First of all, they had an academy in Leningrad where the best agents were trained. They came from Moscow, Kiev, and all over to be trained there. Only the best were selected. They were the officers, not the enlisted men. These were the ones employed against the U.S. Embassy in Moscow. If someone from the embassy left to go to the barbershop, there would be people recruited for positions in the barbershop. If an American were to go shopping, without fail he would be surveilled by other "shoppers." The surveillers could be active or retired people. Everybody in the Soviet Union had a job.

Finally, on 18 September, again in the Aragvi Restaurant, Popov appeared in a neatly tailored uniform of the Transportation Corps and bearing the rank of a full colonel. He was able to pass to Langelle what appeared to be a genuine message, in addition to one that obviously was KGB authored. The authentic message was written in pencil on eight small pieces of paper and rolled into a cylinder about the size of a cigarette. (In the future this message would be referred to as "the cylinder message.") In addition, it was wrapped in cloth, was tied with a string, and carried a pleasant fragrance, like shaving lotion. In this letter, he reported that he had been arrested the previous February and that all of the meetings since had been under KGB control while he was wearing a microphone. The letter revealed the extent to which the KGB did and did not know of Popov's actual cooperation with the CIA. It revealed some technical errors that the KGB had made in its analysis of his situation. It described the KGB plans for future meetings between him and CIA people. It indicated that there was a high likelihood that his interrogators thought he might be the source of the leak of Marshal Zhukov's speech.

The validity of the 18 September "cylinder message" was discussed at length in the chambers of the CIA's Clandestine Services Directorate. At first, it was considered impossible that Popov had smuggled such an item from, for instance, Lubyanka Prison. Moreover, the message itself had suspicious elements. It had been written throughout with a sharp pencil. Would Popov, while incarcerated, have access to numerous sharp pencils or a pencil sharpener? How could he have written such a complete message without having been observed at some time in the process? Yet there were aspects to the letter that indicated Popov and only Popov was its author. Perhaps his incarceration was more benign than it otherwise could have been. Perhaps he was still successfully playing games with his masters. Ultimately, the conclusion was that the letter was genuine. It was much too reflective of Popov's personality to have been a ruse.

George's description of the 18 September Aragvi Restaurant meeting follows. "Well, this long story has a sad and illuminating ending. Not only does it illustrate Popov's ability to execute a most incredible act in the art of clandestine tradecraft, but it also demonstrates the sad, simple naiveté of the man, in that he had so much faith in the propensity of people to do the right thing. Eventually, after they thought they accurately understood his relationship with us, the KGB tried to set him up as part of a gimmicked, double agent, controlled operation. They planned a meeting between him and Langelle in which they endeavored to have him pass more lousy information. However, during the time that he was in jail, he had meticulously, over months, constructed his own message. First, he cut his finger until it bled profusely and had a bandage put around it. Then, he removed the bandage, placed the message against his finger, and reinstalled the bandage. In the middle of the controlled operation, in the men's room of the Aragvi Restaurant in downtown Moscow, completely covered by the KGB watching, our man Langelle and Popov shook hands. Popov then slipped the bandage from his finger and gave the note to Russell. This was undetected by the surveilling KGB."

Although the successful pass of the cylinder message might have given hope that some productive use of Popov might still be possible, a month later on 16 October, a brush meeting between Popov and Langelle on Moscow bus 107 was abruptly and prematurely terminated. Langelle was detained and then sent home persona non grata. Popov was seized and scheduled to be put on trial before a military collegium on the 6 January 1960.[1]

George continued, "When I finally received [the cylinder message] and deciphered it, word by word, it caused me to cry. This guy was a rare jewel, a genuine prince. The note gave us some meaningful intelligence as well as the admonition that the American Embassy in Moscow was completely surveilled. In part, the note sought to confirm to us the fact that he was under the control of the KGB and had been since February. Finally, in the note he pleaded, 'Could you not ask your kind President Eisenhower to see if he might cause restitution to be made for my family and my life?'

"I literally bawled. I remembered the time when his brother, Alexander, had thrown the guy through the oak door and had gotten everyone into the jug, when they had written the collective letter to Kalinin, who took notice and gave them a reprieve. Now, on these slips of paper, in this little note, written in detail, he was once again pleading for help from above. Popov was drawing from that pivotal event of his life. He was grasping at straws. It was so poignant. He hoped that mercy could once again be dispensed. He gambled. He knew that he was in very deep trouble when he passed the note in the restaurant. He had hope, however, and he tried in the best way that he knew for an escape from the inevitable. He had incredible courage and tremendous faith in the belief that things could somehow be made all right. He was a true Russian patriot. Everything that he did, he did for the Russian peasant, not for himself. Of course, nothing could be done.

"There was nothing that any one of us could do. There was no way for the politicians, or any of us, to intervene. He was tried before a military collegium of the Soviet Supreme Court in January of 1960, and then they executed him. It was by firing squad, I believe in June of 1960. They confirmed this to us finally, in 1996. They told us all about it. They couldn't have tortured him for too long; he didn't have that much time. They now tell us something of these things but they may be too embarrassed to tell us the whole truth, even today. There is the rumor that he was cremated alive while a number of junior GRU officers witnessed the spectacle, a lesson to them as to what might be their fate were they to embark upon the path that Popov took. I do not believe that it is true.

"We owe him a fortune in back pay. I have made an inquiry every year from 1985 to 1997, ever since Gorbachev created glasnost and the new government took over. I have tried to get some of his money to whoever is left in his family. I ran into a stone wall. The hierarchy there, the military, would not permit it. They said, 'What would you say if we wanted to pay Aldrich Ames or some other CIA traitor money for his child or something?' So, then, even with our standard, American hypocrisy, we would have to let it go at that. I tried five times in five different years through five different people, all or any one of whom had influence in Moscow. What can I do? I know who the family members are, but the Russians will not say anything more. They are not going to satisfy American curiosity; they don't give a damn. So, that is it."

"Is that it for today?" I ask.

"Yes, that is it."

PART III

Penkovsky

CHAPTER 10

The Letter

At the beginning of 1961 the United States had a new president, John F. Kennedy, who was inexperienced in matters of high command and state diplomacy. When he took office, the nation had a significant advantage in missilery over its Soviet competitor but a disadvantage in intelligence. Both conditions would change on his watch. The missile advantage would dwindle to the point of a stalemate, and the intelligence gap would close, at least temporarily, with the appearance of one man, a Soviet colonel in the GRU. This individual provided the United States with information so voluminous and valuable that the relationship between the two nations would dramatically change. The operation developed by the CIA and its British partner, the SIS (Secret Intelligence Service), to capitalize on the opportunity has rightly been termed the most successful in the history of espionage. Although the Kennedy administration did not take full advantage of all the intelligence provided by the colonel, it did use enough of it to stave off a nuclear confrontation, and Oleg Vladimirovich Penkovsky, the Soviet colonel, would be acclaimed as "the spy who saved the world." George's part in the operation was that of principal case officer and interpreter. He jump-started the operation through personal interviews with the colonel when lengthy personal contacts were possible. As with Popov, George's ability to relate to the prospective agent was the key to the mint, although Penkovsky and Popov were cut from different cloths and came with different sets of motives for aiding the United States.

George's story began soon after he, Ferdi, and their baby, Eva, born in September of 1959 in Berlin, came home to McLean, Virginia, from Berlin in 1960. George had just rejoined his old Soviet operations section, when an intriguing event occurred. One day in August, the Agency received a cable from the U.S. Embassy in Moscow stating that a letter concerning a mysterious activity was to be forwarded. The letter had been dropped off at the embassy in the following manner. A Russian man in Moscow had contacted two American students who were part of a student group touring the USSR. He first made note of the young men at a railroad station in Kiev, where he noticed these two on the platform speaking reasonably fluent Russian to each other and to their neighbors. He realized that they were Americans, by their dress as well as their demeanor. He wished to approach them, but he didn't for fear that the *Intourist* guides, or others accompanying them, might be KGB. The next day he saw the same group in Sokolniki Park in the middle of Moscow, where American goods—tractors, women's clothes, etc.—were being displayed. Soviets were attending the exposition in large numbers, and the two students were curious about how the Soviets might react to the American goods.

The man again focused on the two students, but he didn't approach them because of obvious surveillance by security people in the area. As they left the park to go to their hotel, he followed them at a respectable distance. Later that evening, as they were strolling down the street, he suddenly approached them and offered a letter. He begged them to take it to the American Embassy, knowing that as Americans they could pass by Soviet police and be admitted in the front door by the marine guards. He needed to gain their confidence, so he gave them some information that he knew would interest them and be of value to the people who, he assumed, would hear from them. He talked of the recent Gary Powers U-2 affair and said that he knew its details through contacts that he had. He volunteered that fourteen rockets were fired at the U-2 and that there were no direct hits. Moreover, one of the rockets destroyed one of their own MIG 19s in the area, killing its pilot as he was attempting to shoot down the U-2. At this time, the United States had limited information on the U-2 incident, and Powers was due to go on trial within days. The mysterious Russian also talked of an event involving an RB-47, another U.S. aircraft that had been shot down on an intelligence mission. Publicly, the Soviets had always contended that the RB-47 had been intercepted while gathering data as it flew directly over the USSR. American intelligence personnel, however, were certain that the plane had been destroyed in international waters.

He agreed that it had been. He was very pleasant, yet insistent.

Eventually, one of the two young men gained enough curiosity and courage to cooperate with the man. He accepted a large, thick envelope from the man and assured him that it would be taken to the American Embassy. Abruptly, the man stopped the conversation, saying, "I see a militiaman walking down the street, and he may be curious as to why I, obviously a Russian by dress and so forth, am speaking to two foreigners. So you better go now before someone is too curious. It is not a good thing. As for the letter, just hand it to the marines; that is all you have to do."

The embassy was not far, so that evening, the lad stepped up to the door and knocked. The marine guard appeared and let him in to see the security officer, who was working late that day. The intrepid student handed the letter to the security officer and told him how it had been acquired. The officer cautioned the young man to stay out of harm's way: "You shouldn't be picking up things like that; that is how you get serious problems. Who are you? What is your name?" The student showed his identification. The officer wrote down his name as well as his passport number and, after making positive identification as well as giving him another admonition about staying out of trouble, told him to take care of himself. He then accepted the letter and dismissed the student. The security officer promptly reported the incident to his superiors and gave them the letter. When the letter finally was delivered to the CIA and its contents were viewed, personnel in George's Soviet activities branch made the necessary inquiries and had case officers interview each student. The case officers asked each student about the circumstances of the letter's receipt. Nothing about either student appeared insidious or disturbing, and neither of them knew more about the man who had delivered the letter. Moreover, neither knew its contents.

When George first viewed the letter he considered it an astonishing document. In neatly typed Russian, the anonymous writer spoke derisively of the Soviet government and stated emphatically that he was very much opposed to the actions of that body. He praised the performance of Van Cliburn, the American pianist who had won the Tchaikovsky competition prize. He claimed to know American Embassy personnel in Istanbul, where apparently he had been stationed as a Soviet military attaché. Then he stated, "I offer my services to you and I have some most significant facts to share." Enclosed were two very important items. The first established the writer's bona fides. He knew that the U.S. Embassy personnel often received letters and notes of all kinds in Moscow and that most of them were either pranks or provocations. He wrote, "I know that you have no sound basis for completely trusting everything that I have said to you, so I must prove myself. In order to do so, I am enclosing a list of incoming Military Diplomatic Academy students and their future assignments." The list was for the next class, the one that would graduate three years hence, in 1963. It contained the incoming students' full names, their ranks, a little about their previous education, the language they would be studying at the MDA, and the countries to which they later would be assigned. Most were military attachés but a number of individuals were identified with asterisks as potential illegals. Since illegals are spies who might enter their target country surreptitiously with false identities, and who possibly never are identified by the local security personnel, this was startling. Prominent among the countries designated were the United States, Canada, and Great Britain. The letter went on, "Many of these facts I am giving to you can be checked by you, because a number of these people have already been abroad before and were previously exposed to you. In addition, I want instructions from you as to how I might safely deliver to you some top secret nuclear information. I don't know how to do this securely. I need your guidance and help."

There was no signature on the letter, but its author left a clue by saying, "I send greetings to my first good American friend who I knew in Turkey, Col. Charles MacLean Peeke." He also extended his best wishes to many others who had been in the U.S. Military Attaché Office of the U.S. Embassy in Turkey from 1955 to 1957. He had written their names in English, using ink because he did not know how to translate their names accurately in Russian on his typewriter.

The second important enclosure in the envelope was a group photo. Among those pictured were some of the attachés, including Colonel Peeke, who was, at the time of the photo, the chief American military attaché in Istanbul. A Soviet military officer's face had been neatly excised (perhaps with a razor blade) from the rest of the picture. Only the top of the man's head remained. Near the scalp of the missing face, the writer added the caption, "I am." This was as far as he would go in identifying himself, fearing that the package might fall into the wrong hands. Within a matter of minutes, however, George's group had identified the author simply by reviewing various snapshots and portraits in the State Department's Military Attaché Office until they found a duplicate copy of the whole photograph. The sender was Col. Oleg Vladimirovich Penkovsky, a senior GRU officer in Turkey at one time, who had been replaced after some internal Soviet rumpus. That is all that the CIA knew of him.

Some at the CIA were not convinced that Penkovsky was genuine and thought that he might actually be attempting to penetrate the CIA. The Agency analysts simply did not know much about him. He did not say a lot in his three-page letter and, assuredly, the Agency wanted to avoid any big chance of a provocation. George, however, was convinced of the man's bona fides. He said, "After all, how could anyone present the identities of sixty individuals posted worldwide—all high ranking, all future placements, all strategic intelligence officers—without going too far? The man could not give away the countryside—dog and all—just to prove that he was being cooperative. One does not give away what Penkovsky did as a ploy." Nevertheless, George and his group had to be certain, so they analyzed all that they could about the sixty men from every source they had. They reviewed every historical record of every individual, particularly looking for evidence that some might be intelligence officers, legals or illegals. Some at the CIA worked sixteen hours a day analyzing every scrap of information on each individual. Many of the Soviets could not be identified because they had never left the confines of the USSR, but a goodly number of intelligence officers were recognized. These were previously known to the CIA and had been stationed abroad, serving as attachés. Something else helped confirm this man's validity. Penkovsky had, with asterisks, further identified some of the people as illegals, and CIA analysts knew one such person working in East Germany, by name and by function. He had been quite effective in countering Agency operations from West Berlin into East Berlin. Moreover, independent CIA investigations had previously discovered a number of illegals working in Turkey who were on the list. The Soviets could not reasonably be expected to give away these illegals as a ploy.

But perhaps the most conclusive evidence of Penkovsky's authenticity was demonstrated shortly thereafter. Because the Soviet MDA had a beginning date, every officer in the new class had to leave his respective post or station in order to get to school on time. In every case where it could be documented, this travel did occur. No one in an intelligence service would give away that information as a ploy; such an act would jeopardize too many people in order to make one person look acceptable. George's people needed to know more, however, before they could act.

The letter had one more facet that intrigued them. Its author had described in detail the location of a dead drop in Moscow and what he wished to be placed in the box: instructions for a secure means by which he could pass to the United States a large envelope-sized package, maybe half an inch thick. The envelope would contain detailed information on every operational missile in the arsenal of the USSR: free rockets, guided rockets, conventional armament, and nuclear missiles. He said that he didn't know how to securely deliver this, but he indicated the location of a telephone booth in another part of Moscow where the CIA could provide a signal. At this booth, he suggested, one could place a sign, say a chalk mark, which would indicate that the dead drop had been loaded. He would go by this booth every day and look through the glass to determine whether or not the mark was there. If it were, within twenty-four hours he would go to the dead drop and retrieve his instructions for delivering the missile data.

How to contact him personally in Moscow was still a problem. The Agency had no means. Penkovsky couldn't invite Americans to his house, and he couldn't visit the American Embassy. Needed was a secure means for a rendezvous, completely secure if the man were an intelligence officer. The ball was in the Agency's court. The Agency's position in Moscow at that time was very limited, however. The branch that was to handle Penkovsky had handled the Popov case, but it had lost all of its officers in Moscow as a result of that operation when the Soviets had declared them *personae non gratae* and precipitously sent them home.

The man intrigued his readers to no end. He had approached the students in civilian clothing, one of whom had delivered the package. He had identified himself and had given splendid bona fides, but he had assumed that the CIA had powers that it did not have. It couldn't even, for instance, send someone in a car and invite Penkovsky to throw his package into an open window of the vehicle.

Very quickly, people were recruited for assignment in Moscow under any diplomatic cover that could be arranged for them with the State Department. The Agency felt that their people had to have some kind of diplomatic cover for the personal safety brought about by diplomatic immunity. Joe Bulik was the supervisor of the branch, and he was responsible for obtaining this cover for his people. His job was not easy. Compounding the problem was the way in which the State Department designated all U.S. government personnel who were available for international assignments. If they were not career Foreign Service officers, they were considered Foreign Service Reserve. Such a designation often resulted in an *R* being attached to their names on lists that were overtly published. This tended to suggest that they were CIA personnel. Moreover, if one used State Department cover, he or she also had to follow State Department rules and practices. One State Department rule required the use of the indigenous population for such things as domestics, a practice that tended to bring a fatal flaw of security. Even with State Department cover, Agency activities were limited. Worse yet, the State Department did not readily cooperate with the CIA and, in fact, the security officer at the Moscow Embassy believed Penkovsky's actions to be nothing more than a provocation. He briefed Ambassador Llewellyn Thompson accordingly, telling him this exercise was of no value. The ambassador then was not inclined to enthusiastically support the CIA. After all, the State Department had the almost impossible task of dealing with the Soviet Union, and CIA operations in Moscow could jeopardize the entire diplomatic mission.

The Soviet Division at the CIA considered filling the dead drop with a message asking Penkovsky to throw his parcel over the wall of the American Embassy as he passed by. The ambassador said no. In the meantime, the material from Penkovsky's letter was being studied, and the information concerning those illegals who might come to the United States was given to the FBI. Information related to the British Commonwealth was given to the SIS.

Penkovsky had said in his letter that he would start looking at the signal site three days from the date that he had delivered the letter. Of course, he did not know how the Agency bureaucracy worked. The people there just could not respond in three days. One could not even be expected to do traces[1] in three days. One doesn't do anything in three days within a bureaucracy. George's branch didn't even receive the letter in three days. Penkovsky also wrongly assumed that the CIA had someone in Moscow who could quickly do the traces, establish his bona fides, and develop an operational plan. So, in August of 1960 Penkovsky began walking past that signal site every day. He continued to do so almost until the time he met George eight months later. When they did meet, he asked George, "Why didn't you signal?" All George could do was blush and offer some vague reply.

No one in George's branch could understand the exact status of Colonel Penkovsky. Why had he worn civilian clothes when he approached the American students? He was a Soviet military intelligence officer on duty with the GRU, so he should have been wearing a uniform. As time went by, the branch learned that he was approaching others. In December of 1960, the British SIS reported that some British gentlemen had been on a business trip to Moscow, trying to sell some of their non-embargo items. When they came home, one of them reported to the British Intelligence Service in London that some man named Penkovsky had approached them at the airport as they were leaving. He had asked them to take some information to the American Embassy in London. The businessmen refused to take any of this man's paper. They wanted nothing compromising in their possession while in Moscow or while boarding a plane to leave Moscow. They did, however, take the man's business card, printed in English, displaying his name and position: Member of the State Committee for the Coordination of Scientific Research Work, the committee responsible for scientific and technological liaison with foreign countries. Dzhermen Gvishiani, future premier Aleksey Kosygin's son-in law, headed the committee. Penkovsky wrote his telephone number on the back. He then said, "Please tell the American intelligence people in Moscow to call me at ten o'clock on any Sunday morning, speaking only in Russian. Please ask the Americans to inform their representative in Moscow to have someone do this."

The SIS mistakenly believed that the CIA had previously operated with Penkovsky but was now separated from him. Their precedent was the 1956 occasion in Stralsund, East Germany, when the British had put Popov back in touch with the CIA after he had been separated from the Agency for some months. Assuming a like situation, they informed the CIA of the contact between the businessmen and Penkovsky. When this was reported to George, his reaction was one of shock, fearing that Penkovsky was much too forward in his approaches to the West. George wondered how often the man had tried to make such overt contacts. Now, however, George realized that Penkovsky had a different kind of position in the GRU, one that would allow him to wear civilian clothes, but George did not understand what it was about.

Another extraordinary incident involving Penkovsky occurred soon thereafter. This time it was with the Canadians. George got a call in January of 1961 from an old acquaintance in Ottawa, a Canadian diplomat. He was coming to Washington and he wanted to meet with George personally, because he suspected that his own telephone lines were being monitored. When George saw him, the diplomat described Canadian contacts with Penkovsky in Moscow. The basic circumstances of the contacts had previously been reported to the U.S. Embassy in Moscow and forwarded to George's branch, but George's Canadian friend could expand upon its details, as follows.

In walked a Russian man who had in his arms a large bundle of papers in a large envelope. He met with one of the diplomats, Van Vliet, a commercial counselor. The man started by saying, "I represent a scientific group here in Moscow that has to do with the English-speaking world—the Canadians, the Americans, and the British. You are Canadians. We understand that you are friendly with Americans. I want you to do something for me. This package that I am leaving with you is very sensitive. I want you to deliver it to the American Embassy."

He handed Van Vliet his card along with the package and walked out. A day or so later Van Vliet met with Penkovsky and told him, "Look, Penkovsky, here is your package. We did not open it, we did not photograph it, and we did not give it to the Americans. We are not to be involved in this. Please take your package and leave. We have enough trouble politically now without inviting a total disaster from a provocation. You came to us. We did not go to you."

The dejected Penkovsky left. That was Van Vliet's story to George's friend in Ottawa. The Canadians would not take his package but they did report the incident to the Americans. To George, Penkovsky appeared to be operating in an extremely dangerous way.

Earlier, in the fall of 1960, the CIA had been able to get a lower-level operations officer in place in Moscow. He had moved into America House, where some of the U.S. Embassy personnel lived. The officer looked for a way in which Penkovsky could dispatch his package. George instructed the man to call the number specified by Penkovsky at ten o'clock sharp on Sunday morning and to speak in Russian. The substance of the message was to be: "Please do not try to contact anyone else; it is not safe. We are on top of this but we are still trying to find a secure way to accomplish a safe means of contact. Do not approach anyone else. Contact no Canadians, or British businessmen, or anyone else." Unfortunately, however, the CIA operative in Moscow did not make his call to Penkovsky until February of 1961, and then he called at eleven o'clock instead of ten o'clock as prescribed by Penkovsky. He also mangled the Russian language, forgot or could not say the message that was intended, and improvised his own message, one that made no sense at all to Penkovsky. When George later asked Penkovsky about the phone call, he was sorry that he had asked the question. The CIA wound up looking like fools, judging by how Penkovsky described the message he had received. In George's mind the endeavor was totally useless, and although it didn't cause any damage, it had been dangerous and stupid.

In April of 1961, the British came to George's group with yet another Penkovsky story. A prosperous businessman by the name of Greville Wynne, a salesman of precision machinery, representing seven manufacturers of high-grade non-embargo tools, had organized a visit by a British trade delegation to Moscow. They wished to sell machinery that previously was embargoed. In the process he had run into a man by the name of Penkovsky in Moscow. Penkovsky told Wynne that he was with a scientific group, a committee for the coordination of new technical developments, and that he was assigned to them as their liaison officer. He escorted Wynne about Moscow, wining and dining him, and took the opportunity to make an overture: "I would like to make a trip to London, leading my delegation, or representing it so that I can work more with the British, Americans, and Canadians in matters of scientific commerce. Can you help me?"

Wynne, of course, could make no commitment. At their last moment together at the airport, when Wynne was preparing to leave Moscow for London, Penkovsky stopped him and said, "Look, I have some envelopes in my pocket. Would you deliver them to the American Embassy in London?" Wynne responded, "Look, Penkovsky, you are a likable guy but I want to go to London, not Vladimir[2] or some damn jail place. I want nothing like that on me when I go through your customs. Please, no way, no way!" Penkovsky assured Wynne that there would be no problem with customs and, displaying a number of parcels as if they were playing cards, implored Wynne to "just take one or two." "No; I won't take any of your paper," insisted Wynne. But he did accept a single sheet, a letter addressed jointly to various leaders of the United Kingdom and the United States. He delivered this to the British SIS. When the British told the CIA, George mulled over the situation and thought, "My God, we don't have an operation here; we have a disaster in the making. This guy is going to hang himself sooner or later. This is how many times, four? How many strikes does one have before he's out in a baseball game?"

It had been almost a year since Penkovsky's first attempt to contact the CIA. George was amazed that the man had not yet been caught as a result of making such dangerous, blind approaches. Then, things took a turn for the better. A cable from London informed George that a delegation of six Soviet scientists would be coming to London for a fifteen-day sojourn. They wished to visit British steel firms in London, Leeds, and Birmingham. They probably would have representatives from the KGB and/or the GRU, but their leader would be Col. Oleg V. Penkovsky.

Joe Bulik, George's newly appointed branch chief, declared, "I'm going to go. You go with me, Kisevalter." George spoke fluent Russian and Bulik did not. George had not known of discussions between the CIA and SIS that had culminated in the agreement of a joint operation to exploit the Penkovsky potential. Unaware of the extent of the British involvement with Penkovsky, George was not comfortable with this arrangement. Moreover, perhaps he also believed that he, not Joe, should be the branch chief. George was fresh from his successful operation with Popov, and he felt that he did not need anyone to assist him in debriefing Penkovsky. He thought Bulik could not add anything to the mix and, in fact, might even be detrimental to the process. Nevertheless, George was a cooperative team member. Any personal differences between George and Joe would be put aside throughout the period of direct contact with Penkovsky.

With the near calamities that had transpired with Penkovsky still fresh in their minds, Joe and George went, making additional preparations for security. George had a false identity, McAdam, a Scotsman. Why he was a Scotsman, George did not know. He didn't know a thing about Scotland or Scots idiom. Harold Shergold and

Michael Stokes of British intelligence met them. George recognized immediately that Shergold was very experienced and astute, someone who knew his business inside and out. Stokes was young but seemed capable, smart, and enthusiastic. George and Bulik described to them their past contacts with Penkovsky, and the British reviewed theirs with the Americans.

The British Intelligence Service had recently experienced a most alarming revelation. Only a couple of weeks earlier, thanks in part to Shergold, the British had unearthed George Blake, a Soviet mole burrowed into their intelligence service. He had been a very high ranking member of the SIS. Following his trial, he was sentenced to forty-two years of incarceration at Wormwood Scrubs, the longest sentence ever imposed for espionage in the United Kingdom. He was a high-ranking British intelligence officer and he deserved no less. Fortunately, he could not have known anything about Penkovsky, so he wasn't a hazard. "We want you to know that he confessed in this chair in which you are now sitting, just two weeks ago," Shergold told George. In October of 1966, however, Blake was sprung from prison and went to Moscow.[3]

Since Greville Wynne was planning to escort the Soviet scientific delegation about while they were in London and to have sales meetings with them, he met the group at the airport. Although he wanted simply to sell the Soviets goods from his manufacturers, he was now under the control of the SIS and would be the conduit for overt contact with Penkovsky by the two intelligence organizations. When Wynne returned from the airport, he had with him a letter from Penkovsky, which he promptly turned over to Dickie Franks, his principal contact at the SIS. Franks in turn gave the package to Shergold. No one had a chance to review the material in the letter before the first meeting with Penkovsky, when it was shared with the Americans on the team.

The letter was typewritten in Russian. Originally it had been addressed to President Eisenhower, but this now was scratched out and President Kennedy's name substituted. It also was addressed to former secretary of state John Foster Dulles, then deceased, and his brother, the director of the CIA, Allen Dulles. Penkovsky had added by hand, "And to Her Majesty, the Queen of England's Government." Prime Minister Harold Macmillan's name also was included. The letter read, "I have approached the Americans and offered my services, but this is an opportunity to come to England that I didn't expect. Since I am here, I want to take the opportunity, without denying my American contact, to offer my services jointly to both countries." Along with the letter was the dog-eared package that Penkovsky had been carrying around for more than a year, which contained all of the details about the missiles, the same package that the Canadian Van Vliet had rejected.

The Soviet delegates would not question Penkovsky's movements. He was in charge of their itinerary—the selection of factory visits as well as the various company presentations—but Wynne and the other British set the actual schedule. Wynne assigned the hotel rooms according to a special plan provided by the SIS. All were housed in the Mount Royal Hotel, a huge barn of a building that takes up an entire city block near Hyde Park. Bulik and George were to occupy the safehouse room, a corner room with minimum exposure to contiguous rooms. The two could look out the window across the inner core of the hotel at other rooms. All of the Soviets were on a floor well above them. Penkovsky's room was around a hall corner from the other delegates, so he could come and go freely without passing by any of their rooms. For the first meeting, as a final safety measure, yet another room was engaged on a floor above the safehouse room. In it Bulik and Shergold would have first contact with their prize. Here, in the event something was amiss, Shergold could fix the problem or abort the meeting with minimum exposure to the rest of the team. As yet, they did not know for certain that Penkovsky was genuine.

After the members of the delegation had their dinner, Penkovsky excused himself from the others and went back to his room. From there, by the back stairs, he came down to the designated initial meeting room. Shergold opened the door, introduced himself, and introduced Penkovsky to Bulik. The three of them then came down to the safehouse room to meet Stokes and George. The first meeting would begin.

CHAPTER 11

The Man from the Caucasus

Penkovsky began. "A lot of this is over my head. I am not a scientist. I am an intelligence officer. I only have heard about nuclear materials. I went to a nuclear school but that does not make me an expert. That is one difficult field, nuclear weapons. Do you know about it?" George answered, "No, heavens no. I can say only a few words."

When the two began to talk about inertial guidance systems, semiconductors, and such, the team realized that they had to have a new dictionary for the new words in Russian. What is a space carriage? What is an oblating nose cone? All of these terms had different meanings in different languages. They had to create a glossary for the missile/space language. Getting intelligence was one thing. Understanding technical details was another matter. George did not try to pretend to know any more about nuclear missiles than Penkovsky did.[1]

The group especially wanted to know where Penkovsky had gotten the material he had given them, why it was in his possession, and why he was doing this. To make sense of these things, he had to tell them his whole life story, from the moment he was born to that moment. George's own account of what he learned from Penkovsky follows.

Oleg V. Penkovsky was an only child born in 1919 during the Counterrevolution by the Whites against the Reds, in a small town in the southern Caucasus by the name of Vladikavkaz, meaning "Empress of the Caucasus," like Vladivostok is "Empress of the East." It is in the south of Russia, midway between the Black and Caspian seas. His grandfather was an eminent judge in the tsarist days, presiding in the Stavropol district. The judge had a younger brother,

Oleg's great-uncle, Valentine Antonovich Penkovsky. He was very well known in his own right and had little contact with Oleg. They did meet later in life for at least one very poignant meeting.

Penkovsky's father, Vladimir Florianovich Penkovsky, was a mining engineer in the White Army, a lieutenant who was married to a girl from that area. In 1920 he fought in the region north of the Caucasus Mountains toward the Black Sea. During the fighting, the father disappeared and was never heard from again. This battle was part of the campaign to take Tsaritsyn, later to become Stalingrad (now Volgograd). Joseph Stalin, then a Bolshevik political commissar, fought in the same battle. Thereafter, Penkovsky's mother told others that her husband died of typhus rather than in battle with the Reds, in order to protect the young Penkovsky. She withheld the truth from him as well.

Penkovsky went to middle school for ten years and then to the Second Kiev Artillery School. It was a lower-category military school, something like the American OCS or ROTC. He also joined the Komsomol, the youth Communist organization. According to his own statements, he was an enthusiastic member, in accordance with the propaganda of the times. He was a fine student. In 1939, at age twenty, he was graduated from the artillery school, becoming a junior lieutenant. He became a Communist Party member at twenty-one, the minimum age.

In September of 1939, the Germans invaded Poland. By previous agreement between Stalin and Hitler, the Soviets then attacked Poland from the east. Penkovsky's first military assignment was the occupation of the Lvov-Tarnopol area of Poland. There was minimal fighting in this operation, and he was promptly reassigned that fall to the Ninety-third Rifle Division of an artillery battery in Siberia. In January of 1940, the Russo-Finnish war began. The Soviets presumed that it would be a trivial matter to subdue Finland, but they were disappointed. It was winter and the Finns were adept on their skis, and they exhibited great nerve and tenacity. Penkovsky's division was placed in the Karelian Isthmus, the narrow neck of land in Russia between Leningrad and Finland. The division immediately suffered 90 percent casualties. With more experienced and heavily armed units from Siberia, masses of artillery, and tremendous loss of life, the Soviets eventually overcame the Finnish defenses. Penkovsky was physically unscathed but emotionally traumatized.

At the conclusion of this action, in the spring of 1940, Penkovsky's decimated division was pulled back in order to be reformed. He was temporarily put into a manpower reserve outfit back in Moscow. When the Germans and the Soviets went to war in June of 1941, he was assigned to the Political Directorate of the Moscow Military District. He met a young lady in Moscow, Vera Dimitrieva Gapanovich, who was very high on the social ladder. Her father, Lt. Gen. Dmitri A. Gapanovich, was prominent in the party, the political military chief in Moscow, and a two-star general. Penkovsky romanced her, discreetly and successfully. Now he began to meet important people and to have some influence on them as they had influence on him. His primary duty during this period was to work with the Komsomol.

In mid-1942, Penkovsky was transferred to the Military Council of the Moscow District, into a section for extraordinary missions. By November of 1943, he had seen many people coming from the front with decorations, and he became anxious to see front-line duty. He requested a combat assignment and was promptly sent to the First Ukrainian Front as a commander of a training center for anti-tank regiments. These units were being decimated right and left by very powerful tank actions by the Germans. In March of 1944, after completing his preliminary service with this training unit, he was assigned as the deputy commander of an anti-tank regiment. It was a tough proposition. His regiment of tank destroyers would either destroy the tanks or be destroyed. However, he was effective and he received awards for valor and military competence. He was promoted to major, then to lieutenant colonel. He became the commander of the regiment when its commander was removed for disciplinary reasons.

Penkovsky improvised ingeniously. For example, he realized that the howitzers in his unit were virtually useless against tanks because these weapons, designed for indirect fire over long distances, were not maneuverable in close combat. He had one mounted on mobile steel plates that were stacked on one another and lubricated with the oil from the recoil mechanisms of the guns. The weapon then could be spun around in various directions and the gun barrel depressed to the desired elevation by only two men in a matter of seconds. This idea converts the howitzer from an indirect-fire weapon into a direct-fire weapon, which aims straight away. Thus, howitzers that employ this modification can fire point-blank into the tanks. Penkovsky's improvisation in the field was very effective against German tanks and for this he earned the Order of Alexander Nevsky. He received other awards for inventiveness, valor, and military competence. Altogether, he received eight assorted decorations, four of which were battle orders.

In June of 1944, Penkovsky was hit by an exploding shell while fighting near the Rumanian border. He suffered concussions, his jaw was fractured, and he lost six teeth. He was taken to a hospital in Moscow.[2] In that same hospital was a very prominent man, the commander of the artillery of the entire First Ukrainian Front, one of four major Soviet fronts during the war. These fronts altogether numbered 5 million men.[3] This commander of the artillery, Col. Gen. Sergey Sergeyevich Varentsov, later became a marshal of artillery and eventually chief marshal of all artillery of the USSR. He would play a key role in Penkovsky's life as well as in the value of the intelligence information that the team later would receive from Penkovsky. Varentsov was suffering from a leg injury. He had been in a highway accident involving an American jeep and a Soviet tank. When he heard that Penkovsky, who was a commander of one of his regiments, was in the same hospital, he said, "Get him in here." To Penkovsky he said, "I want to be in touch with all of my artillery in the First Ukrainian Front, so I am appointing you to a new job. You are now my temporary aide-de-camp. When you get out of the hospital, I want you to be the contact between me and the front while I am in this hospital. When I am well enough to go over there myself, we will join up."

To become associated with a general was like a gift from heaven. Penkovsky and General Varentsov would eventually become intimate friends. This chance meeting, however, thrust them into an immediate close relationship. Varentsov had, by his first wife, a daughter, Nina. Although she had his whole heart, she was a willful girl and pretty much did what she wanted to do most of the time. She married someone he referred to as a jerk, even though the man was a major in the army. Varentsov heard that in the capture of the city of Lvov in Poland, her husband had been arrested for black-marketing and summarily ordered shot. He said to Penkovsky, "Go help my daughter, Nina. See what is happening there. They have arrested the jerk."

When Penkovsky got there, the son-in-law had already been executed, but he found the general's daughter and tried to help her in any way possible. She had been working there in a hospital. To his dismay, immediately after he found her she pulled a pistol out of someone's holster, and fatally shot herself. He sold his watch and everything else he had with him in order to provide for a decent burial. He came back with tears in his eyes and told the general what had happened to his daughter. Varentsov embraced him and said, "You acted like a son to me in my moment of woe and tragedy. I will never forget it." They became lifetime friends, which for the CIA and SIS was a godsend.

After the war ended, Penkovsky found himself in Czechoslovakia with the victorious First Ukrainian Front. He was liberating artifacts and china, all sorts of beautiful things, and doling them out to his buddies when Varentsov, now a marshal, called him in. He said, "Penkovsky, look, you're not the smartest guy in the world, although now you already are a lieutenant colonel. You should go to the Frunze Military Academy. It's the highest military school of the USSR."

"How do I get in?"

"I'm a marshal! I'll get you in. Here's a letter."

Penkovsky went to Moscow in 1949 and took an abbreviated course of study from this Russian West Point. He also married his girlfriend, Vera Gapanovich. His father-in-law, Dmitri Gapanovich, was a big political wheel and his good friend the marshal was nearby, so it looked as if he was doing fine. When Penkovsky was graduated from the Frunze Military Academy, however, the marshal again called him in and inquired, "How would you like to go to another academy and really get somewhere?" Varentsov was speaking of the Military Diplomatic Academy, the intelligence school for training GRU.

Penkovsky was graduated from the MDA in 1953, and, although he was not good at it, his language was English. But he now had a second degree and was a senior military officer, a full colonel. Soon thereafter, Marshal Varentsov was promoted to chief marshal of artillery of the USSR, in charge of both artillery and midrange, tactical ballistic missiles.[4] Penkovsky seemed to be sitting pretty. With connections like that, he should get a good a job. So he fished around for an assignment abroad. Naturally, there were problems in one country or another, as to how many people were already assigned to each location vs. what was allowed through diplomatic channels. Pakistan was at first a possibility, but it did not work out.

Eventually, even though he was an English-speaking graduate, he was sent, temporarily, to Turkey as the acting station chief for the GRU. Later he would be replaced by Maj. Gen. Nikolai Petrovich Rubenko, who was to be the permanent station chief, with Penkovsky as his deputy. Rubenko's real name was Savchenko, but he had gotten his hands caught in the cookie jar in Afghanistan and was going by the name of Rubenko in an attempt to conceal his GRU affiliation, which the Soviets feared might have been compromised.

In Turkey, Penkovsky met the American Army attaché, Col. Charles MacLean Peeke. As counterparts, they became socially acquainted and got along quite well together. Vera Penkovsky could speak a little French; she loved the West and all of the Western goods in Istanbul. The Penkovskys were satisfied with the assignment and looked forward to an upwardly mobile career path. Although both Penkovsky and Peeke were charged with finding weaknesses in the other that could be exploited for intelligence purposes, neither made an overt attempt to recruit the other. Colonel Peeke must have impressed Penkovsky favorably, because Penkovsky later said he had thought of approaching Peeke with his services while in Turkey. Peeke abruptly returned to the U.S., however, due to a death in his family, and Penkovsky himself was recalled to Moscow shortly thereafter; so the opportunity never matured.

Unfortunately for Penkovsky, there was a young lieutenant colonel by the name of Nikolai Ionchenko, a good friend of General Rubenko's, also at the Istanbul station. There was a certain rivalry there, and when Rubenko came, there was immediate animosity between Penkovsky and the general. The ill will deepened soon thereafter when the shah of Iran and his wife, the glamorous Soraya, came on a state visit to Istanbul. Cables came in from GRU headquarters in Moscow as well as the KGB saying, in effect, "Lay off all active operations because you are going to be infested with platoons of intelligence people from all countries hostile to the USSR. There will be Savak of the shah who are friendly to Americans, British SIS, Turkish Intelligence, Americans' CIA; all who don't like the USSR are going to be very active during this State visit. Lay off." Ionchenko came to Rubenko and said, "General, I have a problem. I have a Turkish officer who is an agent of mine and I have an appointment to meet with him. I want to pay him certain payments I owe him. He also has ready for delivery certain American Air Force documents, which he has stolen from the Americans. He wants to pass them to me and collect his pay. Can I make the meeting? This hold-down was unexpected." The general said, "Go ahead. Go to Penkovsky, tell him to give you the operational funds you need, make your meeting, and pay off your agent."

When Penkovsky was apprised of this, he made a surreptitious telephone call to Turkish Intelligence informing them of the meeting, thereby setting up Ionchenko for apprehension. Upon being caught, Ionchenko was declared *persona non grata,* and the officer escorting him out of Turkey was Penkovsky. To make matters worse, Penkovsky argued with the general over this and then complained to Moscow, using KGB rather than GRU channels so that the general would not know. The incident reached the Central Committee of the Communist Party; it reached Khrushchev, who said, "Get both of those jackasses in here, both Penkovsky and Rubenko, and we'll thrash this out."

Penkovsky and General Rubenko were summoned before the Central Committee of the Communist Party, he for insubordination and the general for not properly following procedures. The general was removed from his assignment in Turkey, and Penkovsky was put on notice. Penkovsky was not actually found guilty of anything because they did not know that he had made the surreptitious phone call. They suspected something, however, and no general in charge of any big section wanted to have Penkovsky work for him.

Penkovsky had gotten himself into a beautiful doghouse. In addition, General Rubenko began to look for something about Penkovsky that would be viewed in a negative light. There might be something in Penkovsky's background that could be used against him. Evidently he found out that Penkovsky's father was a White Army officer. Did Penkovsky know? Did he not know? Rubenko started rumors. Penkovsky was told to walk the halls until a job was found for him.

To his rescue came Marshal Varentsov, who knew Penkovsky's boss, Ivan Aleksandrovich Serov, the chief of the GRU and the ex-chief of the KGB. Varentsov talked with Serov and had Penkovsky assigned to his school. He was given a nine-month refresher course in the marshal's missile academy in Moscow, the Dzerzhinskiy Artillery-Engineering Academy.[5] This was a scientific course, not an intelligence course, and Penkovsky could have been out of his element. He was, however, pretty sharp in other ways and he dropped hints among the faculty that he was a friend of the marshal's. He then became the major-domo of this little refresher class. He was favored by all of the chief generals of the various departments, such as Fuels, Inertial Guidance Systems, Propellants, Power, Nuclear Devices, Range Activities, and Tactics. The heads of the various departments of the school brought him materials to study and to copy. These materials were a precursor of what he eventually brought to the CIA and SIS. He didn't know at that time what he had in his hands. He didn't understand the details or the value of the scientific aspects of the material. He knew that the material was important, but he was unaware of how valuable it might be to the CIA and SIS. Not even the case officers knew its full importance. Those who did were the air force experts at Wright-Patterson Field near Dayton, Ohio, and analysts at the army's Foreign Science and Technology Center at Huntsville, Alabama.[6]

Penkovsky graduated on 30 April 1959 from the Artillery-Engineering Academy and prepared to return to the GRU. The date would prove to be significant. The ill feelings surrounding the Rubenko brouhaha apparently had blown over, and Penkovsky was assigned back to the Mid-East Intelligence Directorate. He began preparing for an assignment as the new station chief in India when quite suddenly the chief of personnel removed him from that position and confronted him: "We have a problem, Somebody is claiming that your father was a White Army officer. Call in your mother."

His poor mother was dragged in. She pled in every way a mother can. She said that Oleg never knew about his father's service in the White Army. "He was guilty of nothing. He was always loyal. He knew nothing. Why pick on him?" She signed an affidavit to that effect. So, they said, "All right, we'll keep it quiet; we'll find him another job. Penkovsky, how would you like to teach here?"

"Not a chance. I'll just walk the halls some more."

"Don't worry, we'll find something for you."

Penkovsky was put back into the reserves. This is near to the time that he first contacted the CIA through the two students in Moscow. It appears that his experiences with the GRU, along with his personal feelings about the Soviet system, were then weighing heavily on his mind. To get an idea of the solidity of Penkovsky's anti-Communist beliefs, it is useful to recall Oleg's great-uncle, Valentine Antonovich Penkovsky, who as a younger man went his own way. He also joined the Soviet Army. He also progressed. He became a one-star general, but he ran afoul of Stalin during the purges and wound up in a jail. Fortunately, he was not shot as many were. When the war against Germany began, Stalin resuscitated almost everyone in jail. The general thus came out. He went up the ladder to two stars, to three stars. He became a deputy chief to Rodion Malinovsky, the minister of defense. He earned three Orders of Lenin.

The general then got in touch with his grandnephew. They secretly met in a hotel room in Moscow, had a bottle of vodka, and talked. Valentine said, "Okay, Oleg, the curse of that madman Stalin is still around. You are a menace to me—you know about my sentiments regarding Communism and that I was in jail, thanks to Stalin. I am a menace to you—I know about your father being a White Army officer. We are contaminants to one other. Let us never correspond. Let us never meet again because in this miserable society one will threaten the other. I don't care how big you get, it's still that way." They agreed. They drank, they kissed, and they said good-by.

That deputy chief later became the assistant first deputy to Malinovsky, minister of defense of the USSR. He became the chief of the Warsaw Pact Nations, the commanding officer of their joint army, and eventually the first deputy minister of war of the USSR. George displayed a copy of the general's attestat.[7] The document, signed by Brezhnev, Khrushchev and others, had appeared in *Pravda.*

Valentine Antonovich Penkovsky is still well known. His accomplishments in battles during the Second World War were renowned. Valentine also received the Order of Lenin on his sixtieth birthday in 1964 from Brezhnev, first secretary of the party. The sixtieth birthday is a big occasion in Russia today even as it was in tsarist Russia, when a railroad engineer or a high-ranking individual would get a gold watch and some sort of award. The relationship between Oleg and his great-uncle underscores the bona fides of Oleg Penkovsky and everything that he told the CIA-SIS team. The account of their meeting also illustrates that even powerful people in the USSR could hate Communism and still do nothing about it. As George said, "How could one afford to be a hero at the expense of all of his friends and relatives who would be punished, even executed, for his disloyalty to Communism? So, one can see how far it goes, how high it goes. How much higher can one get in political circles? He was a deputy chief to the minister of defense."

In June of 1960, Oleg Penkovsky was recommended for an

important new job, member of the Mandate Commission of the Military Diplomatic Academy. The commission would consist of three people: the chief of personnel of the GRU, the chief of the intelligence school, and him. He would be the sponsor of the incoming intelligence officers' class and, in time, be given the rank of general. As the class sponsor, he would process the incoming students. He would get to know them personally, and he would see them through their three years there and into their initial assignments. He was given a list of the students' names as well as their personal and professional backgrounds, the list that he would send in the letter to the CIA. He was given this job even though there was a cloud over his head. Then, just as suddenly, that job was canceled because of the onus of his father's history. He did not want to teach at the academy, and he was just being bounced around.

In August of 1960 Penkovsky first contacted the American students in Moscow, and in November of that year the chief of personnel called him in again. He said, "We finally have a job for you. Go see Colonel Rogov; he is the chief in the GRU for unofficial cover." Rogov worked under Dzhermen Gvishiani, the son-in-law of Aleksey Kosygin, member of the Central Committee. This unofficial cover organization would be associated with scientific research and development and was loaded with KGB and GRU personnel. It's sort of like the circumstance where the CIA might, if they could (and, most assuredly, they cannot), place someone as an employee with the Coca-Cola Company abroad in order to operate in espionage. The outfit was broken down into units depending upon languages: the English-speaking nationalities, the German, the French, etc. Penkovsky would be in the English section, working for the GRU. He would accompany groups of scientists who actually were scientist/spies for steel works, who were visiting foreign countries with the ostensible purpose of fostering commerce between the nations.

At that time, there wasn't an entity in the USSR that contacted foreigners, either inside the boundaries of the Soviet Union or abroad, that didn't contain an element of the KGB or GRU. This particular outfit had a KGB officer and five GRU officers. Penkovsky was the one with the Anglo-American connection. His committee of scientists was to attend meetings in London and attempt to obtain technical information. Penkovsky also would have to obtain intelligence information, so the CIA-SIS team had to be prepared to provide him with suitable information as his bounty. Later, they would take him to locations where he could take pictures that would add to the scheme. These would be targets that were not of too much value but would impress his superiors.

George and the author, summer of 1997.

George with Eva at the CIA Retirees Dinner, 16 September 1997.

Remembering Ferdi.

Central Intelligence Agency

1947 50 1997 Fiftieth Anniversary

GEORGE G. KISEVALTER

is hereby recognized as a Central Intelligence Agency Trailblazer for your significant contribution to the mission.

CIA Trailblazers

18 September 1997
Date

Director of Central Intelligence
George J. Tenet

Only fifty Trailblazers were chosen; George was the only case officer (spymaster).

George and his parents in Petrograd, 1915.

George at Louisiana maneuvers of 1941.

Searching for a radar site on Unalaska Island, 1943. George is the tall one.

Soviet pilot Major Senchenko signals his readiness for takeoff from Ladd Field. Photo courtesy Michael Gavrisheff.

Major Shevlakov readies his P-40 for the long trip to Krasnoyarsk. Photo courtesy Michael Gavrisheff.

Gen. Reinhard Gehlen in 1945 at Fort Hunt, Virginia, "the Snake Farm." George's ability to empathize with this German paid big dividends. When the CIA later facilitated the establishment of the BND, the West German Intelligence Service, Gehlen became its head and George enjoyed a close association with its leader.

Major Kisevalter, Pentagon 1946.

5. 1. 46.

Dear Mr. Kiesewalter,

we were very pleased about your kind Christmas wishes, and I want to express you my sincere gratitude. We had a quiet and nice Christmas; particularly we had a great pleasure by the different Christmas presents given by Col. Shimkin's officers. Mrs. Waldman had selected and wrapped these presents very carefully and with much skill acting as Christmas anglo. Please let me thank you for these presents, since your name also was signed on the Christmas card which accompanied the presents. They were felt by us as the expression of the friendly spirit and human feeling of the gentlemen we have met in the passed month of work.

With kindest regards from all of us,

Very sincerely yours

R. G.

Letter from Gehlen to George, January of 1946, Alexandria, Virginia.

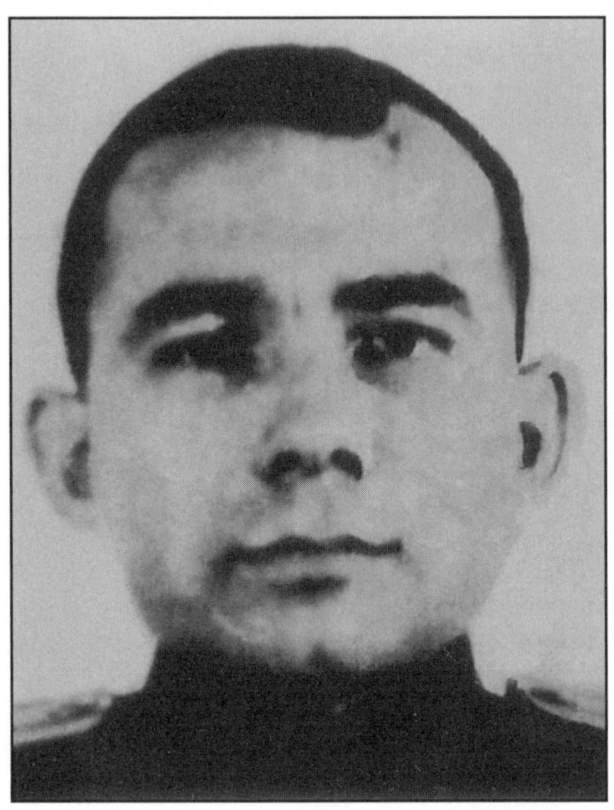

Lt. Col. Pyotr Semyonovich Popov, GRU. Photo courtesy David E. Murphy, CIA.

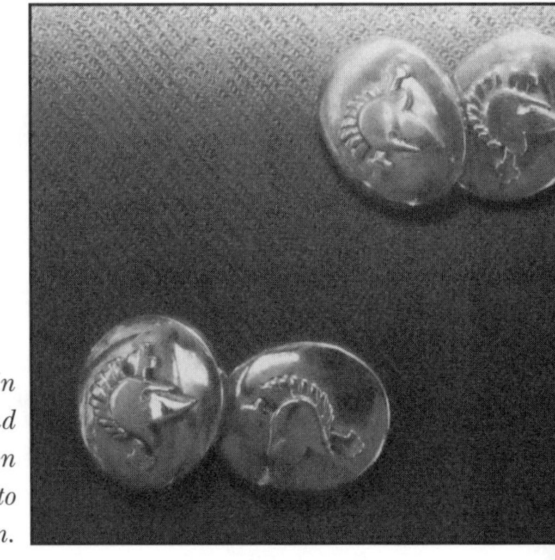

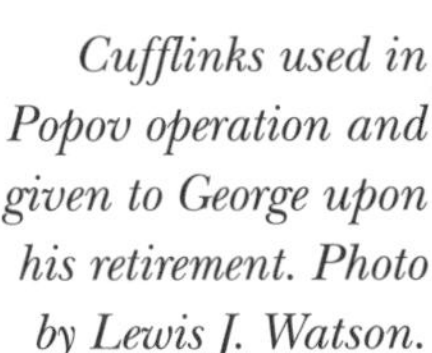

Cufflinks used in Popov operation and given to George upon his retirement. Photo by Lewis J. Watson.

CIA director Allen Dulles (right) presents Distinguished Intelligence Medal to George, 18 May 1959, for his work with the Popov case.

The United States of America

To all who shall see these presents, greeting:

This is to certify that the Director of Central Intelligence has awarded the

Distinguished Intelligence Medal

To

George George Kisevalter

for outstanding service

Given under my hand in the City of Washington, D.C. this 18th day of May 1959.

Director of Central Intelligence

Allen Dulles portrait. Photo courtesy CIA Museum.

Col. Charles MacLean Peeke standing beside Col. Oleg Penkovsky, whose image is excised from the picture. Photo taken at reception in Ankara, Turkey, in May of 1956 and delivered to the U.S. Embassy in Moscow by U.S. student Eldon Ray Cox in May of 1960. Photo courtesy CIA.

Marshal Sergey Sergeyevich Varentsov, good friend and mentor of Colonel Penkovsky. Photo courtesy CIA.

Colonel Penkovsky at the Mount Royal Hotel, London. Photo courtesy CIA.

Harold T. ("Shergie") Shergold, Penkovsky, Michael Stokes, and George at the Mount Royal Hotel, April 1961. Photo courtesy CIA.

Central Intelligence Agency

George G. Kisevalter

Is hereby awarded this

Certificate of Merit with Distinction

for outstanding performance of duty

Given under my hand in the City of Washington, D.C., this 30th *day of* September *1961*

Director of Central Intelligence

Leonard McCoy.

Ted Poling, circa 1952.

Sir Dickie Franks (left), chief of the SIS, with George in London, 1964.

Memento from Richard Helms, director of the CIA, to George, spring of 1970.

Helms (left) congratulating George upon his retirement, April 1970.

A reunion of old friends. George is in the center on the couch. Ted Poling is at top left.

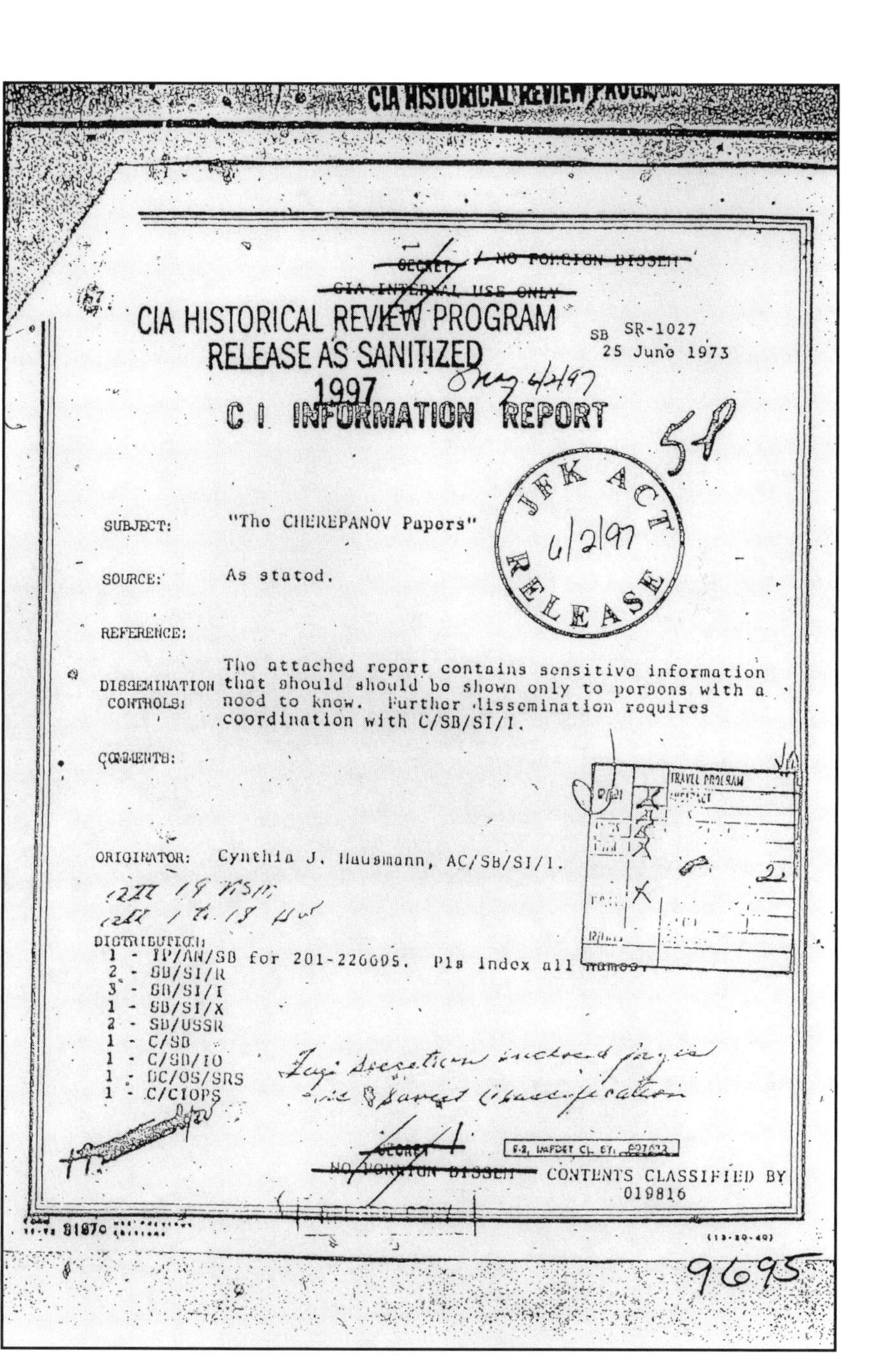
CIA HISTORICAL REVIEW PROGRAM

~~SECRET~~ / ~~NO FOREIGN DISSEM~~

~~CIA INTERNAL USE ONLY~~

CIA HISTORICAL REVIEW PROGRAM
RELEASE AS SANITIZED
1997

SB SR-1027
25 June 1973

C I INFORMATION REPORT

JFK ACT RELEASE 6/2/97

SUBJECT: "The CHEREPANOV Papers"

SOURCE: As stated.

REFERENCE:

DISSEMINATION CONTROLS: The attached report contains sensitive information that should should be shown only to persons with a need to know. Further dissemination requires coordination with C/SB/SI/I.

COMMENTS:

ORIGINATOR: Cynthia J. Hausmann, AC/SB/SI/I.

DISTRIBUTION:
1 - IP/AN/SB for 201-226605. Pls index all names.
2 - SB/SI/R
3 - SB/SI/I
1 - SB/SI/X
2 - SB/USSR
1 - C/SB
1 - C/SB/IO
1 - DC/OS/SRS
1 - C/CIOPS

~~SECRET~~
~~NO FOREIGN DISSEM~~ CONTENTS CLASSIFIED BY 019816

9695

~~SECRET/NO FOREIGN DISSEM~~

~~CIA INTERNAL USE ONLY~~

COUNTERINTELLIGENCE INFORMATION REPORT

SBSR - 1027

25 June 1973

COUNTRY: USSR

SUBJECT: "The CHEREPANOV Papers"

DOI : As stated

SOURCE : As stated

1. On 4 November 1963 Laurence H. MILLER, a librarian from the University of Illinois, turned over a package of documents to the U.S. Embassy in Moscow, with the explanation that A.N. CHEREPANOV, an employee of International Book, had passed them to MILLER's wife with the request that they be delivered to the U.S. Embassy. After photographing the documents, the Embassy, fearing a KGB provocation, delivered the package to the Soviet Ministry of Foreign Affairs the following day.

2. According to a defector source whose information has been reliable,[1] the Ministry of Foreign Affairs turned the package over to the KGB, who identified Aleksandr Nikolayevich CHEREPANOV as the person who had passed the papers to the U.S. Embassy. CHEREPANOV had been a case officer in the First (U.S. Embassy) Department, Second (Internal Counterintelligence) Chief Directorate, KGB until August 1961, when he was forced to retire from the KGB and found employment with International Book. In ca. mid-December 1963 CHEREPANOV was arrested near Baku, where he was trying to flee across the Soviet border. According to another source,[2] CHEREPANOV was later executed.

[1] AEDONOR.
[2] STORAGE. See SBSR 980, 21 May 1973.

WARNING NOTICE
SENSITIVE INTELLIGENCE SOURCES
AND METHODS INVOLVED

~~SECRET/NO FOREIGN DISSEM~~

E2 IMPDET CL BY 019818

3. The documents received by the U.S. Embassy, which have come to be known as "The CHEREPANOV Papers," all appear to have come from the files of the First Department, Second Chief Directorate, KGB during the period 1958 to 1960. A number were handwritten drafts, which would normally have been destroyed once the final copy was typed. Attached is a translation of "The CHEREPANOV Papers."

At Arlington National Cemetery, the flag, at half-mast, stands guard over rows and rows of white tablets.

The final review.

Young Alexander Andreev, ca. 1916. Photo courtesy Alexis A. Andreiev.

Andreev family, circa 1913. Front row, left to right: Natalia (Natasha) Andreev; Yulia (Julia) Andreev; Elena (Lena) Andreev. Center row, left to right: Col. Alexander Andreev's sister, Ksenya (Aysa); Col. Alexander Andreev with Raisa (Raya) on lap; Col. Alexander Andreev's mother; Col. Alexander Andreev's wife, Raisa (Raya) with Michael (Misha); a Kisevalter family relative, Tamara; Boris (Borya). Back row, left to right: daughter of another officer; Alexander (Sascha) Andreev with Yuri (Yura); two of the family housemaids; the nursemaid/governess. The names in parentheses are familiar names, like "Bob" for "Robert." Photo courtesy Alexis A. Andreiev.

CHAPTER 12

Common Purpose

The relationship between George and the British had begun with mutual respect and eventually would develop into one of admiration and friendship. George believed the British to be able, sophisticated, and prepared. He was pleased with their ability to provide backup support for the operation and gratified by their operational capability in Moscow—particularly in light of the CIA's inability to establish the needed resources there. As the case developed, he would discover that Harold Shergold ("Shergie") and Mike Stokes were capable, easy to work with, and likable. The British were delighted to have George on the team. With his Russian background, his experience in the Popov case, and his encyclopedic knowledge of Soviet Intelligence at the GRU, they were happy to leave the running of Penkovsky to him.

According to Shergold, however, George's extensive knowledge of the GRU almost boomeranged at the first meeting. The group had to form an assessment of Penkovsky before proceeding and they had to establish ground rules. George wanted to make it quite clear to Penkovsky that he could not fool the team on anything about the GRU. Accordingly, he overplayed his hand a bit with his vast knowledge of the GRU. In that first meeting the team did become concerned that George was excessive in demonstrating his knowledge. Penkovsky now seemed worried. He may have been wondering, "Am I really with the West? Are these people KGB? This chap knows too much." George not only knew the personalities of the GRU, he knew the buildings, and he knew just how Penkovsky had gotten there. He could mentally walk down the streets of Moscow and that was a bit disturbing to Penkovsky.

While his delegation was to be squired about to various British enterprises, Penkovsky had a dual mission: he would facilitate the delegation's interests in obtaining knowledge about technology in hard metals from the various British firms, and he would gather intelligence information for the GRU. In addition, if the opportunity arose, he would try to spot candidates for GRU recruitment. If he observed such an individual, he would advise his supervisors or the local Soviet Union intelligence personnel, and then step aside as they enlisted some other GRU or KGB operative to actually make the recruitment. This way, his cover would not be blown.

The delegation visited three cities: Leeds, where the steel mills were located, Birmingham, and London. Penkovsky appeared at official lunches in London and side tours in Birmingham that were part of the program. In the evenings and on some occasions for an hour or so in the afternoons, he had meetings with the CIA and SIS case officers. Since he was running the delegation, he could sneak off when the others were asleep and meet with the case officers. Sometimes they would meet at one or two in the morning when all of his "rabbits," as he called them, were asleep. It was also easy for him to break loose from his delegation during the day. Nobody would question either his movements or the time spent away from the delegation. It would be well within the pattern of expected behavior. He controlled the delegation expense account, and when the British would invite them for dinner, the Soviets could pocket their meal allowance. His delegates were naturally content with his easy management style and knew they could be candidates for return trips if he recommended them. He was considerate of them and in the future they might, in turn, recommend him.

Often there was a humorous element with the espionage activities. The team of four usually would send George out if there were a surreptitious contact with Penkovsky, say on the street, to guide him into a safehouse. Otherwise, Penkovsky might not know where to go. He would be told to walk on a certain street at a certain time. George would then sight him and signal to him to follow to the meeting place. George could nod or say a few words to him in Russian and Penkovsky would know just what to do. With English, Penkovsky might be confused, particularly in areas completely strange to him.

George told of one such rendezvous. "So, on a day that was dreary, naturally, we planned to meet. To make things worse, it started to rain cats and dogs. It was a real storm. It was in the middle of a downpour when I found the guy. I said, 'Follow me. Keep going where I go. I'll take you to the safehouse. It's in a hotel.' He followed me. I got to the hotel door. It was a revolving door. He was right behind me. I went through the door. There was a big lobby. It was full of people. They were all sitting around reading newspapers, and it seemed as though they all looked up when I entered. They were curious. It was a full house. Maybe they were salesmen. I don't know what the hell they were, but I had drawn their attention by walking in. Somehow, the instructions to Penkovsky had lost a beat. I was inside and he was still outside. I was standing there like a dope. I waited. I looked around. Everybody was still staring at me. The rain on my wet coat dripped down to the floor and began to create puddles. Finally, I became impatient, so I went outside to pick him up. Simultaneously, he went inside. Now, I was outside and he was inside. I got in the revolving door again and started around. Almost immediately he got in the door. Now we are in together. I'm afraid that he will come out of the building, so I stay in the door as the sector in which I am berthed passes the hotel lobby. He doesn't get out of the door as his sector passes the outside entrance. We are in the fool door going around together. This drew even more attention from the crowd. Finally we got together, somehow, dripping wet, like fools, inside this place. He followed me to what would be our safehouse for the occasion. You might say it happened to be the apartment we reserved. There, the other three guys were ready. I was met with 'What has been keeping you guys? We've been waiting.'

"Some other funny things happened. Once, the local police arrested me. They said, 'You are a Scotsman. This is the time for the ten-year census. You haven't registered! What is the matter with you? You didn't report in for your census, McAdam.' Oh my God, I forgot! The name in the hotel registry is McAdam. I am McAdam, and I am a 'resident.' So, to the laughter of the British intelligence, we had to pause and make restitution. They actually had to spring me, to get me off the hook. I was apprehended and I had no way to explain it. The British intelligence people had to work our way out of it. I was unwittingly violating all of the registration codes by not reporting in. This was in Leeds, England, and I was required to have the Scots registry, whatever that is, because of a certain ten years law, for Pete's sake. I didn't even know my father's name! What a circus we created.

"Even good things happened. What is difficult to understand, though, is why in the world the English, in that day and time, would still have cities with different kinds of electric current, e.g., DC and AC. Eventually, the team happened to hit a place with DC. Our usual recorders there were useless. However, in our weighty suitcases, carried around almost like curses, we had some mobile recorders powered by batteries. We then could tape throughout the entire meeting with Penkovsky without incident. With just a little foresight and by having dragged around these heavy burdens from city to city, we could record."

Penkovsky was not a scientist. He knew nothing about metallurgy or related sciences, but he had a GRU mission to perform espionage to whatever degree he could, as long as it was accomplished smoothly and successfully without tipping off his status. Of course, the CIA-SIS team did not want to compromise military resources, but with the help of the British intelligence and with the modest KF 3 camera the Soviets had issued him, they allowed him to take a few shots of some RAF aircraft. They also gave him pamphlets on British steel technology in order to better fulfill that assignment.

For his part, Penkovsky identified the entire roster of the Soviet intelligence personnel in London for the SIS. He had to meet them officially and he therefore told the team just who these people were. The British were delighted to have this clarification of their records. Additionally, when the case officers showed him thousands of photographs, he identified some five hundred GRU and probably more than two hundred KGB. He often worked twenty hours a day. Outside of meeting for hours with the case officers, taking care of his delegation, and traveling, he had his GRU assignment and had to make reports to his superiors. He met with the team seventeen times, totaling about fifty hours. At the meetings, in addition to relating much vital information, he continuously responded to new requirements that were thrown at him.

The team gave him two German-manufactured Minox cameras and sent a photographer from the SIS to train him in their use. They were reasonably sure of Penkovsky, but just for the record they threw a Minox at him and told him to go ahead and photograph some things, to take pictures of the room, etc. He did so, being careful with each frame. The team had them developed and the photos were perfect. He was so good with the cameras that when repeatedly re-tested to make sure that he was doing things properly, he completely succeeded each time. Similarly, the team trained him in coded radio transmission and he broke the first message they sent to him. The team was using the Russian Cyrillic version of code so that his messages would not need translation. To make sure the KGB couldn't break these messages, George spent several hours writing two that were deeply coded. Penkovsky had them decoded in twenty minutes. He was an amazingly quick study. The CIA-SIS team members were fortunate to have such an able man to train, and this good fortune later paid great dividends.

The radio receiver itself was of Soviet make—not the best but adequate. It would enable him to receive one-way voice broadcasts from points in Western Europe at a frequency and a time known only to Penkovsky and his case officers. The messages would be in the form of a series of cut numbers (numbers expressed in Morse code but truncated for efficiency). He would compare the cut numbers with those on a one-time pad sheet of random numbers designated for that calendar day. A prescribed relationship between the two sets of numbers would generate a third set of numbers. The third set then would designate certain letters in the Cyrillic alphabet that spelled out the intended message. There were only three copies of each pad of random numbers manufactured: one for Penkovsky, one for the SIS, and one for the CIA. The broadcasts could be monitored by the Soviets, but they would have no way of knowing the recipient or his location. Nor could they decipher the messages. Random number codes are virtually impossible to break.

At this point, Penkovsky promptly provided technical information on the new SA-2 anti-aircraft missiles of the kind that had shot down Gary Powers, many types of Medium Range Ballistic Missiles (MRBMs), including the ones that would later be deployed in Cuba, and nuclear stockpiles. In addition, from his conversations with high-ranking Soviet personnel, such as Varentsov, he revealed much about Soviet intentions. For instance, he talked a lot about the ongoing Berlin crisis, the slashing of military pay, food shortages throughout the country, and the ensuing morale crises in the Soviet Union. He revealed that Marshal Zhukov had been retired and was out of favor with Khrushchev.[1] Most importantly, the team heard from him that there were currently no operational ICBMs in the Soviet Union. The ICBMs were still being developed.

Penkovsky was very precise. Anything that his questioners didn't understand he would try to explain to George, and George in turn would try to explain to his colleagues. An interesting aspect of the man was his complete openness. Continuously he talked; continuously the team taped. Ultimately, George would translate more than 140 hours of tape. He also listened to the tapes again at hours when Penkovsky was not available and screened them for important messages that should go immediately to headquarters. True to his own meticulous nature, George forced himself, as he had with Popov, to listen, interpret, screen, and annotate all of the tapes.[2]

The team soon learned something of Penkovsky's motives and his personality. He was disgusted with the Soviet Communist system and wished for it to be destroyed. He wanted to blow up Moscow and thereby destroy the system. His initial vision was to accept from the Americans a suitcase full of atomic bombs, which he would place in strategic places. He described twenty-eight such locations that would be the prime targets. He would put the bombs in garbage cans at these spots and thereby render the whole Soviet Communist apparatus dysfunctional. Pointedly, the garbage cans in Moscow were not private property; they were "Communist" garbage cans. As the trashcans were picked up, the bombs would be distributed throughout the city, with some of the devices wending near the Kremlin. Of course, his theory was useless because the miniature atomic weapons that he envisioned did not exist.

This tells something about Penkovsky's motivations, although the term "motivation" suggests a broad concept by definition. There is almost no such thing as a single motivation. Everyone has multiple motivations with respect to almost anything. Some motivations may be more pronounced than others, and they will vary from to day to day. So, it's sometimes quite difficult to pinpoint someone's motivation about a particular matter, even one's own. In defector situations, the motivations become extremely difficult to grasp, yet they are among the most important aspects of the situation.

Beyond Penkovsky's loathing of the Soviet system, his desire for personal recognition was the thing that most impressed the team. Penkovsky wanted to meet important people, and he insisted upon doing so. He demanded to kiss the hand of the queen. He said, "Look, Yuri Gagarin flies around the world and he has lunch with the queen. What has he done for you? I'm doing more than he ever did for you." The team tried to explain about security and so forth. He then said that he would settle for Lord Mountbatten.

George recalled that the "Brits" tore out their hair over this one while he and Bulik snickered quietly, keeping their sentiments a secret from the "Brits." Then Penkovsky suggested that when he came to the United States, George and Bulik should arrange for him to see President Kennedy. The CIA officers cringed a bit but assured him that something could be worked out. They told him, "Okay, Oleg, someday when you come to the States, all of these things can be handled." They figured that would be easier to accomplish than his demands on the British.

The English finally settled on one man, Sir Dick White, the chief of British intelligence, to placate Penkovsky. He came and told Penkovsky of the great importance of Penkovsky's work and how grateful all of the powerful people were for his contribution. Penkovsky seemed to be impressed, although still somewhat miffed at not meeting the queen. This, however, did not end the matter. He then turned to George and said, "If I get two days off, you could throw me on a U.S. airplane to Washington, D.C. I could meet the president and fly right back."

George replied, "Now, just how could we do this, Oleg?" Oleg's retort floored George. "There's no problem if you want to do this," he said. "You've already done it! You took a GRU colonel to Washington one time and he met Allen Dulles, the director of the CIA. You can do it for me as well."

"My ears lit up," George remembered. "My God! What was he saying?" George then began another of his delicious anecdotes. "Let me tell you how these things affected us by what he said, as he related this story from his past, one that astounded us to no end, right there in front of the British. Now 30 April of 1959 was the date that Penkovsky was graduated from Varentsov's nine-month refresher course in missilery at the Dzerzhinskiy Academy. His association with the generals in the missile academy later had great importance to us. The day after graduation, there was a holiday, the first of May, a good Communist holiday. He and another man, whose name, I believe, was Borisoglebsky, a general at the academy, went for a few drinks out in the spring sun. As they were sitting down, the general congratulated Penkovsky and so forth; then, in a friendly manner, he said to him, 'You know what, Penkovsky, I am a general. Sometimes we are given some damned nasty assignments. We all get these things, don't we? Well, this was a tough one. A few months ago I was made the chief of a court-martial, where we had to condemn a man to be shot for high treason. He was a GRU colonel and an American agent. Do you know, before we caught him, the Americans once flew him back to the U.S., where he met the chief of the CIA, Allen Dulles!'

"Well, when Penkovsky said this, I about fell out of my chair! For Penkovsky to have mentioned this vignette, as it was related to him by the chief of the Soviet court-martial that condemned the guy to be shot, right in front of the British, sent my blood pressure soaring. I'm sure that it raised their hackles as well. ('And who in the hell was this guy that you flew to CIA headquarters in black? You never told us about him.') The truth of the matter was that I was very familiar with such an incident. What he was describing had to be the same case. Both affairs had similar details and both happened during the same timeframe. This, however, was the first time in two years that we had received any knowledge of the final outcome of the man involved in the operation.

"The Soviet agent was an illegal who was picked up in France. My good friend Dick Kovich had doubled him, turning him back against his own people, and was his case officer. I met the man. I met him in Berlin while pretending to be a Frenchman. I spoke French to him and gave him girlie magazines from Paris. He thought that he was teaching me how to drink in Russian. This was a joke, and Kovich was dying from laughter because the poor guy didn't know why I could drink like a Russian.

"Well, as a matter of fact, he was flown black from Berlin. I put him, together with one of our people, on the plane at Tempelhof Airport. They flew toward Frankfurt, then aborted the landing at Frankfurt, swung by Paris, the Azores, and landed at Andrews Airfield. There they were met by some more of our people and taken to CIA headquarters, where they greeted General Cabell, the deputy to our then director, Allen Dulles.[3] Cabell put on his air force uniform in order to impress him, right there in CIA headquarters. He was a four-star general, you know. It was all part of the operation. After all, this was our agent, and a high-ranking one. A few weeks later the man went back to East Berlin, and that was the last thing that we had heard of him until now.

"This guy knew all about dead drops in Karlshorst, East Germany, and had tried to tell us their location. Christ, we were digging up half the railroad tracks and tearing down the station there, looking for the damned things! We never found them. That was one of my ancillary roles there, trying to find out where those places were, while I was stationed in Berlin working with Popov, and that was why Kovich had come to Berlin with the man. Nick Osipoff also was one of our people who worked with him. Nick took him to football games and whatnot in Berlin. So, our agent was flown back to the Agency black for high operational reasons. The transfer and the meeting with Cabell were pulled off successfully, but now we were finding out, two years later, that the poor guy got caught. We found out even later that he was actually done in by some internal correspondence, which was a stupidity with a capital *S*. After some period of not hearing from him, one of our people tried to have him contacted inside the USSR, which was a dumb thing to do. Naturally, the KGB was monitoring the mailbox when the letter was deposited. When Westerners were seen making such deposits, the letters were always routinely intercepted and read.

"Well, this came out of a clear blue sky! Crack, like a lightning bolt striking. Penkovsky was telling us the story for the first time. The Soviets thought that he had met Dulles but it really was Cabell. No matter, they had it close enough. Now, we weren't relating all of the operational history of every asset that we had to the British, for Christ's sake. But the embarrassment, in front of the British, was very extreme. We had to dig up some sort of story to divert their anguish."

Eventually, at one point during the operation, Shergold said, "You know, we don't know when Penkovsky is going to be coming to the West again. We have to have a way of continuously meeting with him in Moscow. What do you have?" Bulik answered, "We have zilch, with a capital *Z*—not a damn thing. It's dangerous there." "We have something," Shergie volunteered. "We would like to exploit it. Here's an idea."

He wanted to utilize Janet Chisholm, at the British Embassy in Moscow. She was living there with her three kids and husband. Roderick Chisholm was a British intelligence officer and known to the Soviets as such. So, with this, Shergold said, "I think that we can use Janet. If Penkovsky can see her officially, with the blessing of the KGB, we will have a resource for passing cassettes or information discreetly back and forth, and this will provide a means of communication in Moscow, right under their noses and with their blessing, for the wrong reason. In the meantime they could initially meet surreptitiously. We'll have to find somewhere that is convenient to them both and would be within the normal routine of both." This was agreed, and it was established that Greville Wynne would deliver to Penkovsky the particulars for meeting Janet the next time he went to Moscow.

It was recognized by all that the best way to transfer information in Moscow would be at official functions and through an intelligence officer sent by one or both of the countries. The CIA officer would be identified to Penkovsky by wearing a special tie clasp, identical to one given Penkovsky, and would further identify himself by saying, "Colonel Peeke sends his best wishes." In the meantime, it was agreed that Penkovsky would not attempt to transact any espionage business with any member of either diplomatic corps.

Then, according to George, there came a very interesting phase of the operation. Penkovsky said, "I have to make some hay for all of my friends when I get back." He came up with a shopping list. "But this was not a list," George said. "This was a book! And in this book, some of it written by hand, was 'my wife, my daughter,' etc. You could see ladies' footprints, shoe sizes, labels, and directions: 'this is Galena's, this is so and so's suit, this is somebody's coat, this guy wants this, this girl wants that.' What a shopping list! The number of hours it took to do this shopping and fulfill anywhere near what this list demanded was really out of this world.

"The mounds of materials required suitcases that, when filled, weighed sixty to seventy pounds apiece, and it took a number of them. But it was going to be a cinch to get them into Moscow because he had in mind a scheme. He didn't want to carry more than he could or should. The next time Wynne came to Moscow, Penkovsky would meet him at the airport. Then, he would pass Wynne right through customs, dump him in his chauffeur-driven car, pass notes back and forth, and eventually take him to his hotel, minus one or two of Wynne's suitcases. Penkovsky would have all of the goodies and there would be no problem. His clothes would arrive later with Wynne! What a list!"

George asked Penkovsky about the materials, with a concern for security. "What does your home look like?" "Oh, I've got a mess of good imported china; it's normal," was the reply. "The personnel man didn't even give me any rubles for stuff like the pens." George told him, "Look, the British give them out as favors at the various factories. You get them for free. They open the drawer and dump them in your bag." So Penkovsky was able to bring back medicine, pens, perfume, lipstick, cigarettes, and special gifts for big people like Varentsov.

After Penkovsky left, the Americans and the British had an incredible amount of work to do: there were the translations, analyses, and distribution of the tapes and many conferences to come. George promptly went back to CIA headquarters after the last meeting with Penkovsky and began the follow-up work that had to be done. It took months to process the tapes even though the Agency and SIS set up a comprehensive task force for the effort.

Within two months Wynne was back in Moscow. He took with him a couple of Penkovsky's suitcases, 3,000 rubles, some cassettes of blank film, instructions for having the first meeting with Janet Chisholm, and a photograph of Janet and her children so that Penkovsky would be able to recognize her. Penkovsky studied the picture but did not retain it. That way there would be no chance of compromising her if it happened to fall into the wrong hands. Wynne also retrieved some used cassettes of film and some notes from Penkovsky during that trip and passed them on to Roderick Chisholm, who, being with the SIS, would subsequently pass them on to the team.

Janet and Penkovsky made their first contact in July 1961 in a park that she routinely visited. He did not approach her at first; rather, he waited until what seemed to be an opportune time, with not too many people around, and none of them suspicious. Then he approached her. He walked by discreetly, said hello, dropped some cassettes and some notes of paper into her open shopping bag, offered a piece of candy to the children, said good day, and passed on.

Penkovsky's notes described the conversations that he had overheard at Marshal Varentsov's homecoming, a celebration in honor of his promotion to chief marshal. The Soviet Union would, Penkovsky heard, sign a separate peace treaty with East Germany in defiance of the Potsdam Treaty with the Allied Nations. (The objective was to require the Allies to recognize East Germany and thereby lay the groundwork for a dominant East Germany, one that contained all of Berlin and one that would be permanently within the sphere of Soviet control.) Penkovsky quoted the defense minister, Malinovsky, as saying that he was going to put up concertina wire in Berlin to stem the flow of refugees to the West. "The Americans would come with their tanks—rubber treads, no less—just stop and stare, and would do nothing," according to Malinovsky.

The second time Penkovsky came to London he didn't have a delegation. He came in July as an assistant supervisor to a Soviet trade exhibition. He did have freedom of movement in the evenings so the members of the team were able to have more or less continual meetings when wished. During this trip, Penkovsky arranged to place himself in good stead with Serov, who was chief of the entire GRU intelligence system. Serov had been head of the KGB but was transferred to the GRU, in part because of the Popov case.

According to George, Ivan Aleksandrovich Serov was a man almost universally detested. He had been with Khrushchev in London in 1956 and was declared *persona non grata* when Lionel Crabbe, a navy commander and frogman, drowned underneath the Soviet cruiser, *Ordzhonikidze.* While the craft was docked at Portsmouth Harbor, Crabbe secretly tried to examine its hull and ancillary components; he accidentally drowned in the process.[4] The British press, in reporting the incident, observed that Serov was aboard and referred to him as the butcher who assisted Lavrenti Beria in executing so many people. They then hounded him out of town, leaving Khrushchev there to salvage whatever relations were left. Thereafter, Serov was never welcome in London.

George continued, "This did not, however, prevent Serov's wife and daughter from enjoying the city of Big Ben. In fact, they decided to go there during Penkovsky's second trip. Before Penkovsky embarked upon the trip, Serov called him in and said, 'Look, while you're there in London, just keep an eye open and make sure my wife and daughter are okay. You know, if they need anything, look after them a bit.' Naturally, Penkovsky made a big production out of the opportunity to ingratiate himself with Serov. First of all, when they arrived in London, the muttonheads at their intelligence station didn't have an embassy car waiting, so he called for one. He got it. He took them to a hotel. He wined and dined them even though the CIA-SIS team pleaded with him not to be too friendly with the attractive, young Miss Serov. He took them shopping. They ran out of money. He gave them money—CIA-SIS money! Serov would repay him when he got home. Penkovsky was making out like a bandit. He was getting them all kinds of stuff: sweaters, shoes, etc. They even wanted to get one of those put-it-together-yourself swings that you use in the garden. They needed a steamboat to haul all of this stuff back to Leningrad. The team members began to see that this was par for the course. 'When you go there, pick me up this and that,' etc. Every secretary got lipstick, etc. Some of these handouts really got to rare proportions. There was some woman for whom Penkovsky was charged to acquire a whole suite of furniture smuggled from Czechoslovakia. A whole suite! One thousand and twenty rubles! I asked him, 'Who the hell is this girl?' 'She's the daughter of the chief of personnel,' Penkovsky replied. Rogov, the chief of Penkovsky's GRU section, wound up with an icebox. Something like the Truman days. Somebody even had false teeth on the list!

"No doubt everybody was happy with these goodies. The assortment was out of this world. But it furthered everything that Penkovsky was trying to do for the Americans and the British. He could do these favors, maneuver people around, and stay on their good side. Actually, just knowing the big people would help, but his enthusiasm was a bonus to the United States and the United Kingdom. He really could get along with the big people. He was making a lot of others jealous, however, and thereby making enemies. This concerned us a bit."

George related an example of Penkovsky's propensity to irritate people who irked him. "To give you an idea of how he could really stick a pin into some body's tail, I'll mention one little episode. During this trip he went to a cemetery in London where there is a grave for Karl Marx. It looked like an outhouse. There were orange rinds, banana peelings, scraps of paper, garbage, and everything else littered about in the little grave enclosure. He photographed the scene. He then sent the photographs, along with a letter, to the Central Committee of the Communist Party in Moscow saying, 'This is how they treat Karl Marx, our national hero, here in London.' Naturally, a great reprimand came to the Soviet Embassy in London. Following that, the station chief was cashiered and perpetual care and attention to the grave of Karl Marx was initiated, all thanks to Penkovsky's jabbing them one."

Since Penkovsky didn't have a delegation to worry about, meeting with him was a lot simpler, and the team had a very nice and comfortable safehouse at their disposal. It was an apartment in Kensington not far from his hotel, which was near the Soviet Embassy. In terms of operational activities, this time there were only thirteen meetings with Penkovsky. Leonard McCoy was the reports officer. It was his job to distribute the take and find out from the customers just what they wanted the team to pursue with Penkovsky. McCoy would brief the case officers beforehand as to what requirements the analysts were especially desirous of having fulfilled, and the team would try to get Penkovsky to respond to those requirements at that time or to make note of them for the future. McCoy would be advised after the meeting of the results, and then if something were of immediate import, he would send a cable back to headquarters describing that information. George described McCoy as being one of the best reports officers in the CIA's history and said that he received recognition from every director for his reports.

When the meetings of this second visit began, Penkovsky was anxious to tell the team about Soviet plans and thinking vis-à-vis Berlin and the gathering crisis there. He set forth Khrushchev's tactic of pushing ahead until he met resistance, then waiting awhile to see a reaction from the United States, then swinging around, perhaps in a different direction, and pressing ahead again. Any concession by the West was regarded as a weakness.

During this trip, the team learned more about Penkovsky's motivations, including his need for personal recognition. If he couldn't get it at home and in his own career, he certainly wanted to be recognized by his case officers. He demanded and got a complete United States Army colonel's uniform. He was very much pleased. He put it on and had himself photographed in it while he experimented with various poses. The British also came up with one of their army colonel's uniforms, and there he was, swagger stick and all. Both were kept for him to wear while he was with the case officers. Shergold and Stokes agreed that, no matter what Penkovsky thought his information was worth monetarily, he didn't have any concept of money in the Western sense. What he wanted was a dignified, comfortable, and secure life. His concept of security was founded more on personal recognition than having money in the bank that might allow him to do what he wanted to with his life. The CIA and SIS were not stingy with him in any way. The CIA agreed to escrow for him a full colonel's pay each month and also to provide him with an additional monetary reward, later to be determined. The British did much the same. He would defect with his family when possible. Before then, he wanted to earn his nickel with the British and the United States by going back to the Soviet Union.

Only a man with Penkovsky's exceptional exuberance for life could have performed so well in this environment. He seemed to thrive on eighteen-hour days, and he found time to do the sightseeing typically desired by all visitors to London. This included visits to the finest restaurants, bars, and nightclubs. The man liked to talk. Moreover, once he got going, he really could carry on.

According to Mike and Shergie, George was the same. The two of them never stopped talking. These were pretty exhausting meetings when the five of them were sitting there for six hours or so in the middle of the night, listening to Penkovsky and George nonstop. The two of them could go on forever. The others' minds would be a bit sore after being hammered about in that way hour after hour. But it was quite important that George do a good job in keeping the confidence of Penkovsky, and it required a lot of delicate handling in order to get him in the channels that the team wished to travel. This was vital and the British maintain that George did it superbly.

Penkovsky came to them wanting to drop atomic bombs in garbage cans in Moscow. They wanted intelligence information. The nuclear-holocaust scenario was prominent in Penkovsky's mind and it was driving him. He would have been content to participate in the elimination of Moscow were the West willing and able to assist him. Shergold stated, "If the team had only given Penkovsky a measure of atomic bombs to toss into the ministry of defense or the ministry of foreign affairs or the Central Committee headquarters or whatever building, he would have been content to go up in ashes along with the rest of Moscow." Penkovsky sorely wanted to get even with the Soviet system, which he thought had been a barrier to his professional progress. He believed that he should have risen higher; he should have been made general by then. When he came to the team in the first round, he really had little idea as to what he was going to do. He came to the first meetings with all of these strange, colorful ideas of miniature atomic bombs, which he could toss down staircases—quite utterly unrealistic nonsense. But this was the way he approached the CIA-SIS team. It was, therefore, quite important to steer his energies into more productive channels, which were, of course, the acquisitions of specifically designated pieces of intelligence information.

Once George got Penkovsky to understand the importance of focusing on the gathering of intelligence information, he began to take tremendous risks toward that end, risks greater than any ever known of by the case officers. When Penkovsky went into the GRU secret library, ostensibly to carry out his studies, he never read any of the material that he photographed. He just photographed it.

He didn't take one Minox camera; he took two so that he didn't have to waste time reloading.

He took risks to enhance his access to top-secret intelligence. Chief Marshal Varentsov was in charge of missiles associated with artillery forces, and this group had a special headquarters. Penkovsky went to Varentsov and, on the grounds that he should keep himself up to date following his studies at the Dzerzhinskiy Academy, asked for permission to take documents from the headquarters building. Varentsov made available to him his own aide-de-camp, General Buzinov, and instructed Buzinov to let Penkovsky have access to the top-secret material there. This, then, was a created access rather than a natural one, and a lot of extremely valuable material came out of that entree, particularly with respect to missile development.

Soon, the case officers had an agent with a burning ambition to do their bidding. Penkovsky was told what was wanted and he went after it in a big way. According to the British, George handled him superbly, getting him into the correct frame of mind, away from his own ideas, while the others sat there and observed. Of course, they discussed things between themselves before they went into the meetings, but George was the spokesman for the team and the handler. Shergold maintained that the British felt quite indebted to George. "None of the other three could have handled Penkovsky the way that George did. It wasn't only the language; it was his understanding of Penkovsky's psychology and his superb background, not only of being a native of Russia, but the Popov experience. He was absolute master of the whole thing. It seemed comparatively easy for him, having had all of those years trucking about the GRU with Popov." There was no question in their minds at all. George was the key to the success. Shergold and Stokes did not believe that their entire service could ever have produced such a man. There were, of course, other vital elements to the operation, but in the handling of the agent, in getting Penkovsky relaxed and producing, George was irreplaceable. The team knew that the main asset in the case (except for Penkovsky himself) was George.

CHAPTER 13

City of Light

In September 1961, George, Stokes, and Roger King, a general factotum provided by the British, took up residence in a Parisian SIS safehouse and waited, but no Penkovsky. Leonard McCoy came and stayed in a hotel nearby. The safehouse was on Beranger Haneau, in a quiet, attractive neighborhood just a few blocks up the hill from the Seine and about ten minutes from the American Embassy. George did not go anywhere near the embassy, which was down the Champs Elysées from the Etoile[1] at the Place de la Concorde overlooking the Seine.

George described his experience with the team in Paris as rollicking: "To drive around Paris, the British brought in Roger King, a case officer and a racecar driver. He could sail through Paris at eighty miles an hour like a damned fool, missing everything, thank God, unlike with poor Princess Diana, and he was at our beck and call. Oh, the British were loaded; they had many safehouses and they had safehouses that really were safehouses! We would come in through the basement. It would be dark. We'd press a button; lights would go on upstairs. An elevator was there for our use. Luckily, I knew a little more about Paris than some of the British, as I had been there many times before. My mother was French, you know, and of course I could speak French. French was my first language. The city happened to be loaded and overflowing. On one occasion, the British intelligence couldn't find a hotel room for a colleague's friend when he came to visit. I went to a little hotel and I told the manager that my mother was from Le Creusot, near Dijon, this and that. It worked like a charm; she said, 'Ohhh, oooh, wonderful, wonderful, wonderful.' She gave me the room. She said, 'Anytime you are in Paris, come see me.' So I had an inside track into the little hotel adjacent to Jardin du Luxembourg, the Luxembourg Gardens, a lovely place but always overloaded with people. Unfortunately, the hotel was next door to a whorehouse."

Penkovsky's arrival at Paris was delayed. French authorities held up his visa for three weeks while the team members waited. They brought Wynne from London to be with them and to front for them, using him as much as possible as an intermediary. Wynne finally met Penkovsky on 20 September and gave him instructions for meeting George and the others. When Penkovsky arrived at the safehouse, he began castigating them for not hurrying up the process. George explained to him, "Look, we did not cut the French intelligence service in on this operation because they are penetrated, so to speak. We have enough problems, for Pete's sake."

The circumstance for Penkovsky coming to Paris was again a Soviet trade fair, an exposition. In addition, he had a mission to find an American or French expert in steel who would give him some new technical information about steel fabrication. An Armco Steel man named George Hook agreed to give him a tour in a fabrication plant, supply him with a big stack of brochures, and personally entertain him a bit. Penkovsky was confident that this would go over well back at GRU headquarters in Moscow. He stayed at a hotel on the Rue de Grenelle near the Soviet Embassy on the Left Bank. It was very difficult for the team to meet with him in Paris. It was a very rough time, politically. As George said, "The Algerians were kicking up. The OAS, the Secret Army Organization, was very active; explosions were all over France. I used to have a drink of wine in a little place near the safehouse. A pretty girl was there, waiting on tables. One day she teased me, saying, 'You were walking down with a very beautiful woman in the morning.' That was Barbara, the British secretary sent to help me do tapes. She was very useful, good, obedient. After she completed her contribution to the Penkovsky operation, she had a long and successful career with SIS. The next day I could not see the little French waitress. The second floor of the building was where the first floor had been before. There had been an explosion. OAS. We actually had heard the roar of the explosion the night before but did not realize its cause."

The team determined that they would use the various bridges over the Seine to their advantage in order to set up their meetings. The first arrangement was to wait for Oleg in the Trocadero Square, right across the Seine from the Eiffel Tower. From the Trocadero's giant staircases they could see a half-mile downtown, thus giving them a remarkable means of surveillance. In order to get to them, Penkovsky would cross the Pont d'Iena and then walk up to a prescribed meeting point where George would be hiding behind a pole. Once contact was made, George would escort him to the place where Roger King was in a car and then let Roger take them to the safehouse. One night George observed two other guys behind two other poles, waiting for some other agent. They were from the OAS. So the team abandoned that plan.

There was a humpback footbridge across the Seine about a block away from the Tuileries Gardens.[2] It was like a shortcut between the Soviet Embassy on the one side and the Tuileries near where the Louvre is on the other side. Penkovsky could walk across that bridge to an opening in the Tuileries buildings, sort of an alleyway. The team members could observe him well during the whole transit, since they could see across the entire river and know whether or not he was being followed. Either Bulik or George would try to arrive early to escort him. When they spotted him on the bridge to the Tuileries driveway, they would walk him to where Roger King would be parked and ready to pick them up in the car and take them to the safehouse. There was only one problem: the Tuileries was also the homosexual meeting place of Paris. George had to take Barbara with him, and Bulik had to find an American secretary whenever he went. That way, they were less likely to be molested. As George said, "you run into the damnedest situations."

Finally, they settled on the Pont de Grenelle, much farther up. This was an automobile bridge across the Seine to the Right Bank, a one-way bridge—the wrong way for them. In other words, Penkovsky would walk across facing traffic and no car could follow him. This bridge connects to an island in the Seine where the little Statue of Liberty sits, the one that was copied in order to manufacture the Statue of Liberty that the French gave to the U.S. So from there, Roger would meet them at the corner and take all of them to the safehouse. Those were the different ways of picking him up, and George volunteered that "it seemed always to be me who was the poor boob who had to do this."

Penkovsky told the team all about the Soviet Embassy in Paris, who the station chief was, etc. This man had just arrived following a major promotion, so he was told by the U.S. Embassy, "You are welcome." The Soviets were shrewd. At a reception in their embassy, they had people on display talking with the wrong people. This was done to fool the French about who was, and who was not, an intelligence operative. The Soviets had penetrations all over France, so the team members were living in a very tenuous situation with regard to security. George said that he never even wanted to look cross-eyed at the American Embassy because he knew that even the Rumanian newspaper seller downstairs there was a Soviet agent.

Penkovsky told the team that when he had returned to Moscow after having squired Mrs. and Miss Serov around London, he was personally invited to their dacha. Someone from Serov's office picked up the phone and told Penkovsky to be at the house at six o'clock that evening. No matter that he was in the doghouse with his people at the GRU. George observed, "Can you imagine trying to fire a guy in this position? How is he going to be bawled out when that kind of call, directly from the chief of GRU, comes right into his office?" Penkovsky went to the house. Serov thanked him and excused himself because he had an engagement a little later, but said his wife and daughter would entertain him. Moreover, the Soviets paid back "his" money, the money that the team had given him in London to "lend" to the Serov ladies, so Penkovsky was doing quite well. He told George about the plush quarters, with guards throughout.

Shergold volunteered that they could arrange to have Janet Chisholm meet with Penkovsky and the case officers the next day in order to plan multiple meetings for the future. True to form, she was there the next morning and they arranged a whole series of meetings. Plan number one would be executed in much the same manner as the initial contact between Penkovsky and Janet. On almost every pleasant day, she would go out of her apartment with her two children and down into the public park. She would sit down. If there were a meeting, Penkovsky would walk by as before, discretely say hello, drop cassettes and notes into her open shopping bag, and offer a piece of candy to the children.

Plan number two was more complicated. There was a place in Moscow called a Kommission store. It was similar to a silver shop, a convenience store of relics and antiques, where poor Russians could sell their earthly goods. They would bring an icon or samovar, something old, something desired by Western people, and present it for sale. Women from the various Western embassies would make a beeline for this store whenever it was convenient in order to see what was newly offered. They would look, they would browse, and usually they would walk out. Most often there was little to see. Nearby was a restaurant/delicatessen where one could browse some more. On Fridays, Janet would take a ballet lesson at the American ambassador's residence and then she would walk to the commercial area, always stopping in one or two stores, including the Kommission store and then the restaurant/deli, thus adopting a recognizable pattern. On certain other days she would leave her home and go directly to either the Kommission store or the restaurant/deli. From within the store or the deli she would be able to see Penkovsky pass by. If a meeting were planned, he'd catch her eye and, without averting his head or otherwise acknowledging recognition, walk by the door of the store or the deli and then down the street. From then on he would be master of the situation. He would direct where to walk in order to make the pass. She discreetly would follow him a block or so. They would meet at a secluded spot such as a covered aperture between buildings. There they could pass things to each other. She would take a bus to go home and he would disappear. The rendezvous locations would sort of alternate, so that if one day it was at the store or deli, then the next meeting would be in the park. In addition, Greville Wynne could continue to serve as a drop for messages.

There was another story relating to Penkovsky rubbing shoulders with big people. During his last visit to London he had required the team to find for him a bottle of very rare cognac, exactly sixty-year-old vintage—vintage 1901. Obtaining such an article is no easy chore. One British officer searched throughout England to no avail. He eventually found one that was shy just a couple of years, however, and the British Technical Services Branch managed to change the date on the label such that the "counterfeit" was imperceptible. This, practically packaged in cotton, was taken back to Moscow. [3]

On 16 September, there had been a birthday party for the recently made chief marshal of artillery of the Soviet Union, Sergey Sergeyevich Varentsov. The master of ceremonies at this affair, held in the home of Varentsov, was none other than Col. Oleg V. Penkovsky. There was champagne and the works. Everybody was whooping it up and congratulating Varentsov, who already had the Order of Lenin and a few other things. Penkovsky lifted up his glass and this bottle of cognac for a toast. As indicated on the label, the cognac was distilled in the year of the marshal's birth. According to Penkovsky, the guest who slopped up most of it was the minister of defense, Rodion Malinovsky. Ivan Tugarinov of the Central Committee was there. He got drunk; he became annoyed with the marshal's dacha and its plethora of roses. He was irked at how these pretenders of the Proletariat could get away with those kinds of goodies at home.

At this party, Penkovsky presented to Varentsov a gold watch from the Penkovsky family with an inscription on the back. The team had a time trying to get this inscribed in London. They couldn't get a legitimate watchmaker who could do the Cyrillic accurately without revealing too much of themselves, and they did not want to get the British intelligence technical resource people involved for fear of blowing cover. So they finally prevailed upon Penkovsky to have it inscribed in Moscow. Another item among the gifts was a huge silver rocket, a beautiful thing weighing more than twenty pounds. When one pressed a button, flame came out to light a cigarette—symbolically quite fitting for Varentsov.

One of Mike Stokes' favorite memories of Paris was the time when the team had the apartment carpeted with enlargements of the Minox pictures that Penkovsky had taken. Penkovsky wanted to see the results of his handiwork because he never knew what was in the articles that he had captured on film. He knew what the titles were but not the contents. When he got to Paris, he handed over the film at the first meeting and was very keen to see his product. One of the first things that the team had to do in Paris, then, was to send the film via a special courier to London. This was highly complicated because it was a holiday weekend. Shergie's secretary in London had to call out the photo technicians and put them to work. This caused a bit of a fuss since it was on Saturday and Sunday, but it was done. The prints were then flown back so that the team could show them to Penkovsky. Shergie laid out photos on the floor until it was totally carpeted with secret intelligence information. Penkovsky was quite impressed with his effort. He hadn't done too badly, but it made the team members wonder about him. He could be a very demanding individual at times, and he expected things to happen in an instant. Shergie commented that there was no patience in the man.

George continued, "Now, my cover in Paris was that of an American living with the British, a tourist. As I was hiding in the British safehouse, I rarely went anywhere else. I would go to meet

Penkovsky, of course, and on a few occasions I went out with Stokes or the others for a short break, but I didn't float around town. We had enough problems without that. Bulik was the one who wanted to do some fast operating. Since I spoke French and knew Paris, he wanted me to help him with some romantic rendezvous for Penkovsky. 'George, buy a hotel room and help me pick up a whore for Oleg.' I refused. No way. I wanted no part of that. I did not want to get mixed up with that sort of activity. Bulik thought he could get in good with Penkovsky by trying to please him. I didn't go out with them. I didn't want to have anything to do with that. He did manage to hire one, somehow or another, somewhere. The British didn't like the idea. They had their own women set up in London, where everything could be controlled. Paris was something else again. You are in deep water. I mean, that is no place to fool around. Bulik wanted to show the British he was awesome, that he was an operator. He did not get along with the British; maybe he was jealous of them. He seemed to keep arguing with Shergold. I wanted out of that whole situation. I didn't like those kinds of politics."

In Paris there was the long, indefinite wait for Penkovsky to arrive. During this period, which turned out to be three weeks, they were all challenged to productively use their time. Then Penkovsky was in Paris for twenty-five days. So, all in all, George actually spent forty-six days more or less cooped up in that apartment. Eventually, the tension building in him would come to a head. Even though George never complained about the circumstances, the living conditions for the group were quite difficult. Mike, George, and Roger King (the housekeeper and driver) were living in a two-bedroom apartment before Penkovsky arrived. Due to his tendency to snore, George was dealt the living-room couch for his bed. After Penkovsky arrived, Shergie also moved in with the group. The place then was like a beehive, since all of the Paris meetings were held in that apartment with all four case officers. Moreover, with McCoy and Barbara also coming and going at intervals outside of the meeting times, there was very little privacy for the residents.

The physical inconveniences and the uncertainties of the wait added to the overwhelming pressure of the mission. Never before, during the entire Cold War, had the West obtained such access to this type and quality of clandestinely acquired, top-secret, eyes-only intelligence information. All parties were anxious for the success of the operation to continue. The pressure was building, especially on

George. Life was not easy for him being virtually housebound. Actually, as the principal interrogator of Penkovsky, he was bearing on his shoulders the weight of the many meetings. Then there was the matter of the differences of opinion between the CIA, as represented by Bulik, and the British on how to handle Penkovsky. With Bulik being his boss, George was right in the middle. Finally, there was Ferdi. George had been away from her for so long, and he was just like a little bird with a broken wing when she was not around to smooth his feathers. He became morose, agitated, and impatient.

Ultimately, these anxieties building in George threatened to fracture the group. After about the second or third meeting with Penkovsky in Paris, George and Mike Stokes went to a bistro to blow off some steam. When they returned, Stokes reported to Shergold that while they were drinking in this rather intimate club, George had been talking loudly with the customers and had created a scene. Mike didn't believe that the security of the operation had been breached, but he was concerned about George's boisterous behavior. Shergold asked McCoy if he would have a talk with George to calm him down a bit. McCoy apprised Bulik of the situation. Bulik concluded that George should be removed from the operation once they returned from Paris to Washington. He also determined that headquarters should be immediately notified of his assessment and asked McCoy to forward the message in a cable.

The interpretation at headquarters was that George needed more personal support than he was getting in Paris. Quentin Johnson, chief of operations in the division, was then dispatched to Paris to ameliorate the discord within the team before it could develop into a serious problem. To that end he a brought a check for $1,000 made out to George. This was a lot of money in 1961. As a further boost to George's morale, Johnson brought him a Certificate of Merit with Distinction. Bulik too was offered an award. He refused it and volunteered that McCoy deserved an award. To both their credits, neither man wanted to detract from George's recognition, and George was the sole recipient of an award. A little ceremony was held on 30 September in Paris, and the operation continued smoothly until Penkovsky left. There was no suggestion of removing George from the operation while in Paris. The team would have been lost without George's Russian as well as his ability to empathize with Penkovsky.

During one of the meetings, Penkovsky mentioned that while he was back in Moscow he had acquired timely and accurate information on the erection of the Berlin Wall before it had gone up but that he had no means of communicating that information to the team. To prevent such a situation in the future, Johnson produced a one-way burst transmitter that he had brought from headquarters. He also provided instructions and a demonstration of the short-range (e.g., 1,000 yards) device, which could send a 300-word message in an instant. No sound, no long transmission time. Penkovsky could have this in his pocket and press a button as he walked near the U.S. Embassy in Moscow. His message would be transmitted immediately, and the Soviets would have only an instant to detect the signal.

During Penkovsky's twenty-five days in Paris, he met with the team twelve times. Again the team had to buy various gifts for him to take home. One of them, a huge picture called *The Sea,* baffled George. They tried to get it off the frame in order to pack it for him. "No, you'll bust it," Penkovsky implored. When they all departed Paris, the case officers as well as Penkovsky were at the airport at the same time, although not acknowledging one another. Then, George saw Penkovsky with "that God-awful picture," preparing to board his plane. That was the last time that any of the case officers ever saw the man.

CHAPTER 14

Missile Crises

As Penkovsky was leaving Paris, the CIA was still trying to put together a Moscow presence. By November of 1961, an operational chief was in place. Paul Garbler, whom George had hired in 1952, was appointed by Richard Helms, then the clandestine operations directorate chief, and approved by Allen Dulles, the director, to be the first chief of Moscow. Nevertheless, the CIA lacked certain essential assets that were needed for a completely effective presence in Moscow, so some innovations were required. One novel scheme was a penetration of the State Department through its Security Office. A State Department clerical secretary routinely met with her CIA counterpart at a designated set of stalls in the ladies' room at the State Department in Washington, and they passed notes back and forth to each other. The notes were extracted from cable traffic between the U.S. Embassy in Moscow and the State Department, addressed to the CIA in a code that was superimposed over the normal State Department code. This amounted to a covert communication channel available to the chief in Moscow for contacting the Soviet activities group at CIA headquarters. The State Department was completely unwitting of this arrangement. The Agency needed this means of communication because their activities were at great odds with the State Department's operations in the Soviet Union.

When Penkovsky got back to Moscow, he had a dozen clandestine contacts with Janet Chisholm. He would give her exposed film cassettes along with written notes. She, in turn, would hand them over to her husband and he would pass everything back to England in a diplomatic pouch. The bag would go to Shergold, who would draft replies to Penkovsky's messages and send copies of his drafts by cable to the CIA for agreement and amendments. A cable then would be sent from the United States back to the United Kingdom and from there another cable would be sent to the British Embassy in Moscow, where it would be translated and made ready for Janet to give to Penkovsky at their next meeting. All of this would have to take place within a week, since Janet could not have the scheduled weekly meeting with Penkovsky without the team responding to his last messages. This frantic pace was necessary in order to keep the case going, but the British conducted the exercise without a glitch. Altogether the team received 103 film cassettes through the British, most of them in this clandestine way through Janet. Of course, the team had to base their communications plan on the young lady's regularly scheduled movements. Any deviation might give the KGB surveillance teams in Moscow cause for concern.

For either the park or the restaurant/deli meetings, the routine followed a procedure always dictated by Penkovsky and designed to be sufficiently varied to avoid creating an easily discernible pattern. Janet would attend her regularly scheduled ballet lesson and then, according to the preconceived plan, would stop by either the store or the deli to briefly look at what was available for sale. When Penkovsky arrived he would endeavor to ensure that he was not being surveilled, then he would see that she had observed him, and finally he would lead her off to the rendezvous. They would walk down the street with her following discreetly behind until he found an apartment block that he believed to be safe. He then would disappear through some door of his choosing and she would follow him in. The door selected may or not be one that they had used at some previous meeting. Once in the hall entrance to the apartments, they would quickly exchange the products of espionage and a few words. He would give to her rolls of exposed films and written messages. She in turn would provide him with fresh cassettes of films, the responses to his previously delivered written messages, as appropriate, and perhaps additional written instructions. She knew a few words in Russian, just enough to follow a little bit; but she did not engage herself in the operation as anything other than a courier, albeit an extremely adept and brave one.

In November, the two of them met publicly while attending an official function at the British Embassy. When Penkovsky advised his GRU superiors that he had met the wife of a British intelligence officer, they gave their endorsement to have contact with her as a potential avenue to her husband. Nevertheless, the two continued their meetings in a clandestine way, just to be extra careful, since the KGB might be snooping.

In January of 1962, immediately following one of their meetings, Penkovsky noted that Janet was being surveilled. He then precipitously chose to abort their next planned meeting. She did not know why he did not appear. She continued her routine but he still did not appear. The team did not know what the problem was. The British and the Americans even considered attempting to find out about Penkovsky's whereabouts through overt commercial contacts. The team sent to Penkovsky a coded message indicating that Mrs. Chisholm would be making rendezvous attempts at selected times and locations, but no response was heard.

Penkovsky wished to transmit to the team why he had broken off, but he had suddenly been assigned the task of accompanying an American paper delegation about Moscow and Leningrad. The task required about two weeks. He approached one of its people as the delegation was leaving Moscow en route to London. He began to explain to his candidate, giving the man a procedure for delivering his message. The message contained the information that a car with "license number such and such had surveilled them." (Penkovsky actually knew the license number.) The message also contained an admonition to Janet: "Be careful. They are watching you all of the time now." This fellow was a former CIA employee but chose not to cooperate with Penkovsky, perhaps thinking that Penkovsky was a provocation. He did not accept any notes from Penkovsky and did not even convey anything of the approach when he reached London.

Finally, on 9 March, the SIS initiated a routine interview with the American who had been in Moscow with the paper delegation. They asked him if he had contact with a man named Penkovsky, whereupon the man cooperated. He told them that Penkovsky had accompanied his delegation in Leningrad and Moscow for more than a week in late January. He gave to them all of the information that he could recall, including the information that Penkovsky wanted to pass on a message to Mrs. Chisholm that she was under surveillance.

So the CIA-SIS team did get the gist of the message, in spite of the man's reluctance to help. Two months had transpired, however;

the calendar already was into March of 1962. Shergold concluded that Penkovsky was in no immediate danger but that Mrs. Chisholm was under surveillance and the contacts should be terminated. A message was sent to Penkovsky advising that the team had received his message through the American businessman.

Penkovsky was invited to a cocktail party at the home of a British scientific attaché on 28 March. The Chisholms were in attendance and Penkovsky was able to pass to Janet a letter and some film cassettes. The letter described in detail Penkovsky's observation of apparent surveillance of Janet at their January meeting and stated his belief that their meetings at the park and deli should be terminated but meetings at diplomatic events should be encouraged. He also indicated that he hoped to attend a number of functions outside of the Soviet Union, including one at the Seattle World's Fair in April. Later on, in connection with his job in the cover-trade organization, Penkovsky was also invited to the queen's birthday party at the British Embassy. At that time he passed through Janet a letter to the team in which he expressed alarm. He was concerned because he had experienced a disappointment at the GRU. He had been told that he would be groomed for a post at the United Nations in New York. In connection with this, he was scheduled for trips to the World's Fair in Seattle and to Brazil in order to observe how the Americans would react to him. The GRU, after all, probably figured that the Americans knew he was GRU from his previous assignment in Turkey. Then, at the last minute, these plans were canceled. The reason, he feared, was the matter of his father's history. Evidently, the neighbors at the KGB had been delving into the details. Since no records of his father's death were available, and no grave could be found, they were suspicious—perhaps the man did not die and was living abroad. Penkovsky added he was sick and tired of this existence, wanted to come out with his family and asked advice.

Although Penkovsky had no more clandestine meetings with Janet, he did meet her on occasion at official functions and they passed tapes and messages back and forth. These opportunities occurred only occasionally during that spring. As time progressed he became more and more concerned about the ever-tightening circumstances that he was sensing. He had been promised trips abroad that had been precipitously canceled: Switzerland in March, Seattle in April. He was concerned as to his future and he wanted to make plans to permanently exit the Soviet Union.

The CIA concluded that a dangerous situation existed and thought that Penkovsky should cease his espionage activities for the time being, getting rid of all incriminating material. The British disagreed. In fact, they believed that the Americans were not leveling with them. *Did the CIA have other information that led them to be afraid, information that was not being shared with them?* The CIA could not convince them otherwise, so a compromise was reached. The Americans and the British would get the appropriate men, under cover, into each of their embassies. If Penkovsky could have regular access to these embassies under the guise of his official cover organization, he would have a perfect reason to meet both people. Both intelligence agencies could then execute all future transfer of materials with ease and security. In June, the CIA finally sent its man, Rodney Carlson, to the U.S. Embassy. Should Penkovsky be invited there for the celebration of some big American day such as Independence Day or Christmas, the Agency was prepared.

The British were not as concerned as the Americans about the potential threat and insisted that Greville Wynne could serve until a replacement for Janet Chisholm could be provided. Janet was to be relieved in any event because she was pregnant again and wished to return home for delivery of her child. In July, Wynne met Penkovsky in Moscow with a new plan for communication. He showed Penkovsky pictures of Janet's replacement[1] as well as the new CIA man, Rod Carlson, and his wife. In addition, Wynne gave Penkovsky a special tiepin, identical to the one Carlson would wear for their initial meeting. Penkovsky told Wynne that he wanted to defect and come to the West. He was worried. He was having trouble with his one-way communication device. He sounded desperate. He wanted to come out, even if he had to leave his family. Wynne noted that his own baggage had been searched in his hotel room and that when he and Penkovsky were together they were watched. Moreover, when Wynne met with the Soviet business committee to make plans for an exhibition, he sensed that he was being grilled.

On Independence Day in 1962, Penkovsky was invited to Spaso House, the American ambassador's residence, and was able to meet Carlson. Both were hopeful that a new phase in the relationship could begin. A few days later Penkovsky officially escorted Wynne out of Moscow. To Wynne, Penkovsky appeared rattled and quite nervous about the surveillance. Nevertheless, Penkovsky had the temerity to make a formal complaint to the GRU. He and Wynne should not be surveilled! After all, he had official reasons to be seeing Wynne!

During the summer, Penkovsky had successful meetings with Wynne but he continued to feel that the world was closing in on him. Finally, on 27 August, he and Rod Carlson executed a successful pass of information, the first for the Americans in all of this time. At that meeting, Carlson also gave Penkovsky an internal passport. This document, forged by the CIA, would permit the holder to travel about freely within the Soviet Union. Otherwise, internal travel was almost impossible in the police state.

Still in August, Penkovsky again met Carlson at a party. Carlson received seven cassettes from Penkovsky and gave him instructions from the team. In early September, Stuart Udall, the U.S. secretary of the interior, visited the Soviet Union and Penkovsky attended a social function in connection with the trip. There he met with Carlson and told him that he would have something for him the next night, 6 September, during the film showing at the British Embassy. No Americans were invited, however, so Carlson was not able to be there. Penkovsky was seen there; but after that, no CIA or SIS people saw him again, even though he was invited to diplomatic functions three times later in September.

In October, the missiles in Cuba were detected. Some had previously warned about this possibility. CIA Director John McCone had advised the president as early as August that he believed in the presence of offensive missiles in Cuba. In August, Sen. Kenneth Keating of New York stated that he had evidence of the entrance of strategic offensive missiles in Cuba. Other senators, Thurmond, Capehart, and Goldwater, berated the president for his "do-nothing" policy vis-à-vis Cuba.

Almost no one within the Kennedy administration, however, believed that the presence of offensive missiles in Cuba was likely. First of all, there was no hard evidence (e.g., photos); secondly, the Soviets themselves had assured Kennedy there were no missiles in Cuba. After some delay, McCone was able to schedule U-2 flights over the island. On the flight of 14 October, offensive missiles were photographed. With the information that Penkovsky had previously provided, the missiles immediately were identified. Moreover, the technical characteristics of the missiles also were available through this material.

Within days, analysis by Agency personnel indicated the missiles' range (more than 1,000 nautical miles) and the extent of the threat. The United States had overwhelming superiority to the Soviets in offensive missiles, as well as superior intelligence, due in no small part to Penkovsky, but there was great concern—even fright throughout the world—regarding the prospect of war over the Soviet presence in Cuba. The concern was warranted. In addition to the incipient missile threat, the Soviets already had a tremendous nuclear capability through their long-range bomber program-one that could have been fatal to the very existence of the United States; and fully operational IL-28 Beagle Bombers were being uncrated in Cuba. More than two weeks of indecision on the part of the Kennedy administration followed.

On 27 October, a U-2 aircraft, piloted by Maj. Rudolph Anderson, Jr., was shot down by an SA-2. Anderson was killed. Tensions rose and the president was pressured to order an attack on Cuba. Fearing, correctly, that such an action might escalate the situation, he made no decision. Meanwhile, other missiles in Cuba, with greater ranges (2,000 nautical miles), were discovered to be nearing operational status. The CIA-SIS team sent a radio message to Penkovsky asking for information on the situation—particularly if an early-warning message were warranted. There was no reply.

Eventually, the crisis was substantially defused with the Soviet proposal to withdraw the missiles in exchange for a U.S. agreement not to threaten Castro or Cuba anymore, as well as its pledge to remove similar U.S. missiles that were deployed in Turkey. Although the Turkish government was unwitting of the agreement, and had previously expressed displeasure at such an action when the U.S. had broached the question (because the missiles were nearing obsolescence), they acquiesced. At least in the minds of the public, the matter was resolved. However, there was no promise on the part of the Soviets to remove the long-range bombers that were deployed in Cuba, so in reality, a dangerous situation still existed. Ultimately, in mid-November, an agreement was reached that the aircraft also would be removed in late December.

Penkovsky could have been the ultimate intelligence asset. With his position as a senior colonel in the Soviet Army, his association with the GRU, and his relationships with people such as Varentsov, Penkovsky could have the capacity to render an early-warning signal if a nuclear attack from the Soviets were imminent. The team, therefore, had devised two procedures Penkovsky could use in such a case, if no personal contact were feasible. In one scenario he would mark a designated lamppost with a dark chalk circle about waist high and then follow that with a call to a specified phone number. If he heard the proper response, he then would blow three times into the mouthpiece and hang up. This would mean "beware; an attack is under way." In case the phones were not operative or the proper response was not obtained when he made the call, he was to mark the same lamppost in the manner as before and then load a dead drop with the message. He also was to call a specified telephone number to indicate that the dead drop had been, or would be, loaded. Other than to signal nuclear attack or that his status drastically had changed (e.g., he had been dropped from the committee or was being posted outside of Moscow), he was not to load the dead drop. Moreover, the dead drop should be used only once.

At 9:00 A.M. on 2 November, soon after the Cuban missile crisis appeared to be settled, U.S. Embassy personnel in Moscow received a telephone call at the designated location. The caller blew three times into the receiver. The embassy cabled this information to headquarters while Paul Garbler and one other person observed the light pole. The mark was there—a circle, waist high, in dark chalk. This meant that the dead drop also had been loaded. The situation was an extreme emergency; perhaps an attack was imminent. The CIA had to clear the dead drop.

George described the next steps. "Jacob, a Dartmouth man and a friend of mine, went with an embassy official, in an embassy car, to a spot not far from the dead-drop location and parked. Jacob got out of the car and walked in a circuitous route to shake any possible surveillance, pausing at appropriate places to observe the scene. Seeing nothing suspicious, he made his way to the dead-drop area. The State Department man, totally unwitting as to what was about to transpire, got out of the car and went in another direction, expecting to do some routine shopping. Jacob stepped into the dead-drop location to clear the drop. He cleared it. There was a matchbox. Important information would be therein. Suddenly, walls broke open! It was a stakeout. Four huge men pinned his arms to his raincoat as they seized him. They literally dragged him to a car, kidnapped him, and took off.

"The State Department guy, seeing what had happened, took off back to the U.S. Embassy. He rushed in and screamed, 'They grabbed Jacob. Protest at once through the secretary of state to Gromyko, Molotov, or whomever. We must spring him. Demand his release; he is our diplomat.'

"In the meantime, Jacob was with the KGB being grilled. Clandestine operations! Illegal activities! Espionage! They tried to pin as much on him as possible and they also tried to see if they could get him to work with them against his own embassy. He had one answer. 'I—want—my—embassy!' They became angry with him. He was like an automaton. He kept saying just one thing: 'I—want—my—embassy.'

"The guy in the back room says, 'Which damned embassy?' They didn't know whether he was American, Canadian, or British. How could they know? It was a joint operation. So finally, it was unearthed that it was the U.S. Embassy, and finally, after whatever, one or two hours, of verbal chastising, but nothing more, the man in charge, the KGB arresting officer, said, 'Their foreign office is calling ours. We're PNGing[2] the man. By international law, we have to release him to his embassy. Tell them to come around.'

"Shortly thereafter, State Department people picked him up and took him back to the embassy. They PNGed him and nine others. Our doctor, who I also happened to know, was PNGed. He was from Atlanta. I used to know his mother and his father; I played bridge with them in Atlanta. He was the American Embassy doctor, Alex Davison. Poor Alex didn't know a damned fool thing about the operation. Anyway, that is neither here nor there. So, Hugh Montgomery, he was PNGed. He had an official job there; he was a recipient of one of the phone calls. Jacob, of course, and the contact man, Rodney Carlson, were also PNGed. In addition, they threw out an 'innocent' State Department employee. He was expelled although he didn't know anything of the affair. Five British as well were sent home. It's funny. I knew all of these guys. Well, anyway, those are the personae; that is how it happened.[3] Later on that day, within an hour or so of Jacob's arrest, Wynne also was arrested in Budapest, Hungary. He was there with his wagon, trying to sell his goods. He was arrested by their secret police and turned over to the KGB, who dragged him to Moscow to be put on trial along with Penkovsky."

Penkovsky had two trials, overt and covert. The overt trial was on 7 May 1963. There, he bravely tried to defend Wynne. He stated that Wynne was a war hero, saying, "He fought the same Hitler that we did." Wynne had been an officer for the British Navy during the Second World War. "His business activity was completely in the blind. He did not participate in espionage or even know what he was actually doing. If he carried anything he didn't know what it was," Penkovsky plaintively, but to no avail, stated. Fittingly, Gen. V. V. Borisoglebsky was the presiding judge. He had been the court-martial judge for Gary Powers as well as for the Soviet who had been flown black to see General Cabell. He was the one who had told Penkovsky of the latter when Penkovsky was at the missile school.

At his overt trial, the Soviets tried to depict Penkovsky as a drunkard. He certainly was not. He drank only a little wine. They could not hide the fact that he had been a most competent military officer—indeed, a war hero. They did, however, succeed in hiding the fact that he was GRU. He got no help from his high-placed friends. By this time, Varentsov was no longer a marshal of the Soviet Union; Penkovsky's father-in-law, General Gapanovich, was dead; and "Serov was somewhere in Siberia, demoted and marching on the Mongolian border," according to George. "There was cashiering coming and going all over Moscow for lack of diligence in watching out for a spy of the caliber of Penkovsky."

Penkovsky was sentenced to be shot. In May of 1963 the Soviets claimed that the sentence had been complied with. "They didn't execute him at once," George surmised, "since they could kill him like a flea at any time. They probably wanted to query him about many of the CIA operations. 'Is so and so one of their penetrations too? What else did you tell them?' How else would they know? Like Ames. We would want to know to what extent he had compromised us." They could have tortured Penkovsky for a long time while trying to find out what information he might have given the team. Evidently, his family did not get penalized. Perhaps he made some deal in order to spare them. Some accounts allege that he was burned alive while a group of new GRU officers witnessed, in order to recognize their own fate should they take the path of Penkovsky. Some say that was the fate of the man who was flown back for a visit with General Cabell. We don't know for sure, but George did not think that was the case with Penkovsky.

Wynne was sentenced to eight years of hard labor but he was traded for one of their spies in much the same way that Gary Powers was exchanged for Rudolf Abel. On 22 April 1964, Gordon Lonsdale, a.k.a. Konon Trofimovich Molody, and Wynne passed each other at Heerstrasse checkpoint in West Berlin. This is the same man that George, at the request of the British, had tried to influence at their April 1961 meeting in London. Then Wynne came home and wrote *The Man from Moscow, The Man from Odessa,* and *Meeting on Gorky Street.* According to George, "He tried to do this and that; he tried to make a big fanfare out of it. He was a little bit odd."

Undoubtedly, this was the most productive U.S. espionage operation of the Cold War. Penkovsky's documentary material came out in English translation to about 10,000 pages. Almost all of it was top-secret information. By contrast, the Popov operation, which previously had been the CIA's most successful clandestine operation, provided about 1,300 pages of comparable material, although none of the Popov information was classified higher than secret. With the Minox and his access to GRU and missile archives, Penkovsky effectively used 110 cassettes of film, producing 5,000 frames, nearly all of which were perfectly readable.

During the last team meeting in London, Leonard McCoy had briefed the case officers on the requirements Penkovsky should attempt to fulfill when he went back to the Soviet Union. One was to obtain a secret version of *Military Thought,* a publication whose existence had been disclosed through Popov. This document was designed to reflect the current opinions of senior Soviet military officers. Popov had given George an unclassified version but in 1959, a Soviet naval captain defector confirmed the existence of a secret version.[4] Penkovsky did not obtain this secret version; rather, he provided a top-secret version, a text that the case officers did not know about. It gave, in detail, the views and intentions of Khrushschev's most senior military officers.

Penkovsky provided the Americans and the British with personal histories of leading Soviet generals and the minutes of Central Committee meetings of the Soviet Communist Party, including some actual documents.

The high-level technical manuals and missile specifications that Penkovsky provided made it clear that the United States was far ahead of the Soviets in military space. But as he told George, the Soviets were "breaking their backs" to close in on the U.S. lead, and they would soon be a tremendous threat to the West.

Penkovsky photographed various Kremlin telephone books, including those of the Defense Ministry, the secure Red line, the

Academy of Sciences, etc. This information gave a means for piecing together a rudimentary organizational chart of those assigned there.

He identified 341 GRU people in Moscow and 192 abroad, and he listed 75 KGB, mostly in London and Paris. These were unique contributions on his part. He also confirmed CIA suspicions about hundreds of other intelligence personnel.

He supplied information about a new tank that the Soviets were creating. So the United States created one to combat it.

He gave the CIA and SIS full knowledge of the SA-2, the surface-to-air missiles that shot down both the U-2s of Gary Powers near Sverdlovsk, USSR, and Maj. Rudolph Anderson over Cuba. Thus, countermeasures were developed. Eventually, he provided the technical characteristics of all tactical missiles and rockets in the Soviet Union.

Most importantly, Penkovsky's information was timely. The team sent reports every day to the White House and 10 Downing Street during the Bay of Pigs debacle in the spring of 1961, the Berlin crises in the summer and fall of 1961, and the Cuban missile crisis in October of 1962. Through personal contacts with Varentsov, Penkovsky was able to tell much about Soviet intentions during that period, something a photograph cannot do. In July of 1961 he stated that the Soviet Union would sign a separate peace treaty with the GDR (East Germany), thereby recognizing them as a separate nation. This forewarning enabled a prepared response from the United States. He also suggested that East Berlin would become a closed zone and added that if the United States objected, the Soviets would relent. Of course, President Kennedy did not act on the information, and the Berlin Wall went up unchallenged.

The Cuban missile crisis became front-page news in October of 1962. The information that Penkovsky supplied long before that date, coupled with CIA's own aerial photography of missiles, gave the type, the technical characteristics, the potential readiness and the capabilities (including their range and destructive power) of the missiles to be deployed. He had provided the manuals on the SS-4, the principal missile deployed there; and when aerial photography identified these as the missiles under construction and ultimately in place, the analysts knew just what coverage the missiles could have of the United States and what threat they might be. Penkovsky also revealed that there were no ICBM forces operational in the Soviet Union at the time, which now gave President Kennedy two aces in the hole during the negotiations. Kennedy, therefore, ultimately reacted to the missiles in Cuba in a more decisive manner than was his custom.

Khrushchev had bullied Kennedy in their diplomatic encounter on June 1961 in Vienna. The Berlin Wall had risen on Kennedy's watch. Khrushchev thought of Kennedy as an inexperienced boy president who could easily be intimidated. Certainly, Kennedy was determined not to be embarrassed by Khrushchev again, and he now knew a nuclear exchange was unlikely. Kennedy also knew from Penkovsky that the ultraconservatives in the Kremlin were terribly frightened by Khrushchev's affinity for freewheeling nuclear poker and might well force Khrushchev to retreat. Therefore, armed with these and other pieces of information and for other reasons as well, Kennedy decided to act. He ordered the naval blockade and the heart of the world skipped a beat, not being privy to the actual circumstances. Ultimately, Khrushchev realized that he had lost his desperate gamble and proposed a solution to end the confrontation.

CHAPTER 15

Reflections

The British case officers, Shergie and Mike, got on very well with George personally and greatly enjoyed working closely with him. They found him to be operationally compatible, someone who agreed with them about the needs of Penkovsky. Bulik wanted to play things more by the book than by the personalities.

Although every significant action taken during the entire operation was done with joint approval of the SIS and CIA, inevitably there would be legitimate differences of opinion between the services as to how the case should be advanced. One such difference centered upon the number of meetings Penkovsky should have with Janet Chisholm. The CIA, represented by Bulik, early on began to be disturbed at the high frequency of the rendezvous. After all, going slowly would certainly seem to be the safe thing to do. Moreover, the intelligence community at one time seemed to be nearing saturation with the type of information that Penkovsky was providing.[1] Perhaps he should have been put on ice and saved for the early-warning notification of a nuclear strike, at least until a safe means of transfer of the clandestine material could be effected.

However, George shared with the British the notion that, in dealing with people of Penkovsky's sort, one has to accept that they are not quite of the ordinary run. That is why they do the things they do. Therefore, one has to go along with their desires and motivations to a degree; one has to be very careful about directing them. Accordingly, the team had to keep Penkovsky's confidence up. On the other hand, there was the matter of his safety. Penkovsky had this burning desire to become the greatest spy in history. He had on numerous occasions said this. Having achieved contact with the West for that purpose, he was not likely to let anything get in the way of that goal. Penkovsky directed that the meetings be frequent. Moreover, the great volume of intelligence justified great risk.

Of course, in the end, Penkovsky did provide an early warning of sorts on the Cuban crises when he provided the vital information that later enabled Kennedy to take the actions that he ultimately did. It may have been the supreme early warning of all time. The information that he had provided to the United States made its position during the crises far superior than it otherwise would have been. So, perhaps he achieved his goal of being the greatest spy of all time. But he would not have done so if the CIA-SIS team had not kept up his morale and motivation. The British continue to believe that the team was correct in playing the act at Penkovsky's speed. Otherwise, he would have lost his confidence in them. In retrospect, and in spite of the ultimate outcome, they maintain that there was no option but to run the case pretty much the way he wanted it run.[2]

George shared some of his personal recollections: "Later I became good friends with the British. Sir Dickie Franks eventually became chief of SIS. He took me to lunch in Bonn, Germany, one day in 1964, when I was dealing with another case. I have about ten pictures of him and his lovely British home with a little lake and a miniature golf course, a wonderful and attractive wife, daughter, and son. I visited with him and took the photos. Sir Dickie Franks, a fine officer. He holds the KCMG: Knight Commander of the Most Distinguished Order of St. Michael and St. George. It is quite an award; it is presented for exemplary service, professionally, and other such things as loyalty and character. He was the case officer separately for Greville Wynne. He kept Wynne under control separately and out of our hair.

"Ultimately Shergie became a very dear friend, and recently made a lecture, praising me to the sky. My daughter, Eva, stayed with him when she was in England. He is intelligent, about my age, retired now and holds the CMG: the Commander of the Most Distinguished Order of St. Michael and St. George. He is a wonderful person who raises and trains seeing-eye dogs for a hobby. His wife, Bevis, just died. She was a great British athletic champion in her youth, a powerful woman. She held the British championship in shot put, javelin, and discus—all at one time—the only one to ever have done that. She competed in the Olympics of 1948 in England. She also was a vegetarian, so he and I had to sneak out of the house at dinnertime for steaks.[3]

"In his book *The Man from Odessa*, Wynne stated that he and Penkovsky had been flown in black to meet with President Kennedy. That is all baloney. The concept wasn't even original. It was stolen from Penkovsky's story about the man flown back black to visit General Cabell. Nevertheless, about twenty years later, this fabrication caused a little heartburn to some of us who were involved.

"The libel laws of England are so peculiar that you would have to stand on your ear to believe them. It is as if the English people cannot say the things they believe. If someone said to you, 'I saw the Second Coming of Jesus Christ yesterday,' and you called him a liar, you'd be subject to libel if you couldn't disprove him. Moreover, you might then be vulnerable to a heavy monetary penalty. Don't ask me why. I cannot explain such a thing. I don't understand these laws at all. That is their society. You can believe it or not. I have it all in writing, right now, everything that I am telling you.

"Rupert Allason, who then was a member of Parliament, and later a noted author of spy thrillers, writing under the pseudonym of Nigel West, called Wynne a liar for stating that he and Penkovsky had flown to the United States, black, to meet with President Kennedy. Greville Wynne instituted a suit against Allason claiming, I believe, 'defamation of character.' The suit could have cost Allason 200,000 English pounds, according to the estimate he gave to me. Allason, of course, wanted me to come over and testify, and he offered to pay all of my expenses. He knew that I had complete cognizance of Penkovsky's schedule and movements while he was with us, and he knew that my testimony would put the lie to Wynne's tall tale. I did not want to get into this argument about money and I did not wish to go to England. I did, however, feel an obligation to help reveal the truth, so I endeavored to assist him without going over there. His lawyer, a woman, came over to my house in Virginia from London and took a deposition from me. I also told her to do her homework. I said, 'We have a Secret Service. They can tell you from the White House log the people who saw the president and whether or not Wynne saw him. They will not tell you what was said between the parties, but at least you can find out whether or not it is conceivable that the dates corresponding to Wynne's bulls— are dates that allow for the possibility of such a meeting. It may be that the president was not even in town on those days.[4]

"Now Shergie, Mike, and their English friends are subject to restrictions regarding the British Official Secrets Act. By saying something that they shouldn't, they could be severely punished. Consequently, they couldn't readily help Allason. Moreover, when Allason asked Len McCoy to help him, all Len could do was to agree with him verbally. McCoy's wife was still at the CIA at the time and it would not have been appropriate or practical for McCoy to get into the fray. Anyway, the lawsuit precipitated by these ideas about black visitations cleared for good, by the grace of God, with Greville Wynne dying in 1990 of cancer. That ended the legal action."[5]

Through personal interviews with Harold Shergold, Mike Stokes, and Yuri Nosenko, a coherent picture of the Penkovsky arrest emerges. Also, some of the elements of this account are attested to in the comprehensive treatment of Penkovsky, *The Spy Who Saved the World*, by Jerrold L. Schecter and Peter S. Deriabin.

The story of the detection and apprehension of Penkovsky is one of sheer serendipity in favor of KGB surveillance, foolish arrogance on the part of Penkovsky, and deserved results for an incredible effort by the KGB "Department of Dirty Tricks." It begins with the series of clandestine meetings between Penkovsky and Janet Chisholm. Everything went perfectly well from the first of these meetings, on 2 July 1961 in Tsvetnoy Park, through the tenth meeting, on 5 January 1962 at the Kommission store. By this time there had been four successful meetings in the park and six successful meetings across town at either the Kommission store or the nearby Praga restaurant/deli. Additionally there had been the November 1961 social event at the British Embassy where Penkovsky had officially met Janet Chisholm.

On 12 January, Penkovsky picked up Janet at the deli and they proceeded down the street as usual. Almost by accident, a KGB surveillance team in the area saw a Russian man enter an apartment door and a Western woman follow him. The KGB team did not know the identity of either person, but they took note of this unusual circumstance, and in short order they identified Janet. It was simply a matter of following her back to a location that suggested her identity, the British Embassy. Then, comparing her surveillance photo with those in their files of embassy personnel, they knew who she was. They did not, however, identify Penkovsky, who took evasive actions that were beyond their means of a successful pursuit at the time. They knew that they had made an exciting discovery. A British Embassy woman was having a surreptitious rendezvous with a Russian who seemed adept in clandestine matters, judging by his ability to escape their track. They resolved to follow up on this curious relationship. If nothing else, they might have an opportunity for blackmail. The next time this couple met, the KGB team would be prepared.

Penkovsky suspected that a surveillance team might have witnessed this meeting. He then did a most brazen thing; he attended the appointed meeting with Janet on 19 January. This ultimately cost him his life. The Soviet surveillance team was in attendance for this meeting with great strength. Rather than the two or three members who attended the first detected rendezvous, they now had members in numbers sufficient to completely blanket the actions of both Janet and Penkovsky. The meeting of the nineteenth was conducted without their awareness of the surveillance, and as they departed, he told her that he would see her on the next planned meeting date. Just then, however, he spotted a car speeding away with the members of a surveillance team. His observation was sufficient to obtain the car's license number. He then knew that he was in jeopardy and resolved not to meet covertly with Janet again.

Janet also saw the car but she was not so keenly aware of the problem. About two weeks later, she waited as usual at the prearranged site at the prescribed time to meet Penkovsky but he did not show. She went to the alternate meeting place. Again he did not show and did not show for several more meetings. She kept up her normal routine, visiting their usual meeting places, hoping to make it appear that nothing was amiss. She changed to days when he would not be expected to appear, however. Now, she did not wish to meet him, suspecting strongly that she was being followed everywhere she went.

The CIA-SIS team sent the coded radio message to Penkovsky expressing their anxiety but got no reply. They later learned that he had not been able to manage the device for the proper receipt of messages. Evidently, George's initial assessment of Penkovsky's ability to use it was wrong. The team was in the dark until March.

When the KGB surveillance team detected Janet Chisholm and Penkovsky at their meeting on 19 January and after the team had identified him by following him back to his office, they still did not know just what they had. Their next step was a full-scale investigation of his associations and habits. They began a full-time surveillance of him. They planted microphones in his apartment and set up cameras to watch his every action within his own home. They placed a camera on the balcony of his apartment during a routine incursion and remotely controlled it from another apartment afar. Initial photographs were obtained.

The KGB then acquired the apartment directly above Penkovsky's for a period of about a month, while that family was given a vacation on the Black Sea. From that apartment a tiny peephole was drilled into Penkovsky's ceiling. A probe with a tiny lens was inserted to scan Penkovsky's entire apartment and witness his every move. After sufficient observation, the search entry into his apartment was planned. While the family was away, Penkovsky was poisoned. He did not eat a poison but contacted a substance surreptitiously placed in his office chair by the KGB. It consisted of a caustic agent suspended in a wax base. His body heat melted the wax, the agent was absorbed into his buttocks, and he then became severely blistered as well as ill. He was taken to the hospital, perhaps unwitting as to the cause of his malady. While there, and with his family not at home, entry into the apartment was attained. Only one entry was required and access to the desk was a trivial task for the much-experienced intruders.

Penkovsky was released from the hospital and returned home. So, the KGB again waited and watched. Finally, on a date sometime in October, he was observed removing from his desk the internal passport that Rodney Carlson had given him. The cameras witnessing his action were of sufficient definition to actually allow recognition of the document. He signed the counterfeit internal passport, thus enabling its use. Fearing that they might lose him, the KGB arrested him. The date was 22 October, the very date that Kennedy spoke to the American public, announcing to them, for the first time, the presence of the missiles in Cuba and that he had sent a message to Khrushchev regarding their removal. It was by mere chance that Penkovsky's arrest occurred amidst the events of that crisis, while both the Soviet Union and the United States were attempting to deal with the missiles that he so completely defined. The timing must have been a shock to Khrushchev, not knowing just what the Americans had learned from Penkovsky and just when they had acquired that information.

There has always been some confusion about the meaning of the telephone signals and the marking of the dead drop. What did Penkovsky do when they arrested him and why? What did he tell them and why? The signals and the arrest, of course, are related.

Some things are clear. He talked and maybe he talked a lot. He probably made a deal, but CIA/SIS analysts don't know for sure. The Soviet press announced that his family was innocent of all misdeeds. This information was printed in the public news, in *Izvestiya.* Evidently, he made a deal that if his family were spared, he would cooperate with the KGB and tell them what he had divulged as well as what he could about his spymasters. It is likely that the KGB had the declaration of the innocence of the family members published in *Izvestiya* in order to assure him that they would honor their agreement. It would have been even more embarrassing to them if they had published such a message and then reversed themselves. They were not above this type of duplicity, but it is clear that they never did persecute the family members in any significant way in the future. They are today healthy and reasonably well off, but reclusive.

It is always standard procedure in such a situation for the offended agency to try to do damage control as well as to turn the agent around for a double-cross operation. So, apart from trying to find out just how much Penkovsky had told the team, they wanted also to take the opportunity to clean out as many embassy personnel as was possible. Penkovsky would anticipate this without a hint from them. He, of course, could not begin to tell them of the volumes of data that he photographed. He didn't know himself. There probably was no reason to tell them too much else of what he knew. He could, however, have had a reason to tell them a number of truths—particularly ones that they could check out for themselves. Such action might gain their confidence that he indeed was attempting to cooperate and thereby might promote their willingness to exonerate his family.

The telephone signals as well as the dead-drop location and procedure would fit nicely in that category of revelations that Penkovsky could share with them to garner their confidence. He probably gave them the location of the dead drop. At any rate, they most assuredly knew it. He certainly told them how to execute at least one of the telephone signals and how to mark the lamppost. He could very well have told them everything about the signals except, most importantly, their true full meanings.

It is worth recalling that after Penkovsky and the CIA/SIS team got to know each other, he related to them various schemes for dropping atom bombs in garbage cans all about Moscow. This passion clearly had been evidenced at the series of London meetings. He was incredibly motivated. No one, of course, knows what was going through his mind when he was first apprehended by the KGB, but one can speculate that the minute he found himself in trouble, he determined that he would play games with the authorities. After all, he was extremely bright and tremendously dedicated to his beliefs.

It is also worth recalling that, if all else fails, the first telephone signal should be interpreted as an early warning. In fact, when the U.S. Embassy received that signal at nine o'clock the morning of 2 November, the people there immediately sent a message to headquarters to that effect. They did not even attempt to service the dead drop until that afternoon. General Cabell had some very anxious moments trying to determine if the Soviets were contemplating an attack on the U.S. Of course, they were not, and there were no other indications from Strategic Air Command or any other alert command. One theory, then, is that Penkovsky decided to cooperate, to a point, and then, by misleading his captors on the meaning of the telephone signals, bring down a rain of nuclear explosions on Moscow, taking everybody and the whole system with him. *Bombs away.*

PART IV

The Reluctant Warrior

CHAPTER 16

Turkish Rondo

Following his active participation in the Penkovsky affair, George was given a promotion and made a special assistant to the Soviet Division chief. He then was assigned the task of developing other Soviet prospects that might appear to the Agency in the West, convincing them to work with the CIA. If one were vulnerable, or could be made so, George would explore whatever opportunities might exist for the Agency. Usually the contact would lead to no benefit, but on some occasions the CIA would gain. Of course, there was always the danger of receiving wrong information from an informant. Sometimes informants were intentionally misleading, as in the case of a double agent; in other cases the informants might lack accurate knowledge of the subject or even be wrong in their assessments of facts. These things can be very confusing. For example, Anatoliy Golitsyn, a KGB officer, defected to the CIA in late 1961. He brought with him a great deal of high-level intelligence as well as false notions and suspicions that ultimately caused so much damage to the Agency apparatus that the CIA would have been better off without his defection.

On other occasions, things might just go right. One of the first such cases involving George came in August of 1961. Mikhail A. Klochko, a well-known specialist in water chemistry, a member of the Academy of Sciences in the USSR, and the head of the Kurnakov Institute of General and Inorganic Chemistry in Moscow, defected to the West. To the chagrin of the KGB, he simply stepped away from a conference in Ottawa. Before Klochko had left the Soviet Union, he had sold his antique grand piano to the president of the Soviet Academy of Sciences in order to arrive in Canada with some cash, not wishing to appear as a beggar when he asked for asylum.

Predictably, the KGB criticized the president of the Soviet Academy of Sciences for not reporting the sale of the piano before the defection. It had never occurred to the president that Klochko was thinking of defection because, as a scientist, he was focused on scientific matters rather than on political ones. The KGB, of course, would never have given Klochko an exit visa had they suspected anything. When he visited Canada, however, it was after his wife had died, so they had lost what they called the "long tail" (leash) on him. Klochko's defection caused Canadian-Soviet relations to remain on edge into early 1962, when another candidate agent appeared. George successfully recruited this new prospect while in Canada, the CIA made arrangements for future contact, and the newly acquired agent went back to his job in the USSR. George's contact was a precursor to a longtime relationship that eventually worked well for the Agency. The man's identity never became known to those outside of the U.S. intelligence community and its cooperatives.

In the spring of 1962, George traveled to Geneva, where a member of the Soviet KGB had volunteered to cooperate with American intelligence and to sell valuable intelligence information. The Agency needed an expert Russian speaker immediately to assess the significance of what was offered. This series of events initiated the Nosenko saga, which culminated in probably the worst failure in the history of the clandestine services group at the CIA.

In late 1962, George went to Ankara to see if he could approach a Soviet officer about whom the Agency knew quite a bit. The man was compromising himself through liquor, illicit relations with women, and activities for which he could be heavily censored by his organization. George recalled, "That involved Malia Natirbov, my old friend from New York City childhood days. He was in here last week. He'll be back in ten days. Right now he is visiting the village in Circassia where his father was born and where his family originates.[1] This small settlement of about twelve thousand inhabitants traces its name and history to the fifteenth century, when it was called Natir Aul. "Aul" means village. Russification of its name today makes it Natirbova. It is near another village called Anapa, on the Black Sea, just east of Yalta and west of Krasnodar. This is not far from Stavropol, where, you might remember, Penkovsky's grandfather was a judge, and Rostov, where his father was killed fighting the Bolsheviks as a lieutenant in the White Army. The people in that village want Malia to return and be their mayor. His father was a government minister there under the last tsar and Malia's great-great-grandfather, Prince Natirbov, founded Natirbova Aul. Of course, Malia's family all left Russia during the last days of the revolution."

I interrupted, "I'm so sorry that I never could convince you to return to St. Petersburg for a visit."

"What would I do, stare at tombstones? They're all dead—the Bolshevik Revolution."

George's story contains a lesson that is not well understood by many. His message, simply, is that the Western world could have an excellent avenue into understanding and negotiating with the Muslim world by utilizing its association with Turkey, a secular state with an overwhelmingly Muslim population. He began to fill me in on the Turkish side of the world. It was late 1962. He was in Ankara, the capital of Turkey, to perform what he called a hatchet job. He was to see if he could subordinate, with appropriate influence, a Soviet intelligence officer working in the Soviet Embassy, by framing him with a lady friend. It should be easy to do this because the man was a bad boy. He had girlfriends when he shouldn't; he got drunk when he shouldn't.

The nature of this operation was pressure from guilt, with an arm twister. It's the traditional way of framing a guy with a girlfriend: *We caught you. We will tell on you if you don't cooperate. Cooperate with us and we will get you off the hook.* Usually it involves a threat and a bit of financial emolument associated with his moment of embarrassment. Sometimes the threat of future embarrassment will be enough to shock the individual into working for the Agency. If he bites, the CIA has an agent. If it works, fine. If it doesn't work—well, an effort was made. George's role in this was to get the man in a drunken condition, frame him in a compromising situation, and then promise to get him off the hook if he cooperated. In preparing the backdrop for this operation, George had the professional benefit of, the opportunity for an education from, and the genuine pleasure of meeting a Turkish gentleman of exquisite bearing and unusual intellect.

As a prelude to the story, George reviewed some of Turkey's background for me, recalling that before the beginning of the First World War, the Ottoman Empire extended right into Egypt. The Turks then ruled essentially all of the Near East, including Syria, Jordan, Lebanon, Palestine, etc. Since Turkey fought with the

Central Powers on the side of Germany during that war, following their defeat they were occupied by the Allies: the Americans, British, French, Italians, and Greeks. The Allies ruled through a set of high commissioners. Sultan Hamid had no powers and was not effective in any way.

In October of 1918, as the war was ending, there was a Turkish colonel by the name of Mustafa Kemal, who was commanding an army down in the region of Syria. Kemal, a word that means perfection, was ordered to return to Turkey, where he found the country in complete disarray. There was no employment. To make matters worse, a million Russian refugees who had just escaped from the Bolshevik Revolution were living there. Kemal also found that a Greek army occupied Izmir on the coast of Anatolia and that Anatolia was to be partitioned by the Allies.[2]

People were looking to Kemal to do something. In time, he set up a provisional government at a location near Ankara and contemplated what he could do. He then issued a pleasant letter to the Allied high commissioners, advising them that he was taking control of Turkey and suggesting that they exit the region. Although this created a little stir, the allied governments agreed to order their forces out of Turkey. There really was no interest in fighting with the Turks now, so almost everybody went home, all but the Greeks.

The Greeks had other plans. They wanted to recapture the former Greek territories, which were then controlled by Turkey. So, as the Allies left, the Greeks collected the equipment left behind and prepared to engage Turkey. Eventually, Kemal reorganized his army, re-equipped it, and augmented it with additional troops. There were a great number of Circassians then living in Turkey who had been part of Wrangel's Army. This whole army had exited Russia into Turkey in November of 1920. Gen. Pyotr Nikolaievich Wrangel, a famous White Russian general, had evacuated his army of about 150,000 men from Novorossiysk, which is on the Black Sea, immediately adjacent to Anapa. These people had fought against Russians before and they had fought in the revolution against the Bolsheviks. They were very good fighters and great horsemen. Kemal enlisted the cooperation of many of these Circassians and incorporated them into his armed forces. Both the Greeks and the Turks fought furiously throughout the Asia Minor Peninsula. After some initial setbacks, the Turks turned the tide, and in battle after battle prevailed. Eventually they dominated the Greeks everywhere. By October of

1922, the fighting was over and Turkey had recaptured the critical regions previously occupied by the Greeks.

Kemal, by then referred to as Kemal Pasha (pasha is Turkish for general), was very pleased with the effective way that the Circassians engaged in the fight. However, because their leader, a General Ertem, had some very big ideas, politically, about his own future in the region, the Turkish general removed him from his command. Sultan Hamid, who Kemal believed had been too quick to cooperate with the Allies, was given his yacht and sent to Egypt. The sultanate, long ago impotent, was abolished. This was in November of 1922. Then, in the next year, the republic of Turkey was proclaimed. Kemal Pasha became its first president.

Kemal Pasha was more than just a president. He actually was a dictator, albeit a benevolent one. He really had the best interest of Turkey in mind, so he did everything practical to change it into a modern, Western republic. Using his vast prestige and charisma, he instituted reforms to create a modern, secular state. He forced every man to shave off his beard. He told the police that anytime they saw a man wearing a fez, they were to knock it off his head. The women were given more freedom; they were allowed to remove their veils. The most significant of the reforms had to do with the language. Up until that time the Turkish language was composed of Arabic characters, written or printed right to left. Following his reforms, the language was written or printed left to right, using the Latin, or Roman, alphabet.

Importantly, Kemal separated religion from the administration of the state. The caliphate had provided for a religious as well as secular head of a Muslim state. Now Turkey would be a secular state, although Islam would remain the predominant religion. In addition, he instituted a few changes that affected the practice of Islam. The Muslim world considers Friday the holy day, while the Christian world considers Sunday to be holy. Thursday in the Arab world is like Saturday in the Christian one: that is, it's usually half a workday. Kemal said, "This is ridiculous. The whole Western world considers Saturday and Sunday to be the end of the week. We need to be on schedule with the West. Therefore, from now on, Sunday is the Sabbath." Of course, the religious groups didn't like it, but he just ignored their concern.

Kemal Pasha ruled as the first president of the new republic from 1923 until 1938, when he died. During that period he introduced numerous reforms: legal, social, economic, military, etc. All of them were Western reforms. He was a very powerful president. He became known as Ataturk, the Father of the Republic of Turkey. As Ataturk, he transformed the social mores of the entire country. He also reorganized the army to be a modern, Western army. But the important thing was as follows. He absorbed as much as he could from the West, but he never trusted the West. He always told his political leaders, "Don't trust the West." As a consequence of this, all of the statues raised to his memory face east. In addition, he told the army, "You are the guardians of this country. Anytime there is a problem, political or otherwise, you have to save the country." Now, these two declarations by Kemal Pasha, formerly Mustafa Kemal and later to be known as Ataturk, are very important to our story.

With this background, George continued, "I was taken to a safehouse to meet with the Turkish intelligence man. He spoke English. I spoke no Turkish. We shook hands and sat down. He was an older man; he was very elegant and very dignified. We respected each other's background. The whole purpose of this meeting was to try and hit it off with him, so I was quite deferential to him.

"He said, 'Look, first let me tell you something of how we fit into the Moslem world, of which we are a part, and how that relates to you Americans. This is important because it is going to be the basis of our cooperation. You Americans must have an understanding of our philosophy, our political motives, our educational and other attitudes and the difference between what you call democracy and what we call democracy.

"'We are part of the Arabic world, as you put it, but we have a violent disagreement with the Arabs as to how to handle this world. Obviously, as you know, there are differences. First, let me tell you what we don't like about the Arabs, especially what we violently oppose. This idea of Allah being everything is not one of our philosophies. We don't think that Arabic is a modern language. We think that it is completely passé. It is religious, you might say. It is related to the Koran like Hebrew relates to the Old Testament and Greek relates to the New Testament. Historically speaking, the Arabic world might dwell on the romanticism of people such as the Persian, Omar Khayyam: *A jug of wine, a loaf of bread and thou.* It is not what we think is important. Specifically, what we don't like about the Arabic state of mind is this: they might think that they have won the battle when the blessing of Allah is dumped upon them as his representative, and they may think that everything else they do will be right. But we don't think so. We think that this is so old-fashioned, so stinking old-fashioned. With that attitude, militarily, one gets pushed aside. One suffers because of it. We are appalled by it and, further, we don't think that it is an accurate reflection of Mohammed. One doesn't win battles because he shouts from the top of a hill that God is on his side. As a further example of our differences with the Arab world, we have removed many of the Arabic words from usage and we have adopted the Latin alphabet as a means of communications. This means we have abandoned the written Arabic language, particularly those of us who are intelligent. Arabic is a cursed, old-fashioned alphabet.' So, these are the fundamentals.

"The Turkish intelligence man was a handsome, nice-looking guy—like Omar Sharif on the screen. He was representative of all of the Turks that put Turkey back on its feet. They have a fine, brave army. They are not going to be pushed around militarily by anybody in the Arabic world, they say; and in every place in the Moslem world, Turkey is the chief republic. They are the dominating force. They have passed laws that make it illegal to have more than one wife anymore. However, they let the men who already have multiple wives live out their lives that way. You wouldn't want them to have to choose which wives to throw out in the street, would you? You particularly wouldn't try to do that to the politically influential ones, now would you?

"My Turkish friend went on: 'Therefore, it's a different kind of society that we have now. It is different even to the degree that, in the American PX, right here in Ankara, you sell those beautiful copper beaten plates to hang up in front of the door entryway, the ones symbolizing *Allah bless us in this house, etc.* We do not buy them. We do not believe the idea that they symbolize to be representative of good military thinking. You do not understand why we Turks, in our ideas of democracy here, consider this a violation of good thinking, but we do. That is one difference between us. Also, that is why we disagree with the Arabs, even though we both are Muslims. You have to understand this and the reasons for it, which I have tried to explain to you.' I said to him, 'That is a point of view, but why are you talking this way to me?' 'Well, you were thoughtful and kind to me,' he continued. 'That is why I am telling you this. Maybe you know this, maybe you don't. So, I'm breaking the law. I'm an old man. I'm writing in Arabic, which is like shorthand to me; and because of this habit, I can take notes no others can.'

"Well, that is where the center of gravity was, and this kindled an understanding that would go a long way toward getting cooperation on both sides of the ball game. I scratched my head and tried to comprehend these concepts so that we could understand each other in order to facilitate our future relationship. This much is fundamental: one doesn't have to be too swift to comprehend that we needed to understand each other before we could be successful working together.

"Now, the execution of these ideas is something else, again. And that was the purpose of my being there, the matter of talking to him in preparation for this frame-up job against the Soviets, of whom we both had a mutual distrust. Honorable relations with the Americans were extremely important to the Turkish. He was satisfied, so we proceeded. When we began preparation for this job, he exhibited a lot of trust in me and allowed me to run the operation in the way that I wanted. We set up a meeting with the Soviet officer within a week. I was completely confident that the operation would succeed when the man agreed to come to our meeting. I knew that he would either cooperate willingly with us or be forced to collaborate because of his love of liquor and sex.

"Incidentally, the operation went down the drain about a week later, by an act of God. The Soviet officer got drunk. He slid down the banister of the stairway in his own home. He hit the newel at the bottom of the stair rail and his kidneys were severely injured. He was taken by ambulance to the airport and flown out immediately to Moscow for hospitalization. End of operation."

When George was ready to go back to the U.S., his old friend Malia Natirbov, at the time stationed in Turkey, was assigned the task of escorting him back as far as London. Natirbov was in security and carried a weapon. Since this was soon after the Penkovsky affair, the Agency people were concerned that George might be vulnerable to retaliation by the Soviets. George and Malia had remained close since childhood in New York. Malia was concerned about George's safety, both on professional and personal levels.

When they got to Rome they had a layover to change flights. Rome has a large airport with shops and restaurants, so the men spent some time looking at ties and so forth in a shop. George then said, "I'm going to go to the men's room." Malia said, "Okay, but don't go anywhere else. I'll wait here." After ten minutes, George had not returned and Malia began to get worried. After twenty minutes Malia went looking for him. He looked in all of the toilet stalls, but no Goga, an affectionate moniker with which he labeled George. He was frightened and wondered, "Should I call the chief in Rome? Should I call the Italian police?" He knew that the revolver in his pocket would be an issue if he did. He ran around all over the airport. He could not find George anywhere. He began to think that his worst fears might have come true. Finally, after about an hour he found Goga wandering lazily through the shops. Malia gave him hell. He was so angry with George that he wanted to hit him. This was typical Goga, he observed. It was just like the time when they were kids living in New York and absentminded George left Malia, without a word of explanation, to languish overnight in New Jersey beside some railroad tracks in the hope of getting a job at a construction site. By the time the pair reached London, Malia had cooled down. They looked at the bears in the zoo before Goga went on to the States and Malia went back to Turkey.[3]

CHAPTER 17

Associations

When he got back from Turkey, things began to work very well for George. He was in the Army Reserves as a lieutenant colonel, and the next year he passed all of the required General Staff examinations to become a full colonel. At the same time, Richard Helms, then chief of clandestine operations and later to become the director of the CIA, called George in and promoted him to the level of GS-16. This was unique. George was the first case office to attain super-grade level based upon work as a case officer rather than as an administrator. This opened the way for other people to do the same. All of George's future assignments, then, came under the deputy director of operations to the director of the Agency, that is, the individual responsible for all clandestine operations. He continued on in special operations, going to Ottawa and Montreal, Boston and Los Angeles. A lot of preparation went into these contacts, and productive intelligence information did not always materialize. In the spring of 1964 he went to Mexico City in an attempt to make contact with a Soviet believed to be a good candidate for cooperation. The man was scheduled to go home, so George had to meet with him promptly. Unfortunately, the timing was very bad. The operation there didn't take place because the man didn't make his scheduled rendezvous with George at a certain music shop as planned.

One of George's last long trips made while he was on active duty with the Agency came in late 1964. He was a guest speaker of the BND, the West German Intelligence Service, whose headquarters were located in Pullach, just outside of Munich.[1] He recalled that this was very difficult for him because his fluency in German was not current. He apologized for his misuse of the German language, but in the arena of intelligence operations, the illustrations that he used were very clear. This trip was particularly interesting to him because he previously had been acquainted with General Gehlen, the chief of the BND. They had met in 1946, right after the war, at Fort Hunt, Virginia (near Washington, D.C.). Gehlen had been the chief of intelligence for the Eastern Front of the German military. George recalled that Gehlen was very gracious to him, excessively wining and dining him.

George then went to several other German institutions—the Coast Guard, the police, the Internal Police in Cologne—and to an American retreat for intelligence personnel in the Alps, where he gave additional lectures. George maintained that he was well received there and it was his hope to be assigned to the area. It didn't work out that way, however, because he later made what must have been a very good lecture "down on the farm," the CIA training facility near Williamsburg, Virginia. His talk prompted the audience to hoot and holler such that his leaders decided he should teach at the prep school there for case officers. George was assigned to the farm for two and a half years, until the summer of 1967. After that, George spent three years back at headquarters, instructing and running courses in officer training. Additionally, he gave lectures about CIA activities to the army, navy, and air force, specializing in the topic of intelligence vis-à-vis the Soviets.

Dating back to its inception, the Agency required that individuals retire at age sixty. So in April of 1970, George's retirement was automatically scheduled. He was given a splendid cocktail party, and Director Helms spoke some fine words on his behalf and gave George one of the two pairs of gold cufflinks that were used operationally during the Popov affair. Following retirement, George continued to correspond with Director Helms, who occasionally asked him for clarification in the transliterations of Russian names that the director would write about in various magazines. George had a warm relationship with Mr. Helms, who, on occasion, invited him to lunch to discuss certain aspects of various operations. When appropriate, he also was used by the Soviet Division for various operational needs. In addition, he continued to lecture for the Agency on a contract basis. The lectures were almost exclusively about Penkovsky. He gave an average of three or four a month, at CIA headquarters; FBI headquarters; Bolling Air Force Base, where the Defense Intelligence Agency was headquartered; the navy premises in Anacostia; Fort Meade, where NSA is located; and occasionally down on the farm.

The lectures usually ran about four hours in length. Security was always maintained, but a special person brought in visual aids from the Agency so that George would not have to be burdened with that task. He of course knew most of the material by heart, but to be effective with the audience, certain things had to be visually presented.

George spoke to me on some of the fascinating associations that he had made throughout his career. He began, "That reminds me of someone. One day, when I was in Washington, at CIA headquarters, I saw Sam Wilson there at a party for somebody's award presentation. I had not seen Sam since the days of our working together in Berlin when I was involved with the Popov case and he was working for Bill Harvey. Sam was the one who, along with his wife, had shared the QP car with Ferdi and me for bingo that night and had the embarrassing event with the condoms in which he was completely innocent but unable to explain himself to his wife.

"Well, time had gone by. Sam had completed his assignment in Berlin and now was a lieutenant colonel. He had moved up. So, we warmly shook hands. To my amazement, he had a new job there at our headquarters. He volunteered for everything. From the CIA he went to Vietnam. There, one of our top generals, Westmoreland, took a liking to Sam. Sam became very well known in Vietnam. He became a hero. Sam became a one-star general. Sam then got his second star and became chief of the Eighty-second Airborne Division, the jumpers. He would jump; he would do anything. Eventually, Sam got his third star. So he came back to Washington and his new assignment was that of deputy director for the intelligence community to Bill Colby, who was by then director of the CIA.[2] Following that, Sam became director of the Defense Intelligence Agency, our top institution for all military intelligence and particularly for battlefield intelligence.

"One day I was sent to lecture at DIA. Sam saw me and said, 'George, my buddy, come here! Have some Irish coffee.' I replied, 'Oh no; I know you, Sam. Look, I have a four-hour lecture which I'll screw up with a capital *S* with your coffee.' Ah, but afterwards we got along fine, and that is Sam Wilson on the cover of that magazine right there on the table in front of you. This is his new retirement address in Virginia. I have been so lucky to know so many interesting people. Associations. Thanks to Sam, when I went to Bolling Field I was able to enter a brand-new DIA building there called Moscow Hall. It was so named because it was all red inside. It is a gorgeous building, an office building, hidden there and classified. You needed ten passes to even look at it, let alone walk in. I lectured there about four times. Courtesy of whoever was there, I walked under the wings of a MIG 25. I walked around a T-10 tank, like the one that I told you about, hidden in that classified barn. I saw it and artillery all over, some of it taken by the Israelis during that six-day war with the Egyptians. Not the MIG; it came by way of a defector in Japan. I understand nothing of these highly technical, super instruments. To walk around and look at them doesn't make me any smarter. Sam Wilson. That's what life is all about. Associations."

Even after his retirement, George helped the Agency from time to time with its operational activities. No one else could quite fill his shoes, and on occasion his unique talents were in critical need. Such was the case in the fall of 1972 when George was asked by the chief of operations to accept a special assignment in Kenya. It is a tale that I refer to as "African Queen." In this instance, his maturity and experience, more than his fluency in Russian, were needed. The target was the longtime ambassador of the Soviet Union to Kenya. The Agency believed that he might be a good candidate for recruitment and cooperation because of recent apparent overtures on his part. In addition, the ambassador had been treated cruelly by the Stalin regime, and Stalin's successors also had hurt the man, perhaps provoking him to turn on them.

The operation involved extensive covert preparations. George's cover was very elaborate. He went to Kenya with a false name, Pershing, and a passport to match. The Agency planners thought that his nom de guerre might make an impression on the ambassador, as Pershing has a Russian connotation. George played the role of a traveling American millionaire-author with a Russian background. Once there, he needed a good personal reference in Nairobi through whom he could make acquaintance with the ambassador. The party the Agency hoped would cooperate, albeit unwittingly, was the world-famous author Joy Adamson, who wrote *Born Free,* the book about the taming of Elsa, the lioness. She was known worldwide for her efforts in the preservation of animals. She was married to George Adamson, who was similarly disposed. George would not meet him, however, because he lived in a different part of Kenya pursuing the preservation of elephants.

In order to approach Mrs. Adamson, George needed an initial

reference, which he presumed to have: his good friend and classmate from Dartmouth, Nelson Rockefeller. The governor did not know this at the time, although George was certain that his classmate would have gone along with the ruse. Governor Rockefeller had supported animal-preservation activities for a long time and had communicated with Joy Adamson in that regard. When George first contacted her, she accepted his phone call as a friend of Nelson Rockefeller and agreed to meet with him.

George then took an elaborate suite at the Hilton Palace, overlooking Lake Naivasha, sixty miles northwest of Nairobi and not far from their intended meeting place. He approached Mrs. Adamson with books she had written and requested her autograph. He also purchased numerous boxes of "Elsa the Lioness" Christmas cards through her. To his surprise and great pleasure, he found out that she had been born in Vienna and had a Viennese maiden name. Since Ferdi had come from Austria, George could speak to Mrs. Adamson in German with a Viennese accent. This, of course, appealed to her immensely.

George knew Mrs. Adamson had an appointment to meet with the Soviet ambassador on the following day. She hoped to discuss with the ambassador the Russian royalties for her books sold in the USSR. George deliberately told her that he spoke fluent Russian. She immediately invited him to assist her the next day during the meeting with the ambassador. George expressed surprise at the invitation and consented. She, of course, had no idea that his approach of her had been orchestrated toward this end.

For the meeting on the following day, the ambassador brought with him a well-known pianist who, like the ambassador, had travel rights to the backcountry of Kenya. He and the ambassador were the only ones in the Soviet Embassy to have such a privilege—no other Soviets had that license. George promptly spoke in Russian to them in order to prevent them from speaking between themselves. He told them that he was an author by the name of Pershing and that he was of Russian descent. Everyone then had a very pleasant brunch. The ambassador explained to Mrs. Adamson that commercial arrangements for royalties were not the custom in the Soviet Union. He did propose, however, that revenues from the sale of her exceptional books on wildlife could be applied to the preservation of wildlife in the USSR. Animals such as the polar bear, the brown bear, the white wolf, and the gray wolf could thereby benefit. Moreover, she would get great publicity from such a covenant. This compromise suited her and the meeting wound up in a pleasant atmosphere. Before departing, George invited the ambassador to an intimate lunch with him later in the week. The ambassador accepted. They would meet in George's hotel suite.

During that meeting, as per standard operating procedure, the conversation with the ambassador was recorded. They spoke Russian. As they began to talk, however, and as the ambassador began to reveal himself to George, the spymaster immediately began to see problems. From his reading of the man, he could see that the ambassador's character and background portended danger for the Agency. Not only would the individual be unsuitable as an agent or a defector, but his desertion from the Soviet Union might cause a furor, if not a scandal, to the embarrassment of the United States. George concluded that his personal problems in the USSR as well as his extreme drinking habits would make him unsuitable for CIA use because the man would be too vulnerable to later coercion from his homeland. Such a likelihood made him totally inadequate for Agency purposes. Without sharing with me the details of his apprehensions about the individual, George simply stated that he foresaw the possibility that the Agency might lose much more than it could gain from proceeding with him. This was to the dismay and disappointment of the local intelligence officers, who had hoped a successful defection operation could occur on their watch, so to speak. George wasn't happy in this conclusion either, but he did not see an alternative. He left Africa shortly thereafter and reported his findings back to headquarters. The chief of operations agreed that George had recommended the proper course and broke off contact. "It is fine to make successful intelligence operations," George told me, "but you can lose tremendously if you misfire in these adventures." It had been an interesting trip. It was also a hectic one, however, one that frayed the spymaster's nerves somewhat, as he continuously pretended to be someone other than himself. I could not help but observe that George's association with his classmate, Nelson Rockefeller, certainly had facilitated a smooth operation and I began to appreciate the importance that George placed on associations.

CHAPTER 18

Cherepanov

As I climbed the steps to the back entrance of Vinson Hall I still had the Popov narrative on my mind. George had been vague about its resolution. Of course, most true spy stories terminate ambiguously, so I could not expect this one to be tied up neatly. Nevertheless, I believed that I should be able to get a better fix on how it ended. After all, this was the centerpiece of George's service to the Agency and he should know everything that the Agency did about the operation. In any event, I would expect that he knew more about this case than anyone else, so I resolved to ask George, once again, to explain to me just where that operation had gone wrong for us. I rang the bell.

"Come in," his familiar voice roared.

"How are you doing today?" I countered.

"I'm hoping for the end. I want it to come soon."

"Don't wish your life away. Are you eating anything?"

"I just don't feel like it."

"Is something wrong with the New York pie that Clara Sue made for you?"

"I just have not felt like eating anything."

"Well, now, you are going to hurt her feelings; she made it exactly according to your recipe. In the meantime, please try to drink this juice."

"Okay, but I cannot taste much now. . . . That's all I can drink."

"That's okay; we'll finish it later. Maybe we'll also eat something. What do you want to talk about today?"

"Whatever. It doesn't matter. I've lived long enough."

"No you haven't. We have to finish this. We have a long way to go. You have to keep on telling me stories. You're Scheherazade."

"Scheherazade?"

"The girl in the caliph's harem who told him a story every evening for 1,001 nights in order to save her ass."

"Oh yes, of course."

"Your Russian friend Rimski-Korsakov wrote some beautiful music about her affair with the caliph, and I want a thousand stories. You cannot die now."

"Oh, Nikolai Andreevich."

"Who?"

"Nikolai Andreevich Rimski-Korsakov was the guy."

"Okay, let's talk about Popov some more, George."

"Popov?"

"Yes, I want you to clear up a couple of things. When do you think that the KGB first could have suspected Popov and what, in particular, brought him down?"

"The first possibility? Hmm, a long, long time before we would have realized that he was under suspicion. There were some important events occurring later on that allowed us to look back and understand what they might have known had they been sharp enough, and what we believe that they actually knew. The first one happened in 1962 when Nosenko came to Geneva. He told us, for the first time, about the Soviet attempts against our Little Guy. He was called 'Ryzhiy' (Redhead) by the Soviets. Nosenko revealed to me how they conducted their game with 'Ryzhiy.' When I found this out I said, 'Jesus Christ! They could have known about the Popov operation through Little Guy. I guess Little Guy could have hurt us more than we had realized!' Remember? He was the fellow that they were trying to frame with the girlfriend in our embassy. They were using her as bait, keeping the hot pants on him and reporting on his every move. Had they been patient enough at the time, maybe they could have observed just who he was trying to contact."

I knew through conversations with George and I would later learn through Nosenko that surveillance people observe patterns in their quarry. If they had witnessed Little Guy going to a signal site and posting a signal, they would have kept constant surveillance on him, the site, and anyone interested in the site. If they had seen Popov going to the site, the KGB would have made a connection between him, the signal site, and Little Guy. Popov would have become a suspect commencing with his first approach to that site. Little Guy, of course, was supposed to communicate with Popov. The KGB did not realize it, but Popov was the man. Of course, had he been suspected, Popov never would have left Moscow to go on to Schwerin, and the CIA never would have been able to continue working with him. Obviously, the KGB did not make the connection.

George continued, "Nosenko also told me that Popov ultimately was compromised by surveillance of our personnel in Moscow. The KGB covered our embassy like a glove. Our people might as well have been in a glass bowl. Everywhere they went they were followed. Almost all of Langelle's contacts with Popov were routinely monitored. But there were opportunities that they had prior to that time that could have alerted them, and there was something later: a set of papers that came to our embassy in Moscow in late 1963. This gave us some more insight into what they could have known, and it also confirmed how they did succeed in unearthing the fact that Popov was our agent. Now, listen very closely. This is very, very important. There was a disgruntled KGB officer by the name of Cherepanov who had a violent internal disagreement in his professional relations with the people for whom he worked and he was fired."

I was to learn that Alexander Nikolaievich Cherepanov was an intelligence officer of the Second Chief Directorate of the KGB. The First Chief Directorate was intelligence; the Second Chief Directorate was counterintelligence; the Third was military counterintelligence; etc. Cherepanov worked for more than twenty years in intelligence. During the Second World War, he worked with partisan detachments. The Soviet Union had contacts with the Czechoslovakian, Yugoslavian, and Polish partisan detachments. Cherepanov was in liaison with them; thus, even when working with the partisan detachments, he was associated with intelligence. After the war he studied at the Military Diplomatic Academy and then went to work in the First Chief Directorate. His assignment in the 1950s was in Yugoslavia. There it appears the KGB counterintelligence people started suspecting him. Little things occurred that created suspicions—rumors that his wife had slept with an American, for instance. It had also been reported that he made an aborted attempt to contact the American Embassy in Yugoslavia. Evidently, however, no one in the KGB seemed sure of this.

In 1961 Cherepanov was recalled and offered a job in counterintelligence, serving in the First Department of the Second Chief Directorate, with responsibilities in the Consulate Department. The First Department was targeted against the U.S. Embassy. He soon became bored and ineffectual in this position, and the KGB decided to throw him out. Surveillance, the Seventh Directorate, wanted to take him and even offered to make him the chief of a section, but members of the First Department, Second Chief Directorate were opposed. Forced to retire in August of 1961 from the KGB, he found a job at Mezhkniga, the state-run enterprise that distributed books. Mezhkniga had an international bookstore that many foreign nationals frequented. Occasionally, Mezhkniga employees were sent overseas to buy books. Since he knew English quite well, the international bookstore wanted to send him overseas. The KGB said no. This made him very angry.

While previously in Yugoslavia, Cherepanov had saved some money, and when he returned to the Soviet Union he bought himself a small dacha, just outside of Moscow. When he had this falling out with his masters he took action on a plan that had been in his mind for some time. Within this retreat he kept several boxes in which he collected various documents describing numerous classified operations of the KGB. One of his KGB jobs had been that of a destruction officer of classified material. Routinely, he destroyed excess classified material, but he had kept some of it for himself. On some of the papers he had written analyses of KGB operations described in the documents. There was no record of these documents within the KGB. They were not registered and were not missed.

In the fall of 1963, a couple from the United States, simply tourists, were visiting the Soviet Union. The man, Prof. Laurence H. Miller of the University of Illinois, and his wife, both librarians, were taken on a tour of libraries. Their guide was Cherepanov. On the last day of their tour, 4 November, there in the Mezhkniga building, Cherepanov thrust upon Mrs. Miller a package and implored the two of them to take it to the American Embassy. His action was not witnessed by anyone. Professor Miller took Cherepanov's package to the embassy and presented it to the consul. The consul took it directly to the first secretary in charge of the political section of the embassy.

George interjected, "Now, as you know, there are jackasses in every profession in the United States, including jackasses in intelligence and jackasses in the Foreign Service of our country. In this particular instance, the jackasses in the Foreign Service took over."

When the Cherepanov papers came to the U.S. Embassy in Moscow, the ambassador at that time was Foy Kohler, but he was out of town. So the deputy chief of the mission, the chargé d'affaires, was in command. He and the first secretary of the political section deliberated overnight, trying to decide just what to do with these papers. The next day, they agreed to return the papers to the Soviets. Moreover, they determined that it should be done promptly. A telephone call went out from the American Embassy to the Soviet Consulate Department:

"I want a meeting with you," said the American.

But the Soviet said, "Hey, we're tied up now. It's too late. We're securing now. We'll be here tomorrow."

"No, no, now; we're coming now. It's very urgent," insisted the Foreign Service officer.

It was at that time that they called in Paul Garbler, the CIA chief, to advise him of what they were going to do. Paul, keenly aware that the American Embassy in Moscow stood like a beacon of hope for those who wanted to help rid the people of their tyrannical government, had made a special agreement with Ambassador Kohler. Essentially it went like this. Whether it be 4:00 A.M. or 9:00 P.M. or whatever time, regardless of what was going on, if anything like this came into the embassy, he, Paul, would be called within one hour and apprised of the situation. Sixty minutes. It was now twenty-four hours later that these two, in the absence of the ambassador, were notifying him. At that instant, the chargé was still clutching the package of papers to his chest. Paul asked, "Can I see that?"

Very reluctantly, the chargé let him see the package. It was about an inch thick and contained extracts from the boxes of material Cherepanov had in his dacha. At a glance Paul could tell that the material must have come from an intelligence officer. It appeared to him to have originated within the Second Chief Directorate of the KGB, the organization responsible for monitoring the activities of foreigners in Moscow and mounting operations against them. It had to have come from a KGB source.

The chargé said, "Well, we're turning it back."

Paul asked, "Why? We'd be giving them back something that is a jewel in the intelligence field. Why give it back to the Soviets? These papers are of significant value. This is what the hell intelligence is all about, looking for things like this."

"It doesn't make any difference," was the retort. "We're turning them back."

"You can't do that," continued Paul. "This is how the Penkovsky case got started. Furthermore, you're sacrificing this guy to the KGB. They'll kill him immediately. They'll find out within an hour who the source of these documents is."

"We are returning it," the chargé continued.

Paul said, "Give me an hour to go over them." He was allowed to take the papers. At the time, the Agency had one photographic duplication machine in the embassy. This was before the days of Xerox. Paul could not get a hold of the warrant officer who worked for the army attaché, one of the few people who could run the machine, so Paul photographed the whole thing manually. He put his copies into his safe and then took the original Cherepanov papers back to the chargé.

Within these papers was information with respect to operations of the KGB against the U.S. Embassy in Moscow. There were a lot of routine data such as the results of monthly surveillance against this or that target and plans to work on other targets. There was also information on the drinking and sexual habits of some of the U.S. Embassy personnel. Much of it was low-grade stuff, kept for possible blackmail purposes. Prominent among them, however, were descriptions of surveillance techniques.

From Nosenko and others, I would learn that the KGB had many means of aiding their surveillance. If, for instance, a known Agency person were housed in the embassy and he had a chambermaid, that maid would be KGB. It would be her duty, among other things, to impregnate the soles of his shoes with a substance that could be tracked. If that individual did not have a maid, then the surveillance people might enter the car that he drove and impregnate the pedals with the substance. The KGB called it Neptune 80. Male dogs readily would detect the odor of this substance because its main component was an extract taken from female dogs in heat. Thus, the target could be surveilled, then released. The target would think that he was no longer being tailed. He would not know that the dogs would shortly thereafter pick up his trail, or that he might be turned over to another team of surveillance agents with other dogs.

Another means employed against CIA personnel involved the

use of an invisible powder sprinkled onto the clothes of embassy residents by their KGB chambermaids. Even in minute quantities, electronic devices could sense it. If the maid sprinkled a little into a jacket pocket, then an object placed in that pocket would acquire a bit of the powder. If the object placed in that pocket were a letter that he intended to mail, then KGB in the post offices would detect the powder. All of the post offices in the Soviet Union had electronic devices that could detect even a microscopic amount of the chemical. Likewise, if an individual were to get the substance on his hands, then everyone with whom he shook hands would bear a trace of the chemical and thereby could be tracked. A TV-like camera—say, concealed in a briefcase—could also detect the chemical. The substance could be placed on the soles of the shoes; it then would leave spots wherever the subject wandered. Thus, once again, the surveillers could follow the target's paths at a distance, never "spooking" the subject. The KGB referred to this invisible powder as *metka.* CIA personnel called it simply "spy dust."[1]

The package also contained information on the Popov case. The material related directly to the discovery of Popov as an agent for the CIA, what the KGB knew about him, and when they knew these things. One document revealed how the KGB had tracked a U.S. Embassy employee to the letter drop where he had mailed a fateful letter to Popov. This confirmed what Nosenko had told George when they met in 1962. Moreover, the subject matter of these papers revealed that Cherepanov couldn't be anything other than a knowledgeable intelligence officer.

The papers were supposed to be taken at noon back to the foreign office, and it was now five minutes to twelve. Paul was in the chargé's office and had the papers in his hands. He said, "Look, you're making a terrible mistake; don't do this."

"Paul, you're beginning to annoy me," replied the chargé.

Paul's response was something to the effect of: "I'll annoy the hell out of you until the end of time if you give these papers back."

"All right," replied the chargé, "I'll call the first secretary and let you talk with him on the secure line."

Paul said, "I don't want to talk with him. I want to talk with you."

"Okay, let's all three go into the secure room and we'll talk," replied the chargé.

In the secure room, Paul raised the first objection to the return of the papers to the first secretary: "You know, you are killing this man."

The first secretary responded, "Well, you guys kill people every day. What's one more?"

Paul then said, "Shut up. Don't say another stupid word. I want to talk to the chargé."

In the hierarchy of the embassy, the first secretary is a very senior guy. He is next in seniority to the chargé. So, he was not supposed to be talked to like that, certainly not by CIA personnel. Eventually, the chargé said, "I'm going to give these papers to the Soviet foreign consul. Our man is going to take them over right now." He called in a courier. The courier came, took the papers, and left. By now it was about three minutes to twelve. Paul immediately pursued the courier. Not wanting to wait for the slow embassy elevator, he ran down nine flights of stairs to catch him. The courier was standing in the courtyard, waiting for the car that would take him over to the foreign consul, when Paul got to him. Paul snatched the papers away from him—right out of his hands—and went back up to the chargé's office. This trip, however, was on the elevator, the creaking old elevator. When he arrived in front of the chargé he said, "Look, over my dead body are you going to take these papers out of here. You can't do it."

The two State Department people then got together for the last time and they decided that there was no alternative to sending them back. They knew of an army attaché in Warsaw who, just a couple of weeks before, had accepted a package from an individual on the street. Some guy had run up to him and handed him a bunch of papers that contained information about missile sites, etc. The moment the attaché had them in his hand, the Polish intelligence people came up and grabbed him. He was then PNGd, disrupting the embassy. That is what the chargé and the first secretary were thinking of.

Paul knew that these papers from Cherepanov could not have been delivered as a provocation, however, since they came right into the embassy and their nature was far too sensitive to be such a ploy. The KGB would never find them because they could not reasonably come into the embassy and search for them. Also, these papers were totally different from those in the Polish incident. If they had been about rocket motor plans, missile sites, or whatever, that's one thing; but these papers were about intelligence operations. The CIA people knew about some of these matters, but they didn't think that the KGB knew that they knew about them. Now, the KGB would know that the CIA knew. Moreover, there were many things contained in the papers that Agency people had not previously known. The embassy had absolutely no responsibility to return them. Eventually, however, Paul reluctantly took the package back down to the courtyard where the courier was waiting to drive off with them. He looked at Paul as if he were some sort of lunatic.

Later, George told Paul that he strongly disagreed with what he had done. George's position on the Cherepanov papers was that Paul should have kept them and locked them up in his safe. Then, the State Department people could not have gotten to them. When he talked with Paul about the matter, Paul explained that if he had committed such an insubordination, the CIA in Moscow promptly would have been closed down. Paul certainly did not believe that it was the appropriate thing to do. After all, he was sent to Moscow as the CIA's first chief and part of his responsibility was to establish a functioning operation that was respected by the ambassador. The chargé actually was a fine gentleman, but the ambassador wasn't there and the chargé didn't want to screw up. The best way to prevent a screwup, he believed, was to give the papers back. In his mind that was the safest thing to do, although the ambassador never would have done this.

I asked George, "How did we know that the Cherepanov package was for real? Was he reliable?"

"He's dead. How much more reliable can you get? This was what got him killed. They had a national internal hunt for him because of our stupidity in returning the documents to the KGB. Not often does the KGB, because of dumbbells like these, receive intelligence leaks by returned mail from our embassy. We had a conflict in acumen in what to do: to return or not to return these things. Our embassy—that is, the chargé—decided to return the package."

When the courier delivered the package to the Soviet foreign consul, he made only one short comment: "Here, it's yours; take it!" Then he left. Not another word was spoken. When someone in their consulate department opened it, he put in a call to the minister of foreign affairs, Andrey Gromyko. Gromyko made a call to the KGB chairman, Vladimir Yefimovich Semichastny, and sarcastically impugned, "Listen, Semichastny, send somebody down to take your documents here, the ones that the Americans just brought in to us. Semichastny then contacted General Gribanov, the chief of counterintelligence of the KGB.

The KGB knew that it had a major screwup. For a short period this was really hush-hush within the KGB because of its embarrassing nature. Within a day or two, however, they knew who had been the perpetrator. Since Cherepanov only recently had left the KGB, since he had been disgruntled when he left, and since he probably was very angry about being turned down in his request to travel overseas, he was the prime suspect. They were afraid to put surveillance on him right away, however, because he had been an intelligence officer with enough experience to recognize such an action. He would be spooked. So they contacted some of his close friends, who they thought would have an easy time talking with him. This ploy backfired. Cherepanov immediately felt that he was suspected and he planned his escape.

Every morning, Cherepanov would go for a walk in his exercise suit. One morning he went out and disappeared. He never returned. The military secured all of the borders of the Soviet Union in order to prevent his escape. The borders into Finland, Poland, or any of the so-called democratic states were monitored, and of course those into Turkey, Iran, Afghanistan, and all over the southern regions were closed.

Why were they concerned? Cherepanov had been with partisan detachments during the war. He could survive in the woods, alone, for long periods of time. They knew that he would disappear if he were not quickly found. On the second day after not seeing him nor hearing from him, they involved the militia. All regular police militia received a photo of his face. These militia and the KGB all over the Soviet Union, particularly the border guards, started a massive search. They went to bus stations, train stations, and dining rooms around all travel stations with photographs of Cherepanov, asking people if they had seen that man. Whenever they would receive some clue from a particular location, they would send out an officer who had known Cherepanov personally, for further investigation. During this process they received many false alarms from all over the Soviet Union.

George went on, "Now, when Yuri Nosenko defected to us in 1964 he told me what had transpired with respect to Cherepanov. Nosenko was important to the hunt because he knew the target, Cherepanov, who had actually worked for him at one time. To people like Nosenko, who were chasing Cherepanov, they gave extra money, temporary promotions, and all kinds of other emoluments.

They provided easy means of transportation, thus promoting clandestine movement, internally, in the search for this target. They were searching for him because they knew that the material was very important to them. It involved Popov as well as the take that the CIA received from Popov. Of course, it was important. For one thing, they revealed information about their operations against the U.S. Embassy and how vulnerable it was. For another thing, they did indicate how Popov was caught."

In mid-December of 1963 the KGB finally caught Cherepanov in the Caucasus Mountains at a small railway station in a very remote area about one mile from the border with Turkey. He almost made it. George said, "This came about only because, like a damned fool, our chargé, for purposes of establishing goodwill with the KGB, had returned those papers to Gromyko. It was a blunder to return them because Cherepanov would have begun working for the CIA as had Popov as well as Penkovsky. Moreover, he would have been good. His experience in intelligence gathering and in counterintelligence would have been quite beneficial to us.

"So, when I heard this one about Cherepanov from Nosenko, I knew that I was getting the true time of day from Nosenko, and no bulls— was going to tell me otherwise. When Nosenko traveled with special passports, which he showed me from his inside pocket, allowing him almost unlimited internal traffic, and which gave him the right to grab this and that, I knew that he was on to something red hot. Moreover, I knew that he was for real, because how else in the world could he know so much about what the hell was going on? Well, that is how you find out what is true and what is not.

"He finally defected to us in 1964. He then just confirmed some things that we already knew about this. When the confirmation was consistent with known facts from the Cherepanov papers and other sources, then I knew that Nosenko was for real. I did, at once. You would too if you were a case officer. Some dumb-asses wouldn't know, but you would. The judgment of a jackass is not what moves the scales. When I say jackass, I say it for the reason that you don't return things blind like that without thoroughly investigating them. You know what I mean?"

"Did the papers indicate a relationship between Little Guy and Popov?"

"That was not a problem. They never saw a connection between Little Guy and Popov."

"Did the release of the information that Marshal Zhukov's speech had been leaked to the West, combined with the knowledge that Popov was in the group that first heard the speech, tend to finger him?"

"No."

"Did the incident about the lady who went over to New York and was encountered by the FBI finger him?"

"It definitely could have but I don't think that it did."

"Why not? After that, the KGB had an investigation about her being surveilled and put a tail on Popov."

"Yes, but they had nothing on him. Moreover, the KGB probably didn't believe all that the couple told them of their trip. The KGB, of course, later could look back and conclude that he could have been implicit in the Margarita Tairova incident, but at the time of its occurrence they couldn't have known much for sure. In fact, one note in the Cherepanov papers made reference to this event. It just confused matters to the FBI and our counterintelligence people. These papers confirmed to me, however, that the thing that finally nailed Popov was the act of somebody sending an internal letter to him, a letter from our own embassy."[2]

CHAPTER 19

The Ukrainian

As George finished his story about Cherepanov, his telephone rang, blasting the room with a noise that immediately destroyed the pensive atmosphere and all hope of concentration. He reached for the instrument. Usually, he would not allow interruptions to our sessions, telling the caller that he would return the call promptly when we were finished, so I stayed in place. This time he continued his telephone conversation in Russian. Since George knew that I had no proficiency whatsoever in the language, I did not feel the need to excuse myself.

"It's Nosenko," he said to me, and continued on the telephone.

George had mentioned this enigmatic individual to me before, but he had never told me the man's complete story. I suspect that it was too painful for him. Even now, I do not know the whole truth about their relationship or the episode. This I do know: the Nosenko saga, with the single exception of the Popov death, grated on George's mind more sharply than any other operational event in his experience. It truly bothered him.

Nosenko's story begins some six months before his appearance in Geneva, with the defection of yet another enigmatic Soviet. In December of 1961, Maj. Anatoliy Golitsyn, a staff officer for the KGB, specializing in counterintelligence matters and stationed in Helsinki, defected to the West. Golitsyn came preaching a most fundamental gospel: the West must be keenly aware of the Soviet penchant for disinformation in order for its civilization to have a chance of survival.[1] He also warned of "Sasha," a Communist spy securely ensconced somewhere within the upper echelons of the CIA hierarchy who already had brought great detriment to the Free World and who threatened much worse.

Golitsyn was very intelligent and seemed to be well informed of Soviet resources. Moreover, he purported an intimate knowledge of a number of KGB penetrations that had long troubled the CIA, and offered to expose them. He did, however, insist that his worth to the Agency as well as to the rest of the U.S. government warranted special treatment, even an audience with President Kennedy. His Agency managers refused him direct contact but did not stop him from writing a letter to the president. He expected it to be forthwith delivered, but the Agency was understandably reluctant for Golitsyn to have direct-mail correspondence with the president. They asked George to attempt to screen and divert Golitsyn's missive if it seemed provocative. In his book, *Molehunt,* David Wise gives George's version of the letter incident:

> "Golitsin was a loose cannon; nobody knew what he would say or do. It was embarrassing to have him write to the President. They sent me to accept the letter; I was authorized to promise to deliver it to the President . . . and if it was not innocuous, to stop it. . . . I was acting friendly," Kisevalter related. "'Let's speak Russian,' I said. 'Let me see your letter.' . . .
>
> "The letter said, 'In view of the fact that the President who has promised me things through his brother, Robert, may not be President in the future, how can I be sure the United States government will keep its promises to me for money and a pension?' . . .
>
> "I said, 'You S.O.B. You're a first-class blackmailer. This is *shantazh!* [the Russian word for blackmail].'"

Wise continues:

> Shaken by Kisevalter's reaction, Golitsin changed his mind and demanded the letter back.
>
> Oh, no, Kisevalter said. You want it delivered to the President, I'll deliver it. Kisevalter grinned as he recalled the moment. "Golitsin jumped up on top of the desk and then jumped down on my side and we began wrestling for the letter. I let him win."[2]

Soon after his arrival, Golitsyn was taken under the wing of the Agency's chief of counterintelligence, James Jesus Angleton, who reported directly to the director of the CIA. Golitsyn and Angleton became close associates, being of the same mind on many things and each providing the other distinct advantages. Golitsyn gave to the CI chief the benefit of his extensive knowledge of recent Soviet intelligence matters. Angleton made Golitsyn aware of numerous U.S. programs, targets, and intelligence resources. He also sent him to England and took him to France, Norway, Holland, Canada, and Australia, where, with Angleton's introductions and endorsements, Golitsyn received the red-carpet treatment from their intelligence services.[3] Soon the Soviet defector knew more about the West's intelligence capability than almost anyone employed by any of its intelligence services.

No matter, concluded Angleton. Golitsyn was now here to help the West. The Western intelligence services had to be observant of all new defections, however, because, as Golitsyn warned, there would be false defectors who would come to discredit him. Thus the stage was set for Nosenko, who, due to the miscalculations of a number of individuals who were misled by Golitsyn and encouraged by Angleton, proved to be the most perplexing, although ultimately one of the most valuable, defectors in the history of the CIA.

In June of 1962, Yuri Ivanovich Nosenko, a handsome, thirty-four-year-old, powerfully built man, appeared in Geneva, Switzerland. He was a member of the Soviet delegation at the seventeen-nation disarmament conference. The conference ultimately would lead to the Strategic Arms Limitations Treaty, which would produce several comprehensive international agreements, including the ABM (Antiballistic Missile) Treaty. Nosenko was the delegation's security officer, a watchdog employed to keep tabs on the other members of his group, always alert for a potential defection.

Yuri Nosenko was born on 30 October 1927 in Nikolaiev, Ukrainian SSR. His father, Ivan Nosenko, was an alternate member of the Central Committee of the Communist Party and had served as the Soviet minister of shipbuilding in the 1940s and 1950s. When he died in 1956, the most important leaders of the USSR, including Nikita Khrushchev, Georgi Malenkov, Nikolai Bulganin, and Klimentiy Voroshilov, formed the guard of honor at his funeral bier. He was buried in the Kremlin wall.[4]

Yuri served in the GRU, working in naval intelligence from 1950 until 1953, at which time he joined the KGB and was assigned to the Second Chief Directorate. The First Chief Directorate had the principal responsibility for KGB espionage and counterintelligence outside the USSR; the Second Chief Directorate was mostly concerned with counterintelligence within the USSR. During his first two years in that job he worked in the American Department and monitored the activities of American correspondents and military attachés in Moscow. In 1955 he transferred to the Department for Tourists, which specialized in compromising and recruiting some of these Moscow visitors. In June of 1958 he was appointed deputy chief of the American and British Section of that department, a job he held until January of 1960. He volunteered that in 1956 and again in 1959 he had been given a special commendation for his work in bringing about compromising situations of various American and British visitors in Moscow, thus allowing the KGB to take advantage of these individuals. In January of 1960, he was transferred back to the American Department, and then in January of 1962 he returned to the Tourist Department, where he was named deputy chief of the department, in charge of operations against foreign tourists. Since February of 1962, he had been temporarily attached to the Soviet Disarmament Delegation in Geneva as the chief security officer.[5]

A few days after his arrival in Geneva, Nosenko approached an American diplomat and asked for a private talk with CIA personnel. The diplomat notified the CIA office in Bern. From there, a CIA intelligence officer was immediately dispatched to conduct a preliminary investigation into the bona fides and potential worth of the prospective agent. This person eventually would become the principal case officer in one of the most vexing episodes in the chronicles of the CIA. Initially, however, there was difficulty in communication, because the CIA officer's poor Russian and Nosenko's poor English prevented an effective connection. At this point, George was rushed over from headquarters to Geneva in order to serve as an interpreter and additional case officer.

George's informal manner, unkempt appearance, lack of pomposity, as well as beautiful command of the Russian language put him in direct contrast with the straight-laced, company-man, former marine who had initially tried to debrief the sometimes hesitant Nosenko. George made a big impression on the Soviet even before he began to question him. From George's face, speech, and everything else about him, Nosenko knew that he was in the presence of someone of Russian heritage. Nosenko also quickly recognized that George was both an able professional and a compassionate human being. From the start, they liked each other.

Nosenko volunteered that he was a major in the KGB, currently a staff officer assigned to the Second Chief Directorate. He was, herewith, available for the CIA's use, offering to sell valuable information for 900 Swiss francs. He declared that he needed the money to replace KGB funds he had squandered on a drinking spree.[6] He added that his daughter, Oksana, had a serious asthmatic condition. He had learned that a special new drug could help her but the USSR could not provide the medication. He wanted assistance in obtaining the potential remedy. The drug was not legally available in the United States, but George found it in Holland. He then had the medication flown in to Geneva.

Nosenko met with his American contacts a number of times in a Geneva safehouse. For these liaisons he chose to employ a rather quaint means of countersurveillance. In order to ensure that he was not being tailed to the meetings, he routinely visited a number of bars on the way, having a drink in each. This usually meant the consumption of a scotch and soda in each of four or five stops. At the safehouse, he continued to imbibe, as he was offered drinks throughout the interviews that George conducted. This excessive drinking would later become an issue in the debate regarding Nosenko's veracity and reliability.

Nosenko promptly disclosed to George the valuable information that William John Vassall—formerly employed as a clerk in the British Admiralty—was an agent of the KGB. He reported that Vassall had provided the Soviets with extensive amounts of embassy documents and pages of microfilmed naval intelligence information from March 1954 until July 1956, when Vassall had served in Moscow in the office of the naval attaché. While in Moscow, Vassall had been caught and photographed by the KGB in a homosexual act. This compromise had led to his becoming a cooperative for the KGB. Moreover, maintained Nosenko, Vassall still was a KGB agent. Golitsyn previously had given information that led in the direction of Vassall, but Nosenko now was pinpointing him. This, in effect, was a bona fide for Nosenko.[7]

Nosenko then said to George, "Oh by the way, I am here also to manage the running of Boris Belitsky against you, the guy that your people believe to be running as your agent. He actually is a double agent under KGB control." Boris was a prominent correspondent for Radio Moscow. He had attended the World's Fair in Brussels in the summer of 1958, where he was recruited by George Goldberg, who began to run him as an agent for the CIA. Goldberg met with him a number of times covertly in various European cities over the next three years. Considering that this could become a very important contact, Goldberg requested assistance in the form of a backup to himself. Harry Young then was assigned the task of serving as an additional case officer for the operation.

Following the fair at Brussels, Agency personnel did not overtly meet with Belitsky until he appeared to them in London during April of 1961. In London, he was serving as the interpreter for the cosmonaut Yuri Gagarin. Goldberg and Paul Belkin, a CIA polygraph operator, met with him in order to administer a polygraph examination, hoping to obtain an objective assessment of Belitsky's authenticity. From the results of the test, both Belkin and Goldberg were convinced that Belitsky was clean. Coincidentally, George also had been in London at this time for his initial meeting with Penkovsky. He was aware of Goldberg and Belkin's activity there with Belitsky, but he was not in any way involved with the Belitsky operation.

Now, in Geneva, Belitsky was again coming out, and, concurrently, Nosenko was telling the CIA the truth about Belitsky for the first time. Nosenko even used the names of the CIA case officers, Goldberg and Young. This revelation stunned George because Belitsky had passed the CIA lie-detector test in the London safehouse with flying colors. The polygraph operator, Belkin, had said that Belitsky was okay, that he was solidly pro-American—so much so that "he could sing the Star Spangled Banner through his a—hole."[8] Young, Goldberg, and George - as well as others at the CIA - thought that they had a good agent, but as it turns out the KGB was duping the CIA. Goldberg and Young were there in Geneva pressing Belitsky for information while he was reporting back to his manager, Nosenko, just what they were about. Nosenko was in turn reporting to George what Belitsky had said. There is a Russian expression for such a circumstance—a *kto kovo*, meaning, roughly, *who's waltzing with whom?*[9]

Upon reporting this revelation to headquarters, George was advised, "Don't tell Goldberg; don't tell Young. We don't want Belitsky to know that we are on to him, and they'll never be able to keep a straight face when talking to him if they know that he is 'dirty.'" For the rest of the Geneva trip, George avoided seeing Goldberg and Young. The unwitting Agency secretary advised Goldberg that George was in town and told George that his friends

Goldberg and Young were in town. George just disappeared, however, and they never understood why until told later.[10]

The revelation about Belitsky provided more bona fides for Nosenko. When queried about "Sasha," however, Nosenko drew a blank. He did not profess any knowledge of a mole planted in the CIA.

Of critical personal importance to George, Nosenko said that the Popov case had been blown by routine surveillance of embassy personnel in Moscow. As he put it, "An American diplomat had been 'tracked' in the process of mailing the fateful letter to Popov. The diplomat had ventured down a small and remote street for posting the letter. At a long distance away, but within view of him, a member of the surveillance team, a woman, saw him raise his hand to deposit the letter in a mailbox. The mailbox was emptied, and the letter, bearing an invisible powder that was sensitive to certain electronic devices, was identified and presented. Retrieval of the note and decoding of its message then led ultimately to the arrest of Popov."

The original case officer cabled back enthusiasm about the information as well as the exciting prospect of a continued dialogue with Nosenko. The Soviet warned them not to try to make any contact with him in Moscow, as he knew of the overwhelming surveillance performed by the KGB there, especially since the Popov affair. All contact would have to be restricted to the times he could come out from the Soviet Union.[11]

In order to arrange a contact procedure for such a time, George called the Office of Security at headquarters, obtained a number of high-security, secret mailing addresses in New York City, and selected one for Nosenko. When he came out of the Soviet Union again, Nosenko then would be able to contact George and the other case officer through this address by cable or mail. Nosenko would use the name "Alex." It was agreed that three days after the date of the cable or letter, Nosenko would stand at 7:00 P.M. underneath the marquee of the movie house whose name was listed alphabetically first in the phonebook of the city from whence the cable or letter had originated. (In the case of a letter as opposed to a cable, "Alex" would date the letter a few days later than the actual date in order to compensate for the longer transit time. The meeting, then, would take place three days after the date indicated in the letter, without regard to its postmark.) Nosenko stayed in Geneva until the fifteenth of June and then returned to the Soviet Union.

After Nosenko's departure for Moscow, George and his fellow case officer returned to Washington from Geneva on separate airplanes, one carrying the tapes recorded during their meetings and the other bearing the handwritten notes, a precaution against losing everything if they were together in a fatal plane crash.[12] Both were delighted that they were working with a high-level KGB officer who was able and willing to divulge significant amounts of valuable information. Moreover, the KGB man would be staying "in place," which made him that much more valuable. When he got home, George tested from time to time the communication channels that he had set up for Nosenko. He contacted the chiefs of stations in selected European cities, asking that both cables and letters be sent to the Manhattan address. This enabled him to predict the transit times for Nosenko's anticipated correspondence from different locations.

On 20 January 1964, Nosenko again arrived in Geneva as part of the Soviet Disarmament Delegation. Leading that delegation was Semyon K. Tsarapkin, who later would come under some scrutiny for what was to occur. The conferences were to be held at the Palais des Nations in downtown Geneva, commencing the next day. Nosenko stayed in the nearby Rex Hotel. Shortly after arriving, he sent a coded letter to one of the New York City addresses. Within hours of its receipt George and the other case officer were winging toward Geneva on separate airplanes.

By this time George had been promoted to a special position in which he received all of his assignments from the director of clandestine services. He nevertheless would continue for awhile as an interpreter and case officer in the Nosenko matter. Likewise, the other case officer had enjoyed two significant promotions within the CIA. First, he had been elevated to the position of counterintelligence branch chief within the Soviet Bloc Division. In this capacity, he had extensive contact with James Angleton, the Agency counterintelligence chief, who advised him that he and Golitsyn both believed Nosenko to be a KGB plant. After having been the CI branch chief of the Soviet Bloc Division only for a short period of time, the case officer then was promoted to deputy chief of the division. Nevertheless, he still was acting as one of Nosenko's two case officers.

The original case officer met Nosenko under the marquee of the designated movie theater in Geneva at 7:00 P.M. three days after the date of the letter. In a brush contact, he gave Nosenko a note specifying the address of the new safehouse located in the suburbs of Geneva. The case officer, Nosenko, and George met together that evening and on five additional occasions during this episode.

Most importantly, Nosenko now wanted to defect, a complete reversal from his desires of eighteen months ago. "Why?" asked George. "Because the KGB suspects me, my marriage is not so good, and I want to make a new life," replied the defector.[13]

"And your daughter?"

"She is much better now. The medicine saved her life. She will be well."

Nosenko talked about Cherepanov, stating that operations described in the Cherepanov papers were known to him, and that he had participated in the nationwide manhunt for the renegade during the previous October. He produced his own travel papers relating to the exercise, including an identification document exhibiting his rank of lieutenant colonel in the KGB. Since the Cherepanov papers dealt mainly with surveillance techniques, they confirmed Nosenko's previous revelations about the KGB procedures. Moreover, the papers' description of the Popov detection dovetailed with Nosenko's earlier story that Popov had first been detected by surveillance.

Nosenko told of the American Embassy being bugged, describing an array of dozens of microphones. Later he pinpointed for the State Department several dozens of locations where these microphones had been built into the walls of the U.S. Embassy in Moscow when it was constructed in 1952. This meant that the Soviets had covertly listened to private embassy conversations for twelve years. Golitsyn previously had mentioned that some microphones were there, but he had not suspected so many nor known of their locations. When embassy personnel eventually opened the walls to remove the microphones, they found many more.[14]

Nosenko gave his own account of how Oleg Penkovsky had been detected, arrested, and forced to participate in the compromise of members of the British and American team who had worked with him. Nosenko mentioned the KGB discovery of the dead drop that the CIA had readied for Penkovsky. The KGB had seen an American Embassy person going there, so they set up shop in the adjoining building. They bored a peephole through the wall of the apartment foyer where the dead drop was located and posted a man there twenty-four hours a day for the next six months.[15]

Nosenko also revealed that the KGB had been in control of an important American source in Paris who had transmitted American NATO military secrets to the Soviet Union. This led to the arrest of Robert Lee Johnson and his friend, James Allen Mintkenbaugh, two sergeants who had served together in the U.S. Army. Johnson had been a sentinel at the heavily guarded military courier station at Orly Field near Paris. The Orly vault contained highly classified material sent to and from the Pentagon as well as various American and NATO commands in Europe. Seven times, from December 1962 until April 1963, Johnson, with Soviet-provided technical aid, defeated three sets of locks, entered the vault, removed the documents, delivered them to the Soviets for predawn, lightning-fast photographic sessions, and then replaced them in the vault.[16]

Finally, Nosenko dropped the intelligence bombshell that reverberated throughout the CIA and other parts of the U.S. government for at least a decade. He declared that he had supervised the KGB file on Lee Harvey Oswald in 1959. At this point in time, January of 1964, only two months after the devastating assassination of President Kennedy and the spectacular murder of Oswald himself, rumors were raging like a virus throughout the North American continent. Some people believed that the U.S. government, including the CIA and the FBI, had been complicit, if not solely guilty, in the killings. Others were convinced that organized crime, right-wing groups, left-wing groups, Cubans, or other foreigners had been involved. Many also considered the FBI to have been criminally derelict in not forewarning Dallas police and the Secret Service of Oswald's background and menace. In an attempt to put an end to such speculation, and to restore faith in the competence of our government, President Johnson convened the Warren Commission to investigate all aspects of the assassination and the murder of Oswald.

Lee Harvey Oswald joined the United States Marines in October 1956 and served at Atsugi Air Force Base, Japan, as a radar technician from October 1957 until November 1958. He was discharged in September of 1959 and defected to the Soviet Union in October, only a month after his release from the marines. He lived in Minsk for two and a half years. While there, on the 30 April 1961, he married Marina Nikolaievna Prusakova, a hospital worker. Her consent to marry him hinged, at least partially, on his promise that he would never return to the United States. In June of 1962 he returned to the

United States, bringing with him his new Soviet bride and their infant child, June Lee Oswald, so named in accordance with the old Russian, then Soviet, law regarding the patronymic.[17]

While back in the United States, Oswald exhibited many attributes of a misfit. Among them was his propensity to campaign for fringe groups such as "Fair Play for Cuba." The FBI was aware of some of his activities but did not consider him dangerous enough to charge him specifically with any misdemeanor or felony. It was later revealed that he had fired his rifle into the home of Gen. Edwin Walker on 10 April 1963. The bullet narrowly missed Walker's head. In September of 1963, Oswald, wishing to return to the Soviet Union, applied to the Cuban Embassy in Mexico City for a visa to go to Cuba, offering his services to "the Cuban revolution" while in transit to the USSR. Cuba would not allow its embassy in Mexico to grant him the visa to Cuba until he first obtained an entrance visa to the Soviet Union. The USSR denied the same. Probably sensing that he was being bumped around, he returned to the United States in October. One month later he shot the president in Dallas.[18]

Nosenko assured his masters, George and the companion case officer, that he had supervised the Lee Harvey Oswald case when the ex-marine had arrived in Moscow in 1959. Additionally, he stated that he, along with a few other officers of the Second Chief Directorate, had decided that Oswald must return to the United States when his visa expired. Oswald subsequently attempted suicide. The decision that Oswald must leave the USSR then was overridden by powers above the KGB. The reason given was the fear of adverse publicity if he were successful at suicide. Such publicity would be worse than any that was likely to arise from his living in the Soviet Union.

After Oswald attempted suicide, two different panels of psychiatrists examined him at KGB behest and each independently concluded that, though quite abnormal and unstable, he was not insane. Nosenko maintained that KGB headquarters had ordered Oswald routinely watched by Byelorussian Republic KGB units of Minsk but not recruited, or in any way utilized. When Oswald returned to the United States in 1962 they were glad. Further, Nosenko insisted that in September of 1963, when Oswald applied in Mexico City for a visa to return to Moscow, the KGB blocked his return. Continuing, Nosenko averred that the KGB didn't want to have any more to do with the Oswalds. He was unstable and "Marina was stupid, uneducated, and anti-Soviet," he reported. "The KGB was glad to see them go when they left for the United States."[19]

Nosenko emphatically volunteered that no one in the Soviet Union had anything to do with the assassination. George and his fellow case officer were curious as to how the man could give total assurance to such a declaration. The informer answered that he and certain other officers were in charge of investigating the question of KGB involvement in the assassination. He maintained that the whole Soviet Union was shocked with the news of the assassination and very much aware of American public opinion. Further, he stated that the KGB was fearful that some maverick officer in the field might have utilized Oswald for some unauthorized purpose, without the awareness of the chain of command. He indicated that anxiety was so great within the KGB that they immediately ordered Oswald's file flown in a military plane from Minsk, where Oswald had lived, to KGB headquarters in Moscow. Nosenko insisted that he was there, along with the others, scrutinizing the document with trepidation as each page was turned, fearing that some relationship might have existed between Oswald and some overly ambitious member of the KGB. If so, the consequence could be devastating to both the Soviet Union and the United States. In addition, he stated that General Gribanov, the chief of the Second Chief Directorate, had sent a squad of investigators to Minsk to question officials on the spot. To emphasize his willingness to cooperate, Nosenko offered to testify to the Warren Commission.[20] The information provided by Nosenko was immediately forwarded to Langley. It later caused great concern and controversy at the CIA among those preparing to assist the Warren Commission.

The provocative agent continued to work for several days with his American handlers and then repeated his previous revelation to them: "I am not going back to the USSR." They, on the other hand, wanted to keep him in place and work with him when he returned to Moscow. He said, "No, I am afraid of counterintelligence. You might have one meeting with me—maybe two—then the KGB surely will catch me, especially after the case of Lt. Col. Pyotr Popov, because they now are very well trained."

It was the end of January and it did not appear to Nosenko that the handlers would accept his defection. He had told them at the first meeting that he was not going back to the USSR, yet still they were not moving. He was afraid that he would be recalled home.

Before he had left the USSR for this trip, his group, the Department for Tourists in the Second Chief Directorate, had been planning a conference of all KGB tourist representatives from all of the Soviet republics where tourists normally visited. He was part of a task force preparing for this conference and he had been told just as he was leaving for Geneva that before the disarmament talks were over he might be recalled. He also knew that the chief of the Second Chief Directorate, General Gribanov, would be coming to Geneva under cover as a diplomat. If Gribanov were to see Nosenko there, he might ask, "What in the world are you doing here?" He then could command Nosenko back home, embarrassing the man. After all, Nosenko was not essential to the group; he had gotten the temporary assignment in the hope that a chance to defect might arise.

Moreover, when Nosenko had come to Geneva in 1962, the KGB deputy *rezident* there was a close friend. Now in his place was another *rezident* whom Nosenko considered very "tough." Nosenko was not drinking during this 1964 trip, but he was repeatedly meeting with his handlers. He was concerned that the new *rezident* would suspect him. Still, the Agency was not moving on his defection.[21]

CHAPTER 20

Sasha

On the morning of 3 February 1964, Yuri Nosenko left his hotel and, leaving his suitcase in the room and taking almost nothing, ventured to the safehouse. There he declared to George and the other case officer, "Gentlemen, I don't know about you, but I just defected now; this day, this hour, this minute, I just defected." The original case officer replied, "No, we are not ready." Nosenko said, "I cannot go back. A cable from the KGB just arrived ordering me back to Moscow. I suspect that it is in connection with the conference that we have been planning for this spring."[1]

That very day, the Warren Commission took testimony from its first witness, Marina Oswald. Other than Nosenko, she was the only person outside of the USSR who could shed any light on the relations that her husband might have had with authorities in the USSR. Nosenko stated to the case officers that he had just been ordered to catch a plane back to the Soviet Union by the next day.[2] Perhaps the call was routine. Perhaps his liaison with the CIA had been detected. He told George that he had no choice: "It is now or never." Nosenko's managers had tried their best to convince him to stay in place. It is almost always desired that an agent do this. Previously, they had believed they could take his testimony about Oswald to the FBI and the Warren Commission without his being present. Now, however, it was clear that the United States had to accept his defection. There was no choice; the Kennedy assassination demanded that it be done.

At this point in time, Richard Helms was the deputy director for plans at the CIA. It was his job to manage the entire clandestine services department of the Agency. He was particularly troubled with the decision regarding the acceptance of Nosenko as a defector. He believed that the potential benefits to the Agency if the man were bona fide had to be fairly weighed against the negative aspects if he were not. If Nosenko's story were true, he might help clear up some uncertainties for the Warren Commission. If Nosenko were sent by the KGB as a plant to ensure that the United States did not suspect an innocent KGB of complicity in the assassination, this could be dealt with, probably with little effort. If Nosenko were just puffing, trying to enhance his own worth as a defector by lying about his knowledge of Oswald, his story definitely would confuse matters, but they also could deal with this situation. Most alarmingly, if the KGB had sent Nosenko because the KGB or someone within that organization was complicit in the assassination, the consequences of such a revelation could be considerably worse than the assassination itself. In any event, it would be better to have the man in custody and attempt to determine the truth from him.

Nosenko was suspected by some, including George's companion case officer, of being a plant, but his testimony could be of paramount importance to the Warren Commission. The CIA couldn't possibly turn Nosenko down, but at the same time they distrusted him and misled him. The original case officer made an employment and monetary proposal to Nosenko and convinced him that he would be formally accepted and treated well. Nosenko agreed and urged the case officer to act quickly. John McCone, the director of Central Intelligence, immediately authorized the acceptance of Nosenko. The director was empowered by Congress to admit, on his own authority but with Justice Department coordination, a limited number of defectors to the United States. On 4 February, Nosenko was given documents identifying him as an American and driven from Switzerland to a safehouse on the outskirts of Frankfurt. Three days later, the CIA's chief of the Soviet Bloc Division met him in Frankfurt. He repeated the promises of money and employment made by the original case officer, but he also believed that Nosenko was lying. After a week of debriefing in Frankfurt, the two of them flew to Andrews AFB, outside of Washington, D.C., arriving on 12 February. Immediately, the chief drafted a memo to the effect that, in his opinion, Nosenko was under KGB direction.[3]

In Moscow the defection of Nosenko was treated as a first-class calamity. He was sentenced in absentia to the "highest measure of punishment."

After Nosenko arrived in the United States, the CIA kept him in isolation, housed in a secret location, with guards, under lock and key. For two months the FBI interviewed him. The FBI had precedence over the CIA in dealing with him because of their investigation into the matters of the Warren Commission. The FBI interrogators were convinced that he was reliable and that he could not connect the Kremlin with the assassination of the president. Unknown to most members of the CIA, the FBI had been using a defector, code-named Fedora, who backed two important claims of Nosenko: his rank of lieutenant colonel and the dispatch of the recall telegram to him while he was in Geneva. The FBI then turned Nosenko back over to the CIA with a clean bill of health. Of course, it was in the interest of the FBI to have Nosenko declared as genuine, thereby attesting that Oswald was not involved with the KGB. Otherwise, the FBI could be blamed for not having been more diligent in their previous investigations of Oswald.

The CIA debriefing of Nosenko, on the other hand, did not go well. The interrogators already were convinced that Nosenko knew more than he had revealed about Oswald, the Kremlin, and the assassination. Moreover, his responses to questions appeared evasive and inconsistent. The combination of their predisposed notions and his apparent lack of cooperation confirmed their suspicions that he was planted by the Soviets to confuse the investigation into the assassination. The more they questioned him, the worse things became. Finally, he asked, "Where is George? I want to see George." George and Nosenko liked each other very much. George was invited over. They had dinner, just the two of them. Recognizing that George did not share their conviction that Nosenko was a plant, Nosenko's antagonists quickly had George removed from the case. After that, Nosenko did not see George for four years.

Nosenko's always-latent fear that the CIA would break its promises to him seemed to be realized. He turned to drink, heavy drink.[4] The interrogators then conceived a new strategy. Perhaps the new defector should have a vacation. Maybe, if he were able to warm up in some southern clime, he might loosen up and be more cooperative. Accordingly, Nosenko was escorted to Hawaii and there provided with luxurious accommodations and amenities. This gambit, however, did not seem to prompt any change in his attitude.

Golitsyn meanwhile voiced more doubts about the genuineness of Nosenko, speculating that the man had come to disparage his own authenticity and that Nosenko, like Cherepanov, was a provocation. The chief of counterintelligence for the Agency, the chief of the Soviet Bloc Division, and the original case officer (now the sole case officer) were all convinced that Nosenko was a KGB plant. Peter Deriabin, the KGB officer who had defected when George was in Vienna on the Popov case, then came to debrief Nosenko. It was not a profitable experience for either former Soviet. Neither trusted the other. The interrogators and their superiors at the CIA continued to be uneasy about Nosenko's answers to many questions. This rendered him unreliable, in their view, to provide information on the association of Lee Harvey Oswald with the KGB.

In an attempt to accelerate the interrogation, on 4 April Nosenko was given the first of three lie-detector tests. It was a charade. They accused him of lying during the test. They tried to intimidate him into admitting the KGB sent him. He then was placed in an attic room in the suburbs of Washington, D.C. The only furniture in the room was a metal bed attached to the center of the floor. A single light bulb burned overhead. He was deprived of sleep, reading materials, adequate food, tobacco, toothpaste, or any other personal amenities. The interrogators forbade him any contact with people other than themselves and constantly badgered him in a hostile manner. He was accorded no fresh air in the hot attic room that summer.[5]

The Warren Commission was pressing to complete its report. Helms met with Chief Justice Warren and told him that the investigation into the Nosenko matter was incomplete and that he could not vouch for the former Soviet's truthfulness. In fact, the CIA did not know whether Nosenko was a legitimate defector or a KGB plant. Their resolution of the quandary was simply to continue trying to break Nosenko into confessing what they believed to be the truth about Oswald. The commission released its final report on 27 September 1964 but did not use information about or even mention Nosenko.[6]

Nosenko had insisted that Oswald had drawn no KGB interest, a contention sufficient to elicit great suspicion from some within the CIA. His statement that the KGB had not even bothered to debrief Oswald upon his entry into the USSR, notwithstanding that Oswald was an ex-marine previously stationed at a U-2 base in Japan and trained in electronics, defied belief for some. After all, U-2 flights had been deployed from Atsugi AFB in Japan more than once during Oswald's service at the base.[7] He must have been at least somewhat aware of the U-2 and its extraordinary program. Soldiers there would have had some opportunity to witness the takeoffs and landings of the incredible aircraft, they speculated. As a radar operator, he surely would have had some awareness of the U-2's radar characteristics.

More generally, Nosenko's assertion about the lack of KGB interest in Oswald was contrary to the historic nature of the KGB as understood by the CIA. The interrogators reasoned, "Why were we so 'lucky' to be in secret contact with one of only a very few members of the KGB who were familiar with Oswald's coming and going? Why did he deny any KGB involvement at all with the assassin? Surely at least some had taken place. Why was Nosenko going to such lengths to convey the impression of no KGB involvement with Oswald? The man must have been dispatched to throw the CIA off the path of Oswald."[8] Nosenko, however, continued to state that he hated the KGB but he could not implicate them in the assassination, for it would be untrue. He maintained that he had been asked to examine Oswald's file and assess the KGB liability in the president's death, that he was familiar with Oswald's attempt in Mexico City to reenter the USSR, and that Oswald was prevented from doing so because there was no interest in him whatsoever by the KGB.

Things then got much worse for the defector. In early 1965, an even more hostile interrogation of Nosenko was conceived by his tormentors and approved by their superiors. The chief of the Soviet Bloc Division, who had met Nosenko in Frankfurt; the director of clandestine services, Richard Helms; and the assistant attorney general, Nicholas Katzenbach, all agreed to the blueprint. Attorney General Robert Kennedy approved the plan.[9] Nosenko's legal status had been that of "on parole" from the Immigration Service. He thus did not have the legal protection of an American citizen. From what followed, however, it could be said that the Justice Department and the CIA denied the man his basic human rights.

The CIA received the final go-ahead from the Justice Department for an incarceration "down on the farm," the CIA training facility that included 10,000 acres of heavily wooded, completely fenced, tidal lands stretching along the York River near Williamsburg, Virginia. Much of it was wilderness. During the Second World War, the camp had been used as a POW detention center for German soldiers. In August of 1965 Nosenko was taken there and put into a newly constructed twelve-foot-by-twelve-foot, windowless, concrete cell. It was outfitted with heavy padding on the walls to prevent him from injuring himself. This vaultlike room was fabricated within a "special-purpose" building, surrounded by double fences and set deep in the woods. There was no terrestrial visibility beyond the second fence. It was his home for more than two years. He was not allowed to exercise at all for almost two years after his arrival, and then finally for no more than thirty minutes a day. He was not allowed any reading material or any "recreational device." When he manufactured the pieces of a chess set from loose cotton strings of his overalls, they were confiscated.[10] He was minimally fed and lost weight. The jailers were instructed not to molest him but not to be friendly with him. They were further instructed to disorient him by varying the clocks, the lighting, and his permitted sleeping hours.

The CIA does not acknowledge administering drugs other than for medicinal purposes. To this date, however, Nosenko continues to insist that he was given hallucinogenic drugs on many occasions, "probably LSD." He believes that on one occasion he almost died from an overdose of some drug. "The guards had to come into my cell and place me in the shower. They then dispensed, alternately, the hot and cold water streams."[11]

Nosenko's main antagonist was the original case officer he had met in Geneva, now the deputy chief of the Soviet Bloc Division. The focus of his interrogation was still the question of Oswald's relation to the KGB, but there were manifold other avenues of query used, with varying degrees of success, in attempts to break down Nosenko and have him admit the "truth" about everything. He interpreted minor discrepancies in Nosenko's story as indications of cunning duplicity, and forced Nosenko to admit that many of his lesser claims were false. Nosenko had said that he was a major in 1962 and a lieutenant colonel in 1964. Then he admitted that he was only a captain.

Nosenko had professed that a cable came to him in Geneva recalling him to Moscow, but the National Security Agency provided cable-traffic analyses demonstrating that Nosenko could not have received such a cable from Moscow on the day he claimed. He then admitted fabricating the tale. Strangely, Fedora, the FBI-controlled defector, had verified these two things, the rank of lieutenant colonel and the dispatch of the telegram. Now, Fedora was suspected by some in the CIA as well as some in the FBI, which ran him, of being a double agent actually working for the KGB. Since Fedora had tried to authenticate Nosenko, some then concluded that Nosenko must indeed be a plant. The KGB must have sent both men.

Nosenko had said that Gribanov, the chief of his directorate, was a close friend and had accelerated his promotions and gotten him special awards from the chairman of the KGB. He now admitted that Gribanov was not such a friend, even though Gribanov had, in fact, awarded him the Chairman's Commendation in 1956 and again in 1959.

Nosenko claimed to have been in the same American Embassy Section of the KGB as Cherepanov in 1960 and to have known him. Cherepanov had been suspected by the KGB of collaborating with American intelligence while serving in Yugoslavia during the 1950s, and then was booted out of the First Chief Directorate. Subsequently, according to Nosenko, the Personnel Directorate of the KGB "felt sorry" for Cherepanov and gave him a job in the Second Chief Directorate Archives. This made no sense at all to the CIA interrogators.

Eventually, Nosenko was forced to recant some of his statements. The apparently exaggerated rank, the overstated relationships with influential superiors, and the confusion with many minor details of his involvement in cases of particular interest to the CIA—especially that of Lee Harvey Oswald—led to the conclusion by some that he must be a KGB plant.

George never accepted the argument that Nosenko was planted by the KGB. He insisted that the USSR would have been crazy to give up Vassall, the British Admiralty clerk blackmailed by the KGB and exposed by Nosenko. Such a course of action would be the death of all future agent recruitment. George also knew of Nosenko's confinement and something of his conditions, but he knew nothing of the "case" against him. Coincidentally, George was stationed down on the farm as an instructor during much of Nosenko's incarceration. He had no contact with him, however, and even if he had known more, he could not have done much about the inhuman circumstances. He was just not the kind of guy who would burst into the chief's office and say, "You are making a terrible mistake and destroying one of the finest agents and operational sources that we have ever had," although it most assuredly would have been his sentiment.

George actually had a reverence for legitimate authority. On the other hand, if he sensed abuse of authority he could be quite contemptuous of that authority. Still, he rarely would tell people of his disdain for them, nor would he pointlessly argue with them.

At first, comparatively few people within the CIA or elsewhere were aware of this harsh confinement of Nosenko, the abusive treatment, and the dubious case against him. Only the Soviet Division management, the Soviet Division counterintelligence officers, some of the Agency counterintelligence staff, a limited number of personnel within the Office of Security who were actually involved in the mechanics of the incarceration, and a few top CIA administrators and their assistants knew anything of this confinement. All of these either believed Nosenko not to be credible or had no knowledge as to his bona fides. Thus, there was no one to make a case for him.

Others were bound to find out, however, and some of them were of the disposition to act in some way. In May of 1964, while serving with the Agency in Vienna, Richard Kovich heard about Nosenko's imprisonment from a high-ranking CIA official. This official volunteered that some Agency personnel now believed Nosenko to be "dirty" and had ordered a hostile interrogation. Kovich has been described as one of the premier case officers of the Cold War, unparalleled in his ability to recruit defectors and elicit information. His immediate reaction to the news about Nosenko was one of shock. He remarked to the official, "This is nonsense. They must be going nuts back there. Evidently, Golitsyn and Angleton must be in on the act. Everybody is paranoid."

Kovich also was a close friend of George and the godfather to George's only child, Eva. In 1965 he paid a social visit to George down on the farm, where George was teaching. George remarked to his friend that he wished he had been there the night before. A member of the Office of Security, one of the guards, had visited with George and had poured out his soul to him. The guard was so upset that he had to tell someone what pained him. He informed George that Nosenko was in solitary confinement and was being mistreated. The officer asked for a drink and threw up; his conscience was hurting him so. After hearing George's story, Kovich concluded that the Agency treatment of Nosenko had turned criminal and that unless circumstances were reversed the Agency would regret the action.

Knowing that Leonard McCoy had a stake in Nosenko's status,

Kovich let him know of the hostile nature of the incarceration. It was McCoy's responsibility to gather intelligence requirements from customers, carry them to the handlers of defectors such as Nosenko, deliver the responses, and follow up on all aspects of the information train. Since Nosenko had first defected, McCoy continually had implored the Soviet Bloc Division chief to allow the publication of some of Nosenko's tidbits of information and to allow further legitimate debriefing of the defector. The chief repeatedly and pointedly had turned down McCoy's requests. Finally, in October of 1965, the chief told McCoy that he wanted to share with him the case against Nosenko, the proof of his *mala fides.* Several hundred pages of raw information and dozens of finished memos were delivered to McCoy on a Friday. Leonard began making notes as he read the material, and he immediately saw analytical errors that had led to erroneous conclusions about Nosenko. On Monday morning the material was abruptly removed from McCoy by the division's new chief of counterintelligence. McCoy forthwith prepared a lengthy and comprehensive memo debunking the case against Nosenko and on the next day delivered it to the Division chief. The memo delineated the errors that he had observed in the analyses of the charges against Nosenko and refuted the conclusions that led to these charges. The chief demanded that all copies of McCoy's memo be immediately delivered to his office.

Three months later, in January of 1966, McCoy's secretary came to him and announced that she had unwittingly kept one copy of his volatile October memo. Since he had heard of no amelioration of Nosenko's status, McCoy took the document to Richard Helms, by then the deputy director of the CIA. This may have been the first substantive step in the vindication of the maligned defector. Because of the powerful controversy still surrounding this issue, however, a lot more investigation into the matter would be forthcoming before Nosenko would have any relief from his plight. McCoy, of course, was in direct conflict with his superiors, the chief of the Soviet Bloc Division and the deputy chief of the division (the original case officer).

In June of 1966 Richard Helms became the new DCI, the first to have come up through the ranks. He had not yet made up his mind about Nosenko. After all, the worst nightmare a DCI could experience would be to have a trusted KGB double agent within the ranks of the CIA. He wanted closure on the matter, so he instructed the

Soviet Bloc Division and the Agency CI staff to review the case and come to a consensus on the man's authenticity.

In August of 1966 Nosenko was administered a second polygraph but it was no more genuine than the first. It too was administered in a hostile manner, the session designed to make him confess to a set of false beliefs rather than to find out the truth. McCoy then prepared another memo to the DCI outlining some of the hazards to the Agency of mishandling Nosenko and recommending that Nosenko be released whether or not he was bona fide. Kovich also was not finished with the Nosenko affair. In the summer of 1966 he had been assigned to teach down on the farm along with George. There the two of them repeatedly commiserated about the fate of the unfortunate man. Kovich resolved to do something about the impasse. In the spring of 1967 he scheduled an interview with the DCI. Helms was unable to keep the appointment but Adm. Rufus Taylor, then the deputy DCI, met with Kovich. By this time Helms had already asked Admiral Taylor to look into the matter relating to Nosenko. Kovich made it plain that he was upset with what the Agency had done. Kovich noted that the admiral was quite attentive and asked Kovich many questions about the case. In September, Helms formally assigned the resolution of the Nosenko question to Taylor. Taylor moved the investigation from the Soviet Bloc Division and the CI staff to the Office of Security, where Bruce Solie began an independent investigation of the matter.

Solie had followed the Nosenko saga from its inception in Geneva. He had been in Geneva in 1962, secreted in a separate location but constantly providing George with questions to ask Nosenko, including questions about "Sasha," the mole.[12] In October of 1967, without informing members of the Soviet Bloc Division, Solie had Nosenko moved from his windowless cell, where he had been for more than two years, to a safehouse near Washington, D.C., and began additional interviews. This time the questioning was conducted more in the manner routinely employed with defectors—that is, designed to elicit information rather than a confession. This time Nosenko took a conventional polygraph.

Nosenko maintained that some of his later statements were contradictory because he had been drunk during the initial meetings. He had no regrets regarding lying about the telegram, saying he had done so in order to encourage the CIA to accept his defection quickly: "They were not moving, and I was concerned that General

Gribanov would soon be arriving in Geneva." He felt justified in his declaration of rank. After all, early in the summer of 1963 the papers for his promotion to lieutenant colonel had been sent to the personnel directorate of the KGB, signed, and approved by all chiefs and Party members. His promotion would have been finalized routinely within months along with other officers in his promotion group. Moreover, as the travel papers of the Cherepanov chase indicated, he had the temporary rank of lieutenant colonel.

By possessing the travel documents for the Cherepanov chase, Nosenko proved the authenticity of the Cherepanov papers. Why else would there have been such a chase? Cherepanov's actions must have been of critical importance to the KGB. Moreover, according to these documents, Cherepanov had worked in the same American Embassy Section of the Second Chief Directorate of the KGB in which Nosenko claimed to have worked, and at the same time. Thus, they verified Nosenko's background and, by implication, some of his bona fides. In addition, these papers confirmed his own story about the entrapment of Popov. Nosenko's claims and the Cherepanov papers were mutually supportive.

The conventional lie-detector test indicated that Nosenko was cooperating truthfully. Nosenko was cleared by Solie's investigation in October 1968. Not until March 1969, however, was Nosenko freed. He then was given his back pay and his resettlement expense money. He had been incarcerated for five years. For 1,277 days he had been held in hostile, solitary confinement. He had been interrogated a total of 292 times. There is no precedent in CIA history for such an incarceration. Presumably, it will never happen again.[13]

For years after Nosenko was released, the Agency used him only a little. The FBI, on the other hand, used him extensively at their Counter Intelligence School at Quantico, Virginia. By 1973 Nosenko was accepted by the DCI. Eventually, the CIA followed the FBI example, hiring him as a lecturer and sending him to dozens of foreign countries to brief case officers and operators.

Throughout all of this time, the myth of Golitsyn's mole, "Sasha," secreted somewhere high within the echelons of the CIA hierarchy continued. This burlesque had been gnawing at the entrails of the clandestine services group since 1962. The calumny assembled was that Sasha had a Slavic background, a last name that probably started with a *K*, a previous station assignment in Germany, and a foreign-born wife. The search for Sasha, conducted principally by

Angleton and his sidekick Golitsyn, terrorized the clandestine services group and the Office of Security. As a result, the Soviet Bloc Division was directed to have no further contacts with Soviets. In effect, they were shut down for a decade.

When I learned of this crippling of the Agency, I had the answer to a question that had plagued me during my years there. As a missile analyst and later as a systems analyst evaluating intelligence collection systems, I had observed very little capability of the clandestine services group against the Soviet missile threat. Almost never, in my experience, had they produced tangible results. There was always the hope that a tremendous cache of intimate, technical details could arrive at any time, perhaps even manuals of the type provided by Penkovsky, but none was forthcoming.

Had there been a real Sasha, he could not have done as much damage to clandestine services group as this phantom Sasha. To make matters worse, numerous case officers were suspected of being the mole. The careers of many were damaged, and some were forced to leave the Agency. Some of those maligned at least had the satisfaction of successful lawsuits settled with monetary compensation and the restoration of their good names, albeit many hard years later. The Soviet Bloc Division chief, the individual who had met Nosenko in Frankfurt and who had continually doubted his credentials, ironically became one of those suspected. To remove him from the scene, he was offered the post of chief in Paris. He accepted the job with some remorse, only to have Angleton, the chief of counterintelligence for the Agency, secretly advise the chief of the French Intelligence Service that the head CIA man in Paris was a Soviet spy. Even Angleton himself was suspected of being Sasha. This has been characterized as the snake finally swallowing itself. George was never seriously suspected of being Sasha, notwithstanding his amazing fit to the Sasha profile. Evidently, he was untouchable.

In 1978, the U.S. House of Representatives formed a committee to further investigate various aspects of the assassination of President Kennedy. They concluded that Nosenko had lied about Oswald. Two years later, the FBI concluded that Fedora was a KGB plant, then reversed themselves. So, in the minds of some, confusion about Nosenko still reigns.

There never was any doubt in George's mind of Nosenko's bona fides. He and George communicated often. There were frequent telephone calls, letters, Christmas cards, and a few visits when the

Ukrainian was in Washington. Nosenko knew that George was a legend at the Agency. George was instrumental in developing two premier sources, Popov and Penkovsky, both of whom were on Nosenko's "watch." He naturally had great respect for George's professional ability. He considered George to be a very intelligent individual and, more importantly, a nonpompous, humble, and caring human being.

After a few minutes George hung up, turned to me, and said, "Nosenko is a good man. I said good-by to him. He was a good friend. I will never see him again." I departed, fearing as to the condition that I might find George in the next time that we met.

CHAPTER 21

Mementos

It was Wednesday, October the twenty-second. As I sauntered up the back walkway of Vinson Hall I could not help but marvel at the gorgeous fall day. The giant hardwoods were almost at their best. One more week would bring in their peak colors. George was fortunate to have such a lovely scene upon which to gaze from the great windows of his end-unit apartment, although he never had acknowledged this to me. I wondered to myself if he appreciated what he had. After all, he never seemed to appreciate esthetics, good music, or fine art. In fact, he didn't like any music, so far as I could tell, even though he probably had considerable knowledge in the classics. He did have some attractive pictures and figures of bears, but aside from these, he did not appear to have much interest in art or things of beauty.

Strolling along, I again reflected on his situation here. He was well liked at Vinson Hall. He was not a joiner, but once the folks here got to know him, they considered him to be warm and dependable. They knew that he was very intelligent and, at first, believed him to be very lucky at bridge. Soon enough, they recognized that he was a bridge genius. He never failed to attend the bridge events and, in addition, he often played in private games. One lady was so grateful to him for playing with her invalid husband each week. I wondered how much lunch money George had taken from that poor soul.

George knew the rules at Vinson Hall and even if he could not make an exact fit to them, he did his best. One issue had to do with the dining room. Coats and ties were required of the men for evening dining. "George had some old green thing that he called a coat," said one of his friends. "With that, he would wear a tie that never matched, in order to conform. But to complement this outfit, he would wear his slippers for dinner." At first, his friends thought the slippers were hilarious, but eventually all got used to the scene and thought no more of it. One evening, George's daughter, Eva, and some of his friends at the home gave him a surprise birthday party. He had no idea it was coming. Knowing of his obsession with bears, many of the attendees gave him bear figures, bear statues, and bear pictures. One of his friends, however, bought him a "God-awful" bright-red Mickey Mouse tie. Amusingly, George liked it and wore it to dinner.

I wanted to review with him his comprehensive photo albums and souvenirs. There were people in his past whom I wished to identify. Most were his relatives and buddies; some were historically notable. I also wanted to ask him about some of his philosophies and personal attitudes. I knew most of these from long-ago discussions, but I wanted to get his most recent take on things. He could be full of surprises, so I wanted to find out now what might be on his mind. I particularly wanted to know if he had changed his outlook on life in light of his illness. I approached his apartment door with apprehension, as I never knew how I would find him. His health was failing and the rises and falls of his spirits were a day-to-day thing. I noted that the doorway was open, so I called out and entered.

"Hello, George!"

"You're right on time."

"How are you?"

"I live as the Lord wishes, from day to day, and I thank him for each pain-free minute. It won't be long now."

"You can't talk like that; we have a lot to do. What can I do to make you feel better?"

"Nothing. The only one who can help me is the one above."

"Well, you know, 'the Lord helps them that help themselves.' Besides, I need your help."

"Okay, I'll try. The last time we met you said that you wanted to see my souvenirs. I have them down. If you will go into the bedroom you will see three boxes on the bed. Bring those, as well as the picture books."

I brought out the complete cache, the souvenirs of a lifetime, and started with a big, dusty, old box. The first thing inside to attract my attention was a small red box with a double-headed eagle, embossed in gold. I said to George, "This is the Russian imperial crown." I opened the box. "Look at that big, red Maltese cross. This medal is beautiful. It must be almost two inches square. I believe that this is baked red enamel inlaid into the gold cross. There is a date painted on the back; it's in Cyrillic. I think it must be 22 September 1782. That was during the reign of the coarse-grained German woman who became empress when her idiot husband mysteriously died, wasn't it?"

"You're right."

"There is a note in the box. It says, 'St. Vladimirs Cross . . . signifying distinguished work for Tsar Nicholas' Army. Georgi G. Kisevalter . . . 1914.' There is no apostrophe on Vladimirs."

"Prince Vladimir died in the eleventh century, before there were any apostrophes. Seventeen eighty-two is probably the date that Empress Catherine commissioned the medal. During that time Russia was at war with Turkey. My father would have received that medal for the work that he did with munitions during the early part of the First World War. It signifies distinguished work."

"Here are some documents written in Russian: a birth certificate, two pages. Aha! This is yours! Let's look at this. Yokohama. Oh, this is the trip to America when you were five years old. I have never seen anybody who had his life so well documented as you do; you have a photograph for every month of your life. This says, 'United States declares war on Germany, 1917.' I can't remember; were you in Chicago or where?"

"New York. How do you like those railroad trains? They really go back."

"Your dad was inspecting railroad cars near Harrisburg?"

"Think of the years. This is around 1917, 1918, 1920. They were developing railroad engines at the same time that they were developing the munitions. When I say munitions, they were developing the cannons as well as the shells. And, in addition, they were developing locomotives. And then they were transporting those across the U.S. to the West Coast and then across the Pacific to Russia."

"Let's go through these papers. Here's one dated 1 November 1918. 'His Excellency Boris Bachmetiev, Ambassador of Russia presents George G. Kisewalter, Mechanical Engineer as Acting Assistant Comptroller, Department of Russian State Control.' And it is signed by Robert Lansing, secretary of state of the United States of America. Okay, this was during the period after the Bolshevik Revolution when the supporters of the Kerensky government were fighting the Bolsheviks. Didn't you tell me that Robert Lansing was the uncle of John Foster and Allen Dulles?"

"You are correct."

"Well, I see that your father's name was spelled with a *w* instead of a *v*. It would be pronounced Kiss-walter, the way that you always pronounced it to me, not Keese-ay-valter as many of your old CIA buddies pronounce the name. Which is correct?"

"It doesn't matter."

"Look at this, George. This must be a special passport: '6 May, 1925, The Russian Consulate General in New York, Madame Rose Kisevalter, accompanied by her son, George, fifteen years of age, traveling to France and Switzerland and returning to the United States. Bearer is a Russian citizen. Consul General Oustinoff.' You went to see your grandfather and cousins in southern France, didn't you?"

"Correct."

"What's this; a beauty contest? That's the ugliest group I have ever seen!"

"This is the Senior French Club at Stuyvesant High School. I was lousy. That made Mother unhappy. She didn't want me to kick footballs until I studied irregular verbs. Now, this photo was taken at the French summer camp in New York. It was a YMCA camp, oriented toward the language."

"Did you learn Latin?"

"I speak a smattering of Greek, no Latin. I stayed away from that like poison."

"Who are these people?"

"There is Malia Natirbov in the group. We said good-by to each other when he was here last week. I will never see him again. I won't be here when he comes back from his trip to Circassia, where he was born."

"Don't talk like that! Keep on saying that you will get better!"

"That's what Malia said to me. I told him that I can say it, but it isn't true."

"This is a patent—12 February 1929. 'G. G. Kisevalter and his Heirs, for seventeen years. Boats.' This is a patent that your father received for the design of the pontoons on Lindbergh's plane."

"You're right. You're absolutely right."

"Here is your soccer team at Dartmouth. Are you in here?"

"I think so."

"Is Rockefeller in here?"

"Maybe. Let me see. I think Nelson is the husky, little fellow. He couldn't hit the side of a barn with the ball. As I said, we stunk."

"Here is another patent. It's dated 23 June 1936 and it's about 'Wind Motors.' Your father did significant work of many different kinds, over an extended period of time. Your dad was all right. He was a mechanical engineer, my kind of people."

"This looks like it's Alaska. Start of the war, World War II."

"It is. We were building a radar station in the Aleutians."

"This is probably a Soviet that you worked with while you were there?"

"Right. We were in Fairbanks. The man's name was Machin. Machin was in charge of all of the Soviets there. He is the one to whom I said, 'Look, you want to make a hit with the Americans? Give them a typewritten recommendation of promotion for their efficiency reports instead of paying them money. They will just blow the money on poker or whatnot.' He appreciated that. He became a general. He later became the commander of all of the Soviet MIGs at a base in Germany."

"Who is that?"

"Gavrisheff, my second in command in Alaska."

"Fancy names. Fancy mustaches too. Fancy everything with these guys. Your friend—the sergeant later promoted to second lieutenant—that's his picture, isn't it?"

"David Chavchavadze. His card is here. He visited me last week. Dedicated man. He sleeps in Buckingham Palace when he goes to London. Why not? His aunt was the duchess of Kent."

"This says, 'Pentagon, 1944.' What is this about?"

"Yes; I'm in Washington."

"And where are you in this group picture? Is this a class or something?"

"There also is a future U.S. senator in there; you can find him."

"I do see you, but there is no way in the world that I am going to recognize whoever the other guy is."

"It's what's-his-name, from Wisconsin."

"Joe McCarthy?"

"No, but you're getting close."

"He is the only one that I know of from Wisconsin. Tell me."

"Well, he's the guy who was giving the sheep prize, whatever."

I realized he was talking about the man who would award a "fleecing" prize to the bureaucrat who had made the most outrageous waste of taxpayers' money. "William Proxmire."

"Right. He was the number-two guy in the class of over a hundred."

"And who was number one?"

"Me."

"Ha, I knew it! What was the class about?"

"The Japanese order of battle. We knew every Japanese division by heart."

"Why Japanese OB? You were working there in Russian intelligence."

"Because that was a side issue at that time, in addition to intelligence on the Soviet Army, as if I didn't have enough to do."

"What are these?"

"We have re-recaptured them from the Germans: Gehlen and company, articles of unknown Soviet and German weaponry."

"These are medals that the Germans collected from defeated Soviets and then you got these from the Germans?"

"Yes."

"But some of these medals are American."

"That's right, that's right."

"It's an exotic kind of collection, here."

"For bravery and so on, the Soviet Army. The Germans got them off dead Russians and Americans; then other Americans got them off dead Germans."

"This gives me a terribly somber feeling to think that some American lad used to wear these. Here are some American's captain bars. There's no doubt a story behind these. Ah, these look very interesting—a lot of words written in Russian and a lot of photographs. These look like passport papers. Why would the Soviets have these kinds of papers? I mean, a soldier wouldn't be carrying something like that, would he?"

"This is part of their gathered intelligence information. These are items of regimental issue and things of that sort. You know, some are from the dead, some are from the living. A lot of it was first-line pickups, documents from dead or captured Soviet soldiers."

"Americans too. '5 January 1946. Dear Mr. Kisewalter'—this is a letter from Reinhard Gehlen, Hitler's 'friend,' thanking you and

Colonel Shimkin for the Christmas presents. And we have 'Kiss-walter' again, with the *w* instead of the *v*. Is it just me, the former secretary of state, and the Nazis who pronounce your name Kiss-walter?"

"Gehlen was the chief of intelligence for the West Germans; he is now dead. At one time he was working for Hitler but Hitler did not like him, nor did he Hitler."

"How did you learn German? I understand that you could speak better German than Ferdi?"

"Dartmouth. The dialect of German spoken by the Austrians is so extreme that one loses all rules of grammar. Now, Ukrainian is a Russian dialect, but they have their own rules of grammar. I also have a fundamental knowledge of Serbian and the languages spoken in former Yugoslavia because they are derived from Russian. It is easier to understand the languages in that part of the world than it is for an Englishman to understand some of those in the British Isles. Welsh, of course, is impossible, and Scots speaking English are almost as bad. I remember one time sitting in an airport, waiting for a plane in Glasgow. There was a group of Scottish soldiers sitting around and talking with one another. They talked constantly. I do not believe that I understood a word that was said in almost an hour."

"Okay, who is this fellow?"

"Henning Christiani. He was the son of Christiani of Christiani and Neilson, famous builders. Do you see how those associations link up?"

"You keep saying that, associations, associations. What is the story here? It has to do with trains."

"I built that factory in Galesburg, Illinois; it was a transfer point for the Chicago-Burlington. This was a mixing and milling station for grain."

"The alfalfa business was quite profitable for you, wasn't it?"

"It is not the financial rewards in life that are important. I spent my life fighting Communism. That was important to me."

"Your father and mother came out of Russia. Who else among the family came to America?"

"Later on my first cousin made it. He was a White Army officer who fought with General Yudenich against the Reds in trying to recapture Petrograd. As you may recall, his father, my godfather, Alexander Alexandrovich Andreev, was a member of Russian hereditary nobility and a general in the Tsar's Army. Andreev also was my uncle, being married to my father's sister, Raisa Georgievna Kisevalter."

I later learned that during the Napoleonic invasion of Russia, at the Battle of Borodino in September of 1812, there was a Russian artillery officer by the name of Andreev. Of course, Napoleon won that conflict, with much loss of life on both sides, and then entered Moscow. After Napoleon was driven out of Russia, Andreev was promoted to general and was made a member of the Russian hereditary nobility as a reward for his exemplary service during that campaign. So, following that, the eldest son of every Andreev, all of whom were named Alexander, then became an artillery officer in the tsarist armies.

George told me, "General Andreev was the commanding general of an artillery proving ground on the island of Poligon, which sits in the harbor of St. Petersburg. Physically, it relates to St. Petersburg similarly to the way that Governors Island relates to Manhattan, in New York." George could vaguely remember visiting the facility when he was a very young boy, less than five years of age. The aunt and uncle had a very large estate with servants, gardens, and animals, much like a large park. In the summertime, the grounds were accessed by ferry; in the wintertime, when the body of water was frozen, one would take a sled mobile to the estate. Men skaters pushed along the sled. Passengers wore great fur coats for warmth as they breezed along very rapidly across the ice.[1]

George's aunt and uncle raised nine children. The oldest was Alexander Alexandrovich Andreev. He was twelve years older than George. By the time of George's departure from Russia in 1915, Alexander had entered the military, first as a cadet, then as a soldier in artillery. He did well in various assignments during the First World War. In December of 1917, right after the glorious October revolution, his mortar battery was dissolved, and in February of 1918 he was demobilized from army service. He returned to his parents' home at Poligon. To placate the Bolsheviks, since they were a threat his parents, he joined the Red Army. He was assigned to the artillery forces associated with an old naval fortress on the island of Kronstadt just outside of Petrograd, in the Gulf of Finland. He served as an assistant to the commander in chief of the facility. A year later, however, his father was executed by the Bolsheviks, who used some trumped-up charges of conspiracy. The general was accused of harboring weapons illegally, notwithstanding that managing the weapons facility was his job. Actually, General Andreev's servants had been soldiers in the Tsar's Army. They lived in a small house next to the general's home, where they kept their rifles, etc. The Bolsheviks found these weapons and accused the general. According to George, under Lenin's orders, his uncle was "machine-gunned down."

The general was murdered in October of 1919. Alexander requested and was granted some time off to attend his father's funeral. While on leave, he deserted the Red Army and traveled south to join the Northwest Army of Gen. Nikolai Yudenich. Again, he served in an artillery battalion. Yudenich, at that time, was in Estonia, attempting to seize Petrograd. With the help of Western allies, his army advanced as far as they could. The British tried to be of aid, but they bungled things. They had agreed to sell tanks to Yudenich's army, but they inadvertently delivered them to the Red Army at Liepaja, a seaport in Latvia, to the rear of the White Army. This paralyzed what might otherwise have been a successful attack by the White forces at Petrograd, and the group retreated back into Estonia in early 1920, never again to be effective. The Red Army wasn't strong enough to capture Estonia, and the allied armies would have stopped them had the Reds tried. They did try to seize Poland, however, but the dictator of Poland, Pilsudski, was very effective in stopping their invasion near the gates of Warsaw. The Reds were chased back into Russia. They then sued for peace with Poland. The agreement reached also ensured the independence of the Baltic States.[2]

George continued, "Aunt Raisa died from a chill, some months after her husband was murdered. All of the Andreev children, except for Alexander, were scattered throughout the Soviet Union into different orphanages and never heard from since. All track of them was lost. Alexander was in Estonia when the army was dissolved. He married an Estonian girl who was working with the Red Cross at the time, a very fine lady by the name of Linda Treff. They had twins. One died at birth; the other was named Alexander Alexandrovich Andreev. A couple of years later they had another son. His name was Alexis Alexander Andreev.

"My father corresponded with Alexander and brought him to this country in 1928. When he entered the U.S., the spelling of his name became Andreiev. He came on a student visa, attended Columbia University, and studied chiropractic medicine. His wife and two sons followed in 1936. They came on a special visa (outside of the quota system), which was obtained through an appeal to Mrs. Eleanor

Roosevelt, who interceded on their behalf. He became a caviar salesman with the Makaroff Caviar Company, and he spent much of his life's work at that enterprise. He labored at many jobs in New York, eventually working in the shipping department of Macy's. He was very accurate in accounting and very thorough; he was very careful with his money. He never smoked and he drank only on special occasions. He lived in Queens, where his boys were raised; all of them were very quickly Americanized.

"In the late thirties, a strange thing happened. Alexander's wife invited her mother to come from Estonia for a visit with them in New York. She came and while she was there, Hitler invaded Poland and started World War II. The Baltic States were partitioned by the Soviets; she could not go home as these countries became doormats for both Hitler and Stalin. So, here she was, with a return ticket in hand. She stayed here until she died. I got a refund for her return ticket in 1946.

"The two boys grew up and, like their dad, joined the army, served in the Second World War, performed well, were discharged after the war, and then used the GI bill to go to college. Alexander studied architecture at Columbia University and Alexis studied electrical engineering at Columbia University and at the Polytechnic Institute of Brooklyn. Their father, Alexander, died in 1971 of a stroke and then their mother, Linda, died in 1972. They would be very proud of their sons. Alexander became a very successful architect in New York and had two daughters; he died just last May. Alexis is the only reasonably close relative that I know who survived that era. I keep in touch with him. He has two daughters and a son. I have met all five of my first cousin's grandchildren. Alexis became a senior engineer with Grumman and was one of the original contributors to the LM, the Lunar Module, Descent Stage of the Apollo program. At the Kennedy Space Center in Florida he was group leader for the LM Support Group, serving from the first Apollo launch through Apollo 17, the sixth and final Scientific Lunar Expedition. This series, of course, includes Apollo 11, during which Neil Armstrong and Edwin Aldrin landed on the moon, while Mike Collins orbited. The members of the launch team signed a document, which was photographed and etched on a copper plate that was left on the moon. His name is now on the moon.

"So, that accounts for all of the relatives that I have in this world—at least the blood relatives from Russia that I know. The rest of these people are difficult to account for because of the revolution, the ravages of war, and the consequences of being non-persons in a Communist country."

"All of your uncles and aunts perished in the revolution?"

"Right, the details of which are totally unknown. How can one know? There are no transcribed details of these actions. They were all, you might say, acts of violence with passion and unpredictability."

"Irrational."

"Well, that oversimplifies it, but when you ask for a specific detail, how can I know?"

"I just thought that you might know of certain ones that did survive for some period of time. I mean, what purpose is there to killing old people?"

"Well, if you can understand mass murder by the Communists of anyone who is not subject to their beliefs, then you can understand why mass elimination has some sort of philosophical value. I don't know of any, but in this world that has happened many times in many areas for many reasons.

"Ironically, it was the revulsion against this sort of thing that precipitated an ill-conceived, pro-Communist campaign called the Cambridge Movement, which is a generic term, meaning nothing specific. It was a protest by intellectual Englishmen such as Kim Philby and others who were famous spies for the Soviets: George Blake, Guy Burgess, Donald Maclean, and so forth. Some of these were homosexuals; most of them were nuts. They were people who would run away from things rather than stay around to fix what might be wrong. All of them had gone to Cambridge or Oxford, had met one another, and had become Communists. Kim Philby went to work for the British Secret Intelligence Service and became their chief liaison with the CIA in Washington for MI 6. He probably would have been made the chief of the British Secret Intelligence Service had he stayed with his job.[3]

"Actually, the Cambridge Movement had its beginnings during World War I by individuals who had great moral objections to the concept of war. The clarion call for their actions, you might say, was the life story of a man who represented the antithesis of their beliefs, a world figure, Sir Basil Zaharoff. This man had controlling stock in the Krupp works of Germany, the famous Schneider works in Dijon and other areas of France, the Skoda works in Czechoslovakia, and the Vickers plant in England. He wore the Victoria Cross and the

Knight of the Grand Cross of England, the Iron Cross of Germany, and the Legion of Honor of France. He was so powerful, making money on munitions, that he had World War I stopped so his train could pass through the front lines while on his way from Paris to visit Berlin. Is that enough influence for one man?

"Well, for this unparalleled wealth in those days we in America had an expression, a 'Pittsburgh millionaire,' meaning that he was in the steel business, making money from munitions. This caricature was the sort of thing that contributed to the establishment of the Cambridge Movement. One specific World War I incident was the most glaring example of all. There was a small plant in a small town in England where guns were manufactured: field artillery, the rolling kind. As the result of a particular very painful and disastrous battle in Belgium, the casualties were very high. Finally, at great cost, the British took a significant position and captured artillery pieces of the Germans. These implements of war were brought home in triumph and mounted in the Town Square as a trophy of war, as if to say, 'Here's artillery, captured from the German enemy.'

"It turned out this artillery was manufactured in that very town in England. It had been sold to the Dutch, who were neutral and not involved with the Germans or the French or the British or us or anyone else in World War I. These materials were purchased through Holland, then resold at a profit, of course, to the Germans, who always wanted extra, heavy artillery. Such an example of the evil nature of people, making money on somebody else's blood in such horrible activities as war, gave credence to the fundamentals of the Cambridge Movement. This incident provided some justification, in the minds of some, for the rise of Communism. They blindly believed that Communism could be a better way, morally, for a civilized world, particularly an Anglo-Saxon world. That was the justification for these traitors' disloyalty. Ironically, Philby, who I consider to have been completely deluded, philosophically, sacrificed his own successful career when he chose this Communist pathway as the correct direction for his life. But there is more philosophical justification for what Philby did, treasonable though it may be to the nth degree, as contrasted with what Aldrich Ames did to our country, which also was high treason. Ames condemned ten men to death, just for the money. Philby and Ames' actions represent a different kind of morality. It is the difference between being a traitor for ideological reasons and selling someone else's life and blood for money, like Judas—Jesus and thirty pieces of silver. Both are evil, both are treasonable, and we detest both, but their nature is not quite the same."[4]

"Did you know Philby?"

"I had nothing to do with him. When he was the SIS liaison man to the CIA he spent his time with James Jesus Angleton, the chief of our counterintelligence, lapping up steaks and martinis at expensive Georgetown restaurants."

"Who is this fellow?"

"Ed Snow. He was an old friend of mine. He was one of the best case officers that we ever had. He died not long ago. These pictures are all in Japan. This is a Russian girl who turned out to be a Soviet agent who was in Okinawa. Snow thought that she was a White Russian. She did him in; got him fired. He became vice-president of a big outfit, however. Allen Dulles got him the job when he booted him from the Agency."

"She really was a Red Russian?"

"Well, she was under subordination. She was protecting her relatives, who may have been White. Of course, the Korean War was on. Before that, a family named Yankovsky came out of the Vladivostok area and came down through North Korea into South Korea. They had originally been in Harbin; they were White Russians fleeing from the Soviets. Snow married one of them. This got him fired."

"What does Harbin have to do with it?"

"Harbin is a city in Manchuria that was occupied by the Imperial Russians for some time. It still shows distinct Russian influence. The city grew up when the railroads in the area were built. Many of them connect there. This was long before the Bolshevik Revolution. All of that area of Manchuria was very Russian at one time. When the White Russians were fleeing Russia after the revolution, many of them went to Harbin in Manchuria, worked there in China for a few years, and then came to America with Chinese passports. Snow's parents were among them. He was born in the U.S. and went to UCLA."

"Point out some of the significant things to me."

"Here is a picture of part of the Berlin tunnel, and these were taken in Munich. I was dropping off something during the Popov operation."

"You really loved that guy, didn't you?"

"We had great affection for, and deep understanding of, one another."

"This is the car that Ferdi was going to drive and get into trouble?"

"Correct; that is a QP car."

"Who is this?"

"This is Dickie Franks; he was the SIS chief for London during the Penkovsky operation. Later he became chief of SIS. I hope that we got that story straight."

"You mean Penkovsky? I'm very confident on that one; I was an analyst with the missiles, you know. This says 1964. What was the occasion for your being there?"

"It was on a trip to Bonn for a lecture that I was giving to the West German intelligence organization, Gehlen's group. I have been very lucky with the people that I know, wonderful associations. This one is of Dick Kovich, a very nice guy; but I repeat myself. I only know nice guys. These are bears at Regents Park in London. You always see bears at Regents Park."

"This is somebody's christening?"

"That is Deriabin and his wife."

"He was Orthodox Christian?"

"Yes he was, but he was KGB also. He's dead now. Deriabin: KGB."

"This is Peer de Silva then, I'll bet?"

"You're right, and this is Saigon. He was our chief of station in Saigon until the Viet Cong bombed our embassy. Ultimately he died because of the wounds that he sustained there. This is Frank Levy and me drinking Molson Beer. These are my Agency medals."

"This is the Distinguished Intelligence Medal: 18 May 1959. You received this for the Popov operation. It says here that this was awarded 'for performance of outstanding services or for achievement of a distinctly exceptional nature in a duty or responsibility.' You did all of that, for sure. Here is a picture of Allen Dulles giving you an award. Is he giving you the Distinguished Intelligence Medal?"

"I suppose so."

"You would have to be dead to receive an award higher than this. Where is the medal for the Penkovsky operation?"

"Rather than another medal, I was awarded a Certificate of Merit with Distinction. I received that and a thousand dollars. Ferdi said, 'Take the money, George.' A thousand dollars was a good bit of money in 1961. We bought a new refrigerator."

"This is a picture of you and Richard Helms; what's happening here?"

"This was my retirement ceremony. It was on the eighth of April

1970, in the conference room on the seventh floor of the headquarters building."

"This then is your Bronze Retirement Medallion: 'For Honorable Service, 1952 to 1970.' And here we have the Trailblazers Award: '18 September 1997, the 50th Anniversary' of the CIA. You were one of only fifty people in the history of the Agency to be selected, and you were the only one selected for activities as a case officer. That is something, George; you have to be proud."

"Thank you."

"Are you getting tired?"

"No, no; we can go on."

"Would you like to lie down while we finish?"

"That would be good. If you could help me to my bed, then we can continue. That would be better."

I helped George up, slowly walked him into his bedroom, and gingerly eased him into his bed. Just as we were completing the move, Eva entered the apartment. She came to the bedside, said hello to her father, kissed him, and mentioned that she was going to buy some things from the grocery store. She went into the kitchen. Moments later she returned with some pills in her hand and began a conversation with her dad.

"Why haven't you taken your pills, Dad?"

"I don't want them."

"You must take them. It looks like you have not eaten anything since yesterday. Is that right?"

"That is correct."

"You have to eat! You have to take your medicine!"

"I do not. It is time; I want to go."

"Do you want to suffer?"

"I want to end the suffering. I've suffered long enough."

"We're just trying to help you!"

"Everybody wants to help. Help is torture. I don't want your help. If you want to help, bring shovels."

"Won't you help yourself?"

"The only help that I want will have to come from above."

"Please, take these pills and drink some juice!"

"I won't do it."

"If you won't do it for yourself, will you please do it for me?"

"No."

"Please! Just do it for me! Do this for me!"

"I wouldn't do it for Jesus Christ."

At that point I intervened and suggested to Eva, "That means he's not going to do it, at least not now. Please leave them here. Maybe I can get him to cooperate while you're out getting the groceries. Try not to get too upset."

She left. George and I continued.

"She gets to you, doesn't she?"

"Yes."

"She and Ferdi are the only ones I have ever known who could get to you."

"You are so right. You have observed correctly. You are very observant. I never knew that you were so perceptive. But you weren't Ivy League; you went to the University of South Carolina."

"Eva said that she had never met Velma. But Eva wound up with all of Velma's clothes. Velma's niece and nephew just wanted to get rid of them?"

"Right. When Velma's family came to bury her there was a slight surplus of clothing, about seven hundred dresses. She was like Imelda Marcos and she never threw anything away. Some of those clothes go back to the twenties. Eva filled up a sixteen-foot truck with them and took it to Athens, Georgia, where she had a store."

"How about this one pill?"

"Okay, but that is it."

"You're getting kind of tired."

"No."

"Yes you are. Is there anything else that you want to tell me?"

"No."

"Okay. We'll put an end to this right now." I propped George up in his bed to make him as comfortable as I could. His eyes promptly flickered shut and he seemed to drift off into a fitful, troubled sleep. I couldn't tell if his rest was comfortable or painful. It certainly was not peaceful. Perhaps, I thought, he was having conversations with Popov, Penkovsky, Cherepanov, or the like.

Eva returned and we put away George's mementos. Together we went to the front desk to photocopy some of the documents that her father had shared with me. Understanding what we were doing, everyone who passed by inquired about George. They all were anxious as to his condition. I went home. Three hours later, at nine o'clock that evening, Eva's good friend, Annie Snyder, called. George had passed away.

When the news gets to you that a good friend has died, it's always a shock—even though you already knew that the word was on its way. I was close to him. Many times he had said that I was like a son to him. I'm sure that he said that to many others. He meant it to all of us. I know.

CHAPTER 22

Taps

Both doors of the vestibule are opened. The two soldiers march forward to retrieve the casket. Click, click, click; the taps on the shoes again reverberate against that hard floor. Grasping the casket handles with strong hands at each end of the bier, they sharply sidestep eight times in unison, rotating the casket 180 degrees. The man at the head of the casket does an about-face. Then, reverently, they follow the chaplain down the aisle with their cargo all the way to the rear of the nave. Click, click, click, then silence. One of the soldiers returns to Eva, again hammering those steel mallets into the ceramic tiles. He escorts her down the aisle to the chaplain, who awaits her at the stationary casket.

I sit and reflect. His life began in tsarist Russia and was abruptly turned upside down with the violent destruction of that dynasty. His family life was tragically altered during the period of the First World War and the years immediately following, as the Communist regime in the Soviet Socialist Republics was being formed. During the Second World War and the ensuing Cold War, he continued to be concerned with the affairs of the Soviet Union. Most of his life's work was dedicated to bringing about the demise of the Soviet regime, the "evil empire." Eventually, he could look back at its collapse and gather great satisfaction in the realization that the focus of most of his life, the task of defeating that corrupt government, was successful. Accordingly, the prospect of our peoples warring with one another was greatly lessened. Thus, George, the antiwar man, could confidently conclude that his life was spent doing *something worthwhile.*

In a sense, George just happened to be in the right place at the right time; and as Adm. "Bull" Halsey once said, "there are no great men; there are only great challenges that ordinary men are forced by circumstances to meet." This, however, implies luck and does not do justice to the merit that should be accorded for one's preparation. Frederick Douglass spoke more to my idea of George: "What we call luck is that moment in life where preparation and opportunity converge." Few men prepare themselves for life the way that George did. He was poised and ready for his challenges and opportunities when they appeared, his unique abilities exquisitely honed to perfection. George was not an ordinary man and he would not rely on luck. He was a most extraordinary man, masterfully prepared for life.

George's basic, innate humility stemmed from his inability to take himself too seriously. But this did not prevent him from being quite self-confident. He was absolutely confident in himself, and this confidence came from his always being prepared. In every situation he always knew that he had paid his dues and was ready. Moreover, he intuitively knew, from his own history, no doubt, that no matter how difficult the task at hand might be, he would persevere until its successful completion. That is the only way that he knew to live. He kept himself alive, through extreme pain, just long enough to give me, through his stories, a reasonably complete picture of himself. In doing so, he demonstrated that there is more to dying than just waiting for the end; he was creative until his last breath.

One feature of George's character that stood out more prominently than others was his untempered demand for integrity. He not only expected it of others, but he absolutely demanded it of himself. He had no patience with those who tended to be less than honest with themselves or with those around them. I believe that this obsession with truth gave rise to his love for mathematics. To him, if the facts in a given situation of life are properly processed, they will add up to the truth, just as in any mathematical exercise. He intuitively knew that things had to be that way.

Eva had noted George's incredible memory, a characteristic that he repeatedly and dramatically demonstrated. But to me, his best trait was the value that he placed on human associations. He loved and enjoyed being with people. After all, the central feature of George's makeup was one of warmth. Indeed, he could have instant empathy with a stranger, a trait so rare yet one so valuable. It was easy for him because he loved people. Almost no one could offend him enough to prevent him from finding a way to recognize that individual's good features and to forgive him. It was all but impossible for George to hold a grudge. There were a few scoundrels that he cursed to his death, but he insisted that even these had positive qualities that he admired. This unusual capacity for forgiveness, especially in light of his incredible memory, makes him a rare individual. I thank God that I knew the man.

Outside the chapel, the sunny bright courtyard provides stark contrast to the somber array of soldiers and funeral implements. Two additional elements have joined the funeral escort: a caisson drawn by six horses and a caparisoned (riderless) horse. The caisson horses are matched in their dark brown color and aligned into two columns of three; soldiers are mounted on the left three. The caparisoned horse is stygian black. A sword is strapped to its English riding saddle; a pair of boots are reversed and fitted into the saddle's stirrups. This horse is one of only three such horses at Arlington. All are black; all are specifically trained for this task and perform no other.

The lieutenant commands, "Escort, atten-*hun.* Present *arms.*" He strikes downward with his saber, all members of the escort raise their rifles, in salute and the band begins to play. The casket team carries its burden to the waiting caisson. The band completes its hymn.

The lieutenant again commands, "Escort, atten-*hun.* Right *face.* Right shoulder *arms.* In slow cadence, forward *march.*" The two rifle platoons snap to attention. All in the formation briskly spin to the right and shoulder their weapons. The assembled train, including the mourners, commences its sorrowful motion and passes through the cemetery gate. A muffled drum metes out a slow ceremonial cadence. Near the end of the train come the six horses pulling the caisson. It is flanked, four on each side, by the members of the casket team. Trailing last is the caparisoned horse and its guide.

The band strikes up the first notes of "The Battle Hymn of the Republic." Down Garfield Drive, crossing Farragut Drive, onto McPherson Drive we progress. Jackson Circle is on our right. There, we see the Confederate Monument, a bronze female figure looking south and holding a plow stock. The statue symbolizes a sentiment that I often heard expressed by George, the biblical passage in Isaiah: "They shall beat their swords into plow shares." Around the monument lie a number of Rebel soldiers. Their tombstones, unlike the others at Arlington National Cemetery, which are rounded on top, are pointed; this is to ensure that "damnyankees would not deem to sit upon them." Next, on our left, is the Rough Riders Monument. Now the procession bears left onto Porter Drive and we can see the Nurses Memorial. Prominently just beyond it is the mast of the battleship *Maine,* the monument to the Spanish-American War. The remains of 215 martyred sailors from that ship are here, marking the first time in history that the United States exhumed and brought home for re-interment the remains of servicemen stationed abroad. Immediately beyond the mast is the unassuming grave of Audie Murphy, the most highly decorated soldier of World War II. Modestly, and so fittingly, the grave of this hero who thought of himself as just another soldier is indistinguishable from the vast majority of others at Arlington.

The band begins "The Army Song," formerly known as "The Caissons Go Rolling Along" when it was the song of the Field Artillery.

Over hill, over dale, we have hit the dusty trail,
And those caissons go rolling along.
Countermarch! Right about! Hear those wagon soldiers shout,
While those caissons go rolling along.

Down the hill we continue. Many in the gathering are walking, as if taking advantage of the magnificent fall day and appreciating all that it offers. We smell the acrid aroma of the autumn leaves.

The sky is absolutely, perfectly azure. The maples are at their peak: bright yellow, brilliant red, and rust brown. The dogwoods have already advanced beyond magenta and are a deep garnet in color. The red oaks have completely turned to various hues of crimson, but the white oaks are mottled, with some of their leaves brown, some crimson, some yellow, and some still green. Their complete transformation will come later. They are tough, like George was; they do not die easily. Off to the left, placed upon a hillside, flying high and set against that beautiful sky is a magnificent American flag. It is one of only two permanent flags in Arlington Cemetery. Both are always raised to half-mast one-half hour before the first scheduled funeral of each day and lowered one-half hour after the last one of the day is completed. Although this one soars about sixty feet above the ground, at that moment it seems to be higher than its ten-story mast could allow. Beyond the flag can be seen the amphitheater, where services are held each year on Memorial Day, usually with the president. I remember taking my boys to the service early one Memorial Day, and I recall reading of the origin of the touching ceremony. The first commemorative celebration was on 30 May 1868; Generals Grant and Garfield, both later to be presidents, attended. Set next to the amphitheater is the Tomb of the Unknowns, where the Third U.S. Infantry maintains an around-the-clock vigil. Just below that is the tomb of Joe Louis (Barrow), the heavyweight champion boxer. On up to the top is Arlington House, the former "Custis-Lee Mansion," where the other permanent flag at Arlington flies and where tourists are viewing the skyline of the nation's capital city.

In 1861, the Union Army seized Arlington House, the home of Robert E. Lee and his wife, Mary Randolph Custis, who had inherited the estate, including 1,100 acres of land, from her father, the grandson of Martha and George Washington. In 1864, the Union completed the confiscation of the property and commenced to use about 200 acres of its land surrounding the mansion for burying Civil War dead. Those lands later were augmented with others, and now there are 612 stunning acres of green hills and vales in the cemetery. Currently, the bodies of more than a quarter of a million souls are here interred. Their common bond is service to their country. The undulating grounds, bedecked with rows and rows of white marble and gray granite stones to mark the repose of the fallen heroes, provide a fitting tribute to the sacrifices made.

As the procession enters the intersection of Grant and Jesup drives, the band begins to play another solemn march; I'm told it is "Departed Comrades." Finally, the steep hill reverts to a gentle slope. As we cross Eisenhower Drive, Porter Drive becomes Bradley Drive. The trees, mostly mature willow oaks at this point, are less frequent and thousands of the hallowed stone grave markers now come into view. We continue down Bradley Drive, passing its intersection with MacArthur Drive on the right, then we advance to section sixty of the cemetery on our left. The firing party, already in position a hundred yards into the graveyard, comes to attention when the escort approaches. The captain is standing in place on the grass just off the road. He had gone before the procession to ensure that all will be prepared for the cortege. As the caisson nears his position, he raises his hand in salute. When it reaches him he drops his hand, halting the progress of the last elements in the procession. The rest of the column ahead continues down the road a hundred feet, and then executes a left turn, leaving the pavement. As they mount the curb and advance across the grass, the members of the escort assume the "port arms" position with their rifles. The band as well as both platoons move across the plain and begin to configure the appropriate formation. The mourners remain on the pavement.

The gravesite is about two hundred feet into the rows of tombstones. Ferdi is buried here; George will be laid to rest with her. The music stops. All elements of the cortege halt. The escort is now in place a hundred yards off among the tombstones. The casket team moves to the caisson and prepares to remove the casket.

The lieutenant strikes his saber downward and the band plays yet another old favorite. Upon hearing its first notes, the casket team removes the casket from the caisson. The chaplain faces about and leads the casket team as well as the mourners forward. The casket team gently lowers the casket in place on the elevator mechanism that hovers over the freshly dug grave. The music stops.

The lieutenant commands, "Order, *arms.* Parade, *rest.*"

All of the mourners assemble on the south side the grave and face the casket. As I gaze beyond the coffin and off to the northwest I can see the escort, standing 100 feet away. To the northeast, 200 feet away, is the firing party. Two soldiers stretch taut the flag that has been draped over the wooden funeral box since the beginning of the ceremony. The air is still, save for the murmur of an airplane descending to National Airport beyond the Pentagon off to the southeast. The chaplain steps to the head of the casket, gathers himself, and begins:

All that the Father giveth me shall come to me; and him that cometh to me I will in no wise cast out. . . .

He throws a bit of dirt onto the wooden box and continues:

Unto almighty God we commend the soul of our brother departed, and we commit his body to the ground; earth to earth, ashes to ashes, dust to dust.

On he goes, but I find it so hard to remain completely focused at a funeral, even one so impressive and so personal to me as this one. My eyes and my thoughts wander. I see the soldiers off to my left, standing at attention. Splendid men they are, like many here, living and dead. I have children in the service. My oldest son served in the paratrooper reserves. My second son, like me, was air force, but unlike me became a career military man. My fourth son, a West Pointer, is preparing to leave for Korea and the DMZ. He might very well have been a classmate of the lieutenant who is leading the escort there before me. My third son is preparing to go into the ministry. He and the chaplain here will become brothers in the cross. Splendid men, all of them. Yet, in their military aspect they are symbolic of all nations' failure to live peacefully with one another. After all, as soldiers, they are instruments of war. Even the chaplain suggests that failure; he represents the need for order and ritual to amend the ruins of war. George had a militarily heritage, yet he so hated the wake of war. He knew all about weapons and famous battles, but he often took the opportunity to condemn those politicians he believed to be warmongers. He had seen enough war and he was unrelenting in his criticism of those who did not understand its consequences. In time, I found myself agreeing with him.

I turn my head and I see a glorious ground cover formed by acres and acres of Kentucky bluegrass sprinkled with brilliantly colored leaves. Thousands of the sacred, white tablets pierce this green carpet in row upon row of various geometric patterns.

The chaplain steps back from the casket. The company commander replaces him, then raises his hand in salute. Off in the distance the lieutenant gives another command and drops his saber in salute. Seven soldiers raise their rifles and simultaneously fire, pause, fire again, pause, and fire a third time. Then without any other order, without a hint of a prompting, come the first few tormenting notes of "Taps" from a solo bugle. They echo across the sunlit cemetery as they have many thousands of times before. This time, however, they are for my friend, George. As I listen to the familiar, mournful tones from that solitary instrument, I recognize once again how excruciatingly painful yet beautiful and appropriate is this most touching of all bugle calls. It conjures up visions of faraway barracks at nighttime, distant trenches away off in Europe, hillsides on remote volcanic islands of the Pacific, and ancient battlefields in Spotsylvania County of old Virginia.

The band starts another hymn as the casket team folds the tautly held flag into an ever-so-neat right triangle. The men are so painfully deliberate in the maneuver that it takes them nearly two minutes to execute the moving, traditional task. The music stops. The captain drops his salute and receives the flag as the casket team leaves the gravesite; he then faces about, hands the flag to the chaplain, and renders a salute, this time holding his hand to the bill of his hat for a full three seconds. He turns and assumes his position at the head of the casket. The chaplain presents the flag to Eva and offers his sympathy. The Arlington Cemetery representative then offers condolences in the name of the chief of staff.

Eva departs the gravesite and the others begin to disappear. An elderly lady dressed in black momentarily stays behind. She straightens the flowers around the casket, selects a bright red one, and strolls away with her memento. A lone soldier, a senior sergeant, commences his solo vigil, standing erect and awaiting the interment. Off in the distance, the escort platoons, the band, and the firing party silently march off the burial grounds and on to their next solemn task. One soldier is left behind to collect twenty-one brass shells.

Epilogue

George continually and emphatically maintained that none of his family members in Russia was alive or traceable. He rebuffed me every time that I suggested that he travel to St. Petersburg and investigate. "What would I do, stare at tombstones? They're all dead or disappeared." The only survivors of the clan he could locate were the descendants of his first cousin, Alexander Alexandrovich Andreiev, and he faithfully maintained contact with this residual branch of the family tree. They lived in the United States. The family in Russia was lost forever. Or so it seemed.

Among many other benefits to mankind, the fall of the Soviet Union enabled communications that exposed the truth to this terribly wrong pronouncement. In 1997, a member of the Kisevalter clan of St. Petersburg, while working abroad, came across the name George Kisevalter in the book *Molehunt,* by David Wise. Three years later, another member of the family, Georgi Dmitrievich Kizevalter, born in Moscow in 1955 and then living in Canada, investigated the curiosity. Georgi is the son of Dmitry Sergievich Kisevalter and the grandson of Sergei Georgievich Kisevalter. Sergei was George's uncle; thus Georgi would be George's first cousin, once removed. Georgi was in the process of constructing a history of his family. Using the Internet to find addresses, he wrote letters to David Wise, George Kisevalter, and the Central Intelligence Agency. There was no reply. Again using the Internet, he found Eva's Washington, D.C., telephone number and called it repeatedly, not knowing whether or not she was George's daughter. There was no answer, as Eva had moved to London. Eventually, however, the CIA dutifully forwarded to Eva the letter Georgi had sent to them. She sent him an e-mail in

October of 2000, confirming the relationship of her father to the St. Petersburg family as well as the news that George had died three years earlier.

Eva also sent Georgi an early draft of this book, *CIA SpyMaster*. He read the draft, translated part of it into Russian, and forwarded his translation to family members residing in Moscow. Georgi then contacted me and forwarded numerous comments regarding the manuscript from various members of the family. Some of these challenged a number of George's statements. "How could a child of less than five years remember such things?" asked one. But the family was astounded at the text's description of the Andreev family chronicles. Those in St. Petersburg had long ago lost contact with Alexander Alexandrovich Andreev, assuming that he was dead or lost in a Russian diaspora.

Likewise, it was a thrill for Alexander's son, Alexis Alexander Andreiev, something like a male Anastasia, to be reunited with his clan. Now, these parties are actively making acquaintance with one another, tracing lineage, reflecting on the deaths that have occurred, and reconstructing personal histories. When I asked Georgi Kizevalter to name those living at the time of George's death, he listed a retinue that includes two first cousins, sixteen first cousins once removed, and twenty-six others whose relationships were more remote. I like to think these people would have been thrilled to meet George if I had been successful in prompting him to take the trip and look around. Russian family ties are strong, especially among those who have long suffered. The Kisevalters, like most other Russians, have experienced great hardships—even numerous tragedies—over the last century.

One of George's traits, that of a packrat, the same trait that made much of this work possible, must have been acquired from his father. George Sr., for whatever reason, retained many of the letters that he received from the homeland. I found 120 of them—unsorted, unlabeled, and piled pell-mell in an old box among his son's belongings. They are dated from 1915 to 1937. All but three are in Russian. The three in French are from George's mother's people. These reveal the sad times in France experienced by Rosa's uncle, with whom she had briefly lived before marrying George Sr.

The 117 letters from Russia proved to be the Rosetta stone of the Kisevalter family history as well as a microcosm of the Russian intelligentsia during the revolution and the two decades that followed.

The heartbreak experienced by these people, as their homeland descends into chaos and hardship, is touching. The maelstrom can be traced letter by letter with the writers' descriptions of disappearing comforts as well as through their thinly veiled sarcasm regarding their new Communist masters. Their plight, when juxtaposed with the life of the Kisevalters and Andreievs in America, even in the days of the Great Depression, is unremittingly bleak. One letter indicates that George Sr. yearned to return home as early as 1916—as soon as his primary mission in the United States was accomplished. "No, stay there; things are uncertain here," his brother replies. In the spring of 1917, with the abdication of Tsar Nicholas II, there is much hope at home that, at last, freedom for all is at hand. This, from people who were in the tsar's court and among the favored of the realm, is surprising. When the Bolsheviks steal the revolution in October of that year, there is great apprehension, even fear. Ultimately, even the hardship of the Great Depression in the rest of the world cannot compare with the pain experienced by one cousin who writes that a loved one has been declared "an enemy of the people." The letters dwindle in number as the family members die. During the purges of Stalin, other relatives are executed or disappear into oblivion. Finally, in 1937, at the height of the purges, the letters cease.

The most dramatic revelation in the letters occurs in 1928 with the very subtle (and coded) acknowledgment that the family in Russia is aware of the safe arrival of Alexander Alexandrovich Andreev (changed to Andreiev when he entered in the United States). Sadly, there is never an indication that this man ever communicates with his siblings or other relatives in Russia. His son, Alexis, advises me, "Since he had sabotaged Bolshevik installations and had fought with Gen. Nikolai Yudenich in the White Army against the Reds, he was a marked man. If the Communists recognized any association between him and a family member, nothing but trouble for that person would follow. Therefore, he never communicated with any of them."

Four pieces of mail are dated 1915. These deal mainly with financial reports and the latest family news. Interestingly, the family had a "Friendly Savings Bank" where its members could take a loan, receive some income (interest) according to their ownership shares, and buy some stocks or even land. Gen. Alexander A. Andreev was its chairman, and Vasiliy, one of George's father's older brothers, was the secretary. The relatives express envy of George Sr., George Jr., and Rosa regarding their trip to America.

Fifty-nine letters and postcards are dated 1916. Some deal with financial settlements within the family but most tell of the war. The death of Jacob, a.k.a. Fyodor K. Ezet, George's favorite uncle, a close friend of all the family, who was the adopted son of George's grandparents, is reported. These letters reveal that all of the brothers (Sergei, the oldest; Nikolai, the railroad engineer; and Vasiliy, the accountant), as well as General Andreev and others, were passionate card players. Many nights they played vint and preference (derivatives of bridge) until dawn. Also, these letters indicate that all family members were very much engaged at the stock exchange. They bought and sold shares all the time and were members of different cooperative societies. George Sr. often sent money to Russia so that Sergei could use it, without interest, if he wished. Rosa and George Jr. had funny nicknames: Zitochka and Ozya.

There are twenty-six missives from 1917. Here are extracts from one written by railroad engineer Nikolai to George Sr. It is translated by Georgi Kizevalter; notes in brackets are mine.

Petrograd,
November 14-15, 1917

. . . Now that the German spies [Bolsheviks] have seized power in Petrograd it will be hard to get out of here due to the nationwide disorder. The deposed Kerensky government had already decided to terminate passenger traffic on the railroads because of the fuel deficit starting on November 10; but they had proposed keeping the mail trains running. Now, after only one week of the Bolsheviks' "reign," the disintegration of the economy has spread much further. Last spring, on the invitation of Sergey's friend, S. I. Makhov, Sergey's family went to live in a cottage house in a village only five km from Yaransk, Vyatka Province. This move was done purely for economics. Since the February revolution, life in Petrograd has been unbearably expensive and inconvenient. There has been a shortage of necessary articles of survival, mainly milk. By summertime they realized that there was no sense in returning to a starving Petrograd, which "the benefactors of the Russian people," the leaders of the Bolsheviks, had decided to grant to Wilhelm [Kaiser Wilhelm II and the Germans]. Bronstein (a.k.a. Trotsky) has described the Kronstadt [island in the Gulf of Finland] hooligans as "the gem and pride of the Russian revolution," but this also refers to all Bolsheviks, i.e., to those benighted hordes and sly tsarist security guards led by Lenin, Trotsky, Zinoviev and other German spies. Sergey spent August with the family and then transported them to Yaransk for the winter where he had rented an acceptably furnished apartment for them. It cost about 37 rubles per month and he was able to rent a rather good grand piano for 10 rubles a month. It looks as if life there is really much cheaper than in Petrograd. Moreover, the necessities of life, i.e., foodstuffs, are available there.

Now I will write about my job. I am still in charge of the technical office. After the revolution I was given a bonus of 105 rubles to my salary under the decision of the Central Council of head employees in the Petrograd factories. So, now I receive 405 rubles [a month]. If we take into account that the present value of a ruble, in terms of purchasing power, equals approximately one former ten-kopeck coin, I now have an absolutely beggarly salary. Currently, even an incompetent worker here makes that much. Fortunately, my rent has increased by only 10%: I pay 75.50 rubles per month, which includes a yard keeper but no firewood.

Before the [February] revolution, things at the factory were going very well. Then conditions started to decline. As the workers began to take control of the factory, they gave themselves many increases in pay and raised the prices of their products. In May they refused to be paid by their output, demanding daily wages. It happened not only at our plant, but also at all factories in Petrograd and perhaps elsewhere. Their demand was satisfied, but their productivity immediately fell by fifty percent. During the month of June the factory lost a half-million rubles. The board declared that on August 1 new, lower, rates would be introduced. If they were not acceptable to the workers, the factory would be closed. The workers did not accept the new rates, and the board did not carry out their threat. This process has been repeated every half-month up until now.

Today, the news about the victory of Bolshevik armies over the Cossacks near Gatchina, and the flight of Kerensky, who led the Cossacks, has resulted in our factory workers declaring that the factory is now socialized. Mr. Gunst abdicated his managerial powers even before the Bolsheviks' mutiny. He did so partly because of the statements made by irresponsible workers against him. Once he was nearly taken out from the smithy on a wheelbarrow. On the other hand, Gunst has categorically refused to put into practice the Board's requirement to accept the rates, since he himself considers these rates insufficient.

What "socialization" at our factory will consist in, I don't yet know. But, it is possible to say that if the workers took the factory in hand and remunerated themselves from the sums netted over one month—taking into consideration the present tempo of work, the cost of materials and hydro energy—they would not receive even 20% of those crazy earnings to which they have become accustomed. Smart workers are already anticipating this, and one may hear it more and more often said that many are going to leave for villages in good time, now that their bootlegs are crammed with money. They also say that already now there is enough tension among the workers; what will transpire with "socialization" is foreboding. What status the white-collar employees will get—I have no idea. The workers will probably require some of the white collars to leave. No good should be expected, either for business, or for the white collars, or for the workers.

However, not all workers equally understand this "socialization." At the state-owned Obukhovsky factory, for example, the workers are now busy with making the cost of the factory public. They consider themselves within their rights to refuse work at the plant in the event that the government gives them the present value of the factory. When they receive this amount, they—just imagine!—will share it and set off for their homes. This is the poverty of ideas that ignorant people can reach! And such "socialists," indeed! They provide support to the leaders who were at one time our intelligentsia, and who now are selling our Fatherland to Germans.

And it goes from bad to worse. Anarchy has already reigned in Russia for a long time. But the real horrors have just begun. What awaits us tomorrow, whether we die from famine, or whether some "socialists" finish us off or cripple us, we don't know.

I think now it is already clear to you why I began this letter expressing joy concerning your stay far from here during these difficult days. And imagine that now I feel almost no worry while thinking of the violence and deprivations that are still awaiting us. You cannot picture yourself how quickly [after the February revolution] the joyful mood, which had embraced all Russian people who love their Fatherland, gave way to doubt in the expediency of the Government's actions under the direction of self-appointed councils. Then came fear for the future and, at last, full despair. I personally went through this gradation of feelings in the first two months after the revolution. Then apathy set in, which I seem now not to be able to rid myself of until I die. At the beginning of May I was again convinced that all the recent developments lead Russia to destruction; all was done to the benefit of Germans. It was done so diligently, though the masses did it unconsciously, that a whole regiment of Wilhelms could not have concocted anything better. But enough of that.

Now, my dear sweethearts, I want to give you friendly advice not to speed up your return to Russia until order sets in here. I believe that sometime, maybe in five or ten years, it will come. Certainly you, Georgy, will have to find a means of subsistence in America; but you are not the kind of person to fail. If not in America, settle down somewhere in Europe, in France, for example. But, really, it's not worth your while coming back to Russia. Now on every corner you hear that it is a shame to be Russian. Yesterday's newspapers reported that Shingarev is going to become an English citizen. [Shingarev was the leader of the Constitutional Democrats and a member of the provisional government in 1917. He was arrested in November for anti-Soviet activities and murdered by sailors in a Petrograd hospital in January 1918.] . . .

I kiss and embrace warmly you and Rosa,

Your brother, Nikolai

Then there is an inexplicable absence of letters during the ten-year period from 1918 until 1927. When the letters resume in 1927, their character and tone do not suggest that a break in the exchange of letters had occurred.

Five letters are dated 1927. Here is one from Rosa's father in France, translated by Eleanor J. Riles, Ph.D.

Semur en Brionnais
February 21, 1927

My Dear Daughter and my dear Georgi,

I received your letter which gave me great pleasure and especially the contents of 120 francs. I thank you with all my heart. I would like to know if you are in good health. Please write to me about this. For me, my health is well enough, but my legs give me trouble with walking. I don't go too far for fear that I won't be able to return. That's why I still go gently to St. Foi, a small village 3 kilometers away. I go and have a drink at St. Foi and I come back. It is always the same life, but here everything is out of price and I don't dare buy anything except a box of matches of 5 centimes that they sell for 40 centimes and all the merchandise is the same. Money brings practically nothing. Let's hope that changes. It has been a long time since I went to Marcigny, because of my legs. Let's hope that that will come back. I believe that my little Georgi is growing big now.

All the best to you from your father who loves you with all his heart.

Charles Ernest Grillet

The one sent in December observes that no letters from George Sr. or Rosa have been received for a period of seven months. The death of Boris Andreev, son of Gen. Alexander Andreev and first cousin of George, is reported. *He died in a lunatic asylum . . . didn't recognize anyone.* Oddly, there was never any previous indication that he was ill. Vasiliy writes Rosa about other Andreev children: "Lena left in September for Siberia, works there as teacher. Raya has entered the Geography department of the University; she lives in a hostel and receives a stipend. Misha studies at a vocational school in a metal-working plant; there the students study for four hours and work for four hours each day. Ksenia lives and studies in a boarding school. Julia works temporarily as a typist at my office. Natasha works at a plant too; but I haven't seen her since Boris's funeral." Vasily reflects on the news from America that *Rosita works at a fashion store/boutique, as George Sr.'s salary is not enough for the family, and George Jr. tries to earn his own money, too, and he's doing very well.* He also discusses the family's observation that Rosita has purchased a Ford automobile—"Oh, what a brave and energetic woman you are!" Poignantly, he notes, "Leningrad is decorated to celebrate the 10th anniversary of the Revolution."

Seven pieces of correspondence have a 1928 date. The last Domnins in Luga, Russia, acknowledge financial assistance from George Sr. In the letter of July 8, Vasiliy congratulates George Sr. on an addition to his family: "Wish the newborn to get strong and make a nice career." The letter is recognizing, in its own personally coded way, that the family is aware that Alexander has arrived in the States and that George Sr. will look after his welfare. Another letter mentions the new living-accommodations norm in the USSR since October: ten square meters per person. Earlier, the norm had been fourteen square meters per person. Also Sergei spreads the news that Maria, his spouse, and two of their kids had visited Maria's sisters in Riga, Latvia, and Arosa, Switzerland.

Three letters bear a 1929 date. They mention additional financial assistance to the Domnins from George Sr. They also tell of diseases that are prevalent in the new Communist nation and the introduction of a continuous working week for the USSR—without breaks on Sunday. There will be a total of five public holidays a year.

Only two letters are from 1930. "Vasiliy has visited Sergei's family in Moscow. Again, no letters have been received from George Sr. for seven months. An economic 'boom' in Russia: everyone gets a job very quickly."

Three letters from 1931 are found: one from Frida Demikeli in Arosa, Switzerland, to George Sr.; another from Sergei to Elsa Philipp in Riga, Latvia; and the last from Elsa to George Sr. They discuss the world crisis, life in Moscow, Riga, Arosa, and Leningrad. "Problems are everywhere." Elsa exclaims: "This damn war made us all disperse and suffer!"

Four letters were received in 1933. Evidently, there had been a two-year-long break in the communication. Two letters were from Vasiliy, one from Sergei, and one from Frida in Arosa, Switzerland. Frida: "Poor, poor guys in Russia—it's so hard for them to live there at old age!" The others report, "The powers in Leningrad and Moscow allow the West kin to provide help for the Russian part of the family. Vasiliy and Nikolai are seriously ill. Vasiliy lives in a communal apartment with seventeen other people, having one room for his family. Dmitry, Sergei's son, is still forbidden to enter the Institute of Geology, being a son of a civil servant and not a Komsomol member."

Frida in Arosa sends a postcard in 1934. It reports the death of Vasiliy in Moscow. No other correspondence is evidenced that year.

In 1935, one letter from Sergei to Elsa in Riga is forwarded to George Sr. It reports that Sergei is ill and that a new Soviet language is recognized, one mixing ostentatious praise to the new regime with Russian.

A solo letter from Frida in Arosa is sent in 1936. Swiss life and the spouses' intent to visit the USSR in the summer are discussed.

The farewell letter of Sergei comes in 1937. Foreseeing his own end in the near future, he passes the title of family elder to George Sr. The death of Elena, Vasiliy's widow, in 1936 is noted. The latest news from Moscow and Leningrad is also reported. "So far, everyone was doing well."

Reflections on these letters give rise to several conclusions. It is obvious that the family was decidedly anti-Communist. Moreover, the hardships faced by those in the Soviet Union, and surreptitiously related to their American kindred, probably had an effect upon George. From my observation, George was as anti-Communist as any rational person could be. In addition, it is clear that the family was close, loving, and loyal to one another—traits that no doubt did a lot to facilitate their survival through wars, revolutions, anarchy, and the attendant deprivations of these scourges. George too had these same traits of devotion, love, and loyalty to his family. These tendencies perhaps troubled him in a way that is hauntingly ironic. Remembering his oft-stated reluctance to attempt to search for his Russian kin (*What would I do, stare at tombstones?*), I must conclude that George made a painful decision for their benefit. Because of his association with the Central Intelligence Agency, like his first cousin, Alexander A. Andreiev, George never sought contact with his Russian kin, in the belief that harm would come to them if he did—even after the fall of the Soviet Union.

Notes

Chapter 1

1. In a 5 June 1999 letter to the author, John Lavine describes the actual events leading up to the gaffe. "The miniature radio transmitter that I planned to use operated on a very narrow band of the Ultra-High Frequency (UHF) range. As I recall, we were looking at something between ninety and ninety-five MHz for this particular transmitter. I could set it to transmit at any frequency within this band. We were not going to transmit very far in distance, so the wattage was set very low. I specifically recall asking the local technician, my counterpart, whether there was anyone occupying this band segment in the area: that is, the police, the transit authority, or anyone else eligible to use this frequency—public or private. He said *no.* He forgot that the public state TV was using this band portion for the transmission of the voice signal of their TV broadcast. The particular MHz that I selected ended right upon the center frequency of the public TV's sound channel."

2. The term requirements refers to the set of intelligence information objectives agreed upon by analysts and other customers of the CIA, as well as other intelligence organizations, and requested of collectors. They can be very broad and ill defined or they can be precisely specified. The degree of specificity typically relates to how much is already known about a particular subject.

Chapter 2

1. *A Life for the Tsar* was first presented in St. Petersburg in 1836. Glinka was driven to compose something "that was genuinely Russian and that would be comprehensible to every Russian."

2. George William Norris (1861-1944) served in the U.S. Senate from 1912 until 1942. The first dam of the TVA system was named Norris Dam in his honor. His autobiography, Fighting Liberal, was published posthumously in 1945.

Chapter 3

1. The Japanese captured Kiska and Attu in June of 1942 and held them until August of 1943.

2. Commissioned in the spring of 1942 under Lt. Comdr. Howard I. Gilmore, the *Growler* made its first patrol in late June from Dutch Harbor. On July 5, she torpedoed three Japanese destroyers, sinking one and severely damaging the other two. During the period between the last week of August and the first week of September that year, the boat sank four freighters off Taiwan. She sank one ship in the Solomon Islands near Guadalcanal in January of 1943. In February, while making a surface attack on a Japanese gunboat, the gunboat turned to ram the *Growler*. Gilmore ordered his boat to "come about" in an effort to ram the gunboat; then, after receiving heavy machine-gun fire and sustaining bullet wounds, Gilmore ordered the boat submerged without delay, leaving himself in the conning tower. He was posthumously awarded the Medal of Honor for this brave, unselfish act. See Lincoln P. Paine, *Ships of the World* (Boston: Houghton Mifflin Co., 1997).

3. After more than a year of active planning, the Alaska Siberian Route, ALSIB, struggled its way into existence on 6 October 1942, when ten A-20 bomber aircraft crossed the Bering Strait into Siberia. One of the planes returned to Nome because of a problem and one of the aircraft was forced to land in Siberia. Eight of the planes eventually reached Krasnoyarsk, the ALSIB terminus 3,500 miles over tundra, mountains, and virgin forest from Fairbanks. The flights of aircraft continued until 2 September 1945. See Otis E. Hays, Jr., *The Alaska-Siberia Connection* (College Station: Texas A&M University Press, 1996).

4. In July of 1940 Brigadier General Buckner was appointed commander of U.S. troops in Alaska. He made major general in 1941 and was promoted to lieutenant general in 1943. Later in 1943, troops under his command drove off the Japanese forces that had gained a foothold in the Aleutians. At Attu, with no evacuation feasible or planned, the Japanese garrison of about 2,350 soldiers fought to the bitter end, as they would in every forthcoming Pacific encounter. In the end, only 29 of them survived. In June of 1944 General Buckner was given command of the Tenth Army in the South Pacific. In April of 1945, four army and four marine divisions under his command landed in Okinawa. Fighting continued until 21 June, at which time the Americans secured the island. Tragically, with victory at hand, Buckner had fallen on 18 June after having received a mortal wound from a piece of stray shrapnel.

5. The Air Cobra (P-39) was replaced by the King Cobra (P-63) in February of 1944. Hays, *The Alaska-Siberia Connection*, 110.

6. The actual number accepted by the Soviets in Fairbanks, Alaska, and delivered across the ALSIB route was 7,924. Within that number were 1 C-46 and 707 C-47 Transports, 1,363 A-20 Light Bombers, 733 B-25 Medium Bombers, 54 AT6-F Trainers, 2,618 P-39 Fighters, 48 P-40 Fighters, 3 P-47 Fighters, and 2,397 P-63 Fighters. Hays, *The Alaska-Siberia Connection*. Others were also taken in over a more polar route into Murmansk and some through Iran. The aggregate number is on the order of 15,000.

Later versions of the measure of the program and its effect on the Soviet war effort, published in Soviet Newspeak, present different impressions. The official Soviet Union assessment of the effect of lend-lease was that it amounted to about 4 percent of the materials that they themselves produced. Their propaganda maintained that this was hardly enough to play a decisive role in the outcome of the conflict. Their own report of the numbers involved, however, belies that assessment. They acknowledge the receipt of 18,000 aircraft, 11,000 tanks, and 400,000 cars and trucks. Moreover, they ignore the fact that the U.S. was engaged in a full-scale war with Japan, which the Soviets were not, when these shipments were accomplished. See William J. Spahr, *Zhukov: The Rise and Fall of a Great Captain* (Novato, Calif.: Presidio Press, 1993), 41.

7. The Soviet Union lost 27 million dead and 25 million were left homeless. Destroyed were 1,710 cities, 70,000 villages, 32,000 factories, 98,000 collective farms, 1,878 state farms, and 2,890 agriculture

equipment parks. *World War II Through Russian Eyes: Time Line of the War on the Russian Front* (Traveling Exhibit of the Central Military Museum and Archives in Moscow, 1998-99).

8. Michael Gavrisheff, like George, also came from a distinguished Russian family. His great-grandfather, Login O. Gavrishev, was a rear admiral in the tsar's navy and the last Russian lieutenant governor of Alaska until it was sold to the U.S. in 1867. Boris Gavrisheff, Michael's father, also was a highly decorated tsarist naval officer until the Bolshevik revolution. Michael was born in St. Petersburg in 1917. The family left the Soviet Union in 1918 and eventually reached the U.S. in 1932. Michael grew up in Texas, attended Texas A & M, and learned surveying and related civil-engineering disciplines from his father. Also like George, Michael had fluency in more than one language. He could translate between Russian, Spanish, and English. Gavrisheff died on 18 May 1999. Michael Gavrisheff, interview by author, Silver Spring, Md., 16 April 1999.

9. Chavchavadze denies this bit of hyperbole (or, perhaps, mass confusion) on the part of George. There are three people in question: (1) Grand Duchess Xenia, who was the sister of Tsar Nicholas II; (2) David's mother's sister, who also was named Xenia; and (3) the duchess of Kent, who was born Princess Marina of Greece and who actually lived in Kensington Palace. He explains that his mother was Princess Nina, born in St. Petersburg, the daughter of Grand Duke George Mikhailavich of Russia and Princess Marie of Greece, not the grand duchess; and that she was a favorite cousin of the duchess of Kent as well as a cousin of Tsar Nicholas II. However, neither his mother nor Grand Duchess Xenia, sister of Tsar Nicholas II, had ever set foot in Buckingham Palace or married an Englishman. Chavchavadze himself did visit the duchess of Kent in Kensington Palace, but he never spent the night there.

10. David Chavchavadze, interview by author, Washington, D.C., 20 May 1998.

11. Odessa was under occupation by German and Romanian troops for four years.

12. Maj. Gen. Edwin Luther Sibert was a close associate of Allen Dulles, who then was the chief of the Office of Strategic Services (O.S.S.).

13. The Germans had captured a number of Soviet military intelligence officers (GRU), whose mission was to traverse Germany and then penetrate the American and British lines in order to investigate

the supposed plans of Eisenhower and Montgomery to prepare an attack on the USSR. Because of this, Gehlen was convinced that after the defeat of Germany there was to be a war between the U.S. and the USSR. As the war in Germany was coming to an end, he and two of his senior associates moved extensive files, records, and German plans to a remote location in the Bavarian Alps. There they dug deep holes into the mountainside to secure their cache and waited for the right opportunity to negotiate a defection to the U.S. rather than be taken captive by the Soviets. Gehlen and three of his chosen officers were flown out of Germany on 22 August 1945, all disguised as U.S. Army officers, and taken to Fort Hunt. See E. H. Cookridge, *Gehlen: Spy of the Century* (New York: Random House, 1972), 110, 115, 125.

14. *Bundesnachrichtendienst.*

Chapter 4

1. Carotene is a yellow-orange- to red-colored hydrocarbon occurring in many plants that converts to vitamin A in the animal liver.

2. Mrs. Wayne Allen, letter to author, 19 October 1999.

3. See Peer de Silva, *Sub Rosa: The CIA and the Uses of Intelligence* (New York: New York Times Books, 1978), 57. Peer de Silva was the CIA mission chief in Saigon when the U.S. Embassy was bombed. He suffered considerably from wounds inflicted and eventually, according to George, succumbed to them.

4. Lt. Comdr. Edward Dean Spruance was himself awarded the Silver Star during World War II. See *Current Biography* (Bronx, N.Y.: H. W. Wilson Co., 1944).

5. Rositzke was a former English teacher and later an author of books on the CIA, the KGB, and the Soviet Union.

6. See David Wise's book, *Molehunt* (New York: Random House, 1992), 220-24, for interesting accounts about Snow, his wife, Nata, and Nata's stepfather, Andy Yankovsky.

7. "Pork Chop Hill" (so called for its shape) was officially named Hill 255, for its elevation in yards. It is located some forty-five miles to the north-northeast of Seoul. It lies within a region defined by the three legs of a triangle drawn between the locations of Pyongyang, Chorwon, and Kumhwa, where extensive fighting occurred at places named Pork Chop Hill, White Horse, T-Bone, Spud, Alligator Jaws,

Old Baldy, Arsenal, and Erie. In November of 1952 Pork Chop Hill was held by the Thailand Battalion attached to the U.S. Army Second Infantry Division and came under heavy attack by Chinese Communist Forces. The hill was fought over many times up until the end of the war in July of 1953. Today, part of it lies in North Korea and part of it is in the Demilitarized Zone.

Chapter 5

1. Andrei A. Vlasov commanded the Thirty-seventh Army of the USSR during the defense of Kiev in 1941, the Twentieth Army in the defense of Moscow, and the Second Shock Army in 1942. At that time he was captured by the Germans and eventually turned against Stalin. He commanded the Russian Liberation Army, commonly know as the Vlasov Army under German command, in its futile attempt to combat Bolshevism in 1944 and 1945. Vlasov was captured by the Soviet Army in May of 1945 and hanged on 2 August 1946.

2. George also played chess very well. In an 11 March 1998 interview in Great Falls, Va., with Joe Skura, Joe stated, "Everyone knew that George was a champion chess competitor and that he won prizes in New York at a young age. Bill Hood, who was the chief of operations in Vienna, thought of himself as being a good player, Bill continually challenged George to matches and George continually defeated him. George often joked, 'Bill tried to get me drunk so that he could beat me; but I could beat him even though I was drunk.' George was a character."

3. George received a per diem for more than the first six months of his stay in Vienna. This shocked headquarters management when they learned of it in late 1954.

4. Under cover, using a fictitious name, identification, etc.

5. Some publications have reported that George and Popov engaged in "drinking bouts" at these meetings. In an interview of 7 May 1999 in Great Falls, Va., Ted Poling confirmed to the author that this never happened. "The two of them did, however, have Russian capacities for drink," he said.

6. The amount was approximately two hundred U.S. dollars per month. George meticulously entered the sums into an escrow account register, which he showed to Popov at each meeting. The

record was communicated to headquarters and obligated in the records of the Finance Department. Poling, interview.

7. The GRU was the Chief Intelligence Directorate for Military Intelligence, roughly equivalent to the U.S. Defense Intelligence Agency. The KGB was the Committee of State Security, the principal intelligence organization and apparatus of the state. It included elements of counterintelligence activities, secret police activities, and foreign intelligence.

8. The school was named for the well-known World War I-era Red Army commander Mikhail Vasilyevich Frunze.

Chapter 6

1. A Quasi-Personal car was one owned by the Intelligence Services but registered in an individual's name and used both for personal and operational activities.

2. George loved his bathrobes. During the last years of his life he spent most of his days in them, rarely dressing.

3. Peter Sergeyevich Deriabin was born in the Lokot area of Siberia in 1921. He was well educated and bright. He had arrived in Vienna in September of 1953. His assignment was that of KGB Chief of the Soviet Colony (Sovietskaya Koloniya), replacing the Soviet consul who had been recalled during a shakeup the previous June. He was responsible for assuring the security and political reliability of Soviet officials and other citizens abroad in Austria.

4. In William Hood's *Mole* (McLean, Va.: Brassey's, 1993), 119, Deriabin recognizes Ted as his counterpart during this initial interview. (Ted is Captain Olson in *Mole,* but he actually used Captain Peterson in Vienna.) In fact, Deriabin knew nothing of Ted Poling's role in Vienna until told by others later, after he had become an asset of the CIA. Poling, interview.

5. Poling, interview.

6. George's cover name for the Popov operation was Herr Grossman.

7. Dead drops are locations where secretive transfers of clandestine materials can be accomplished. Ideally, they should be located in public facilities, where the participants in the transfer can reasonably be expected to frequent, yet they should be hidden spots that are not likely to be accidentally discovered by others and will not

be vulnerable to the vagaries of weather. Typically, they are loose bricks in a wall, a small area behind a radiator in a public but remote hallway, etc. The idea is for one participant to leave an item in the location and for the other to retrieve it. Dead drops should rarely be used more than once. Brush contacts are exchanges of materials between two individuals—"live."

Chapter 7

1. Yuri Nosenko, interview by author, 10 May 1998.

2. Schwerin was one of five major GRU "intelligence points." Schwerin was number 1; Berlin was number 5, etc. Poling, interview.

3. The CIA code name for the gentleman was Cabrilla 19.

4. William King Harvey was one of the most colorful characters in the history of the CIA. Among Harvey's numerous rollicking adventures was his assignment as the CIA's "point man" for the Kennedy attempts to assassinate Fidel Castro. See David C. Martin's *Wilderness of Mirrors* (New York: Harper & Row, 1980), 219. The details of this episode are from an interview with Ted Poling and others.

5. In an interview with the author in April 1998 in Washington, D.C., Chavchavadze proposed, "The Agency would have been quite foolish to let George go because of some silly marriage rule. George was the only guy with whom Popov would talk."

Chapter 8

1. Some in the Soviet Union were aware of the tunnel operation, having been tipped off by George Blake, a Soviet mole placed high in the hierarchy of the British SIS. The USSR did not reveal this awareness for fear that the U.S. and U.K. would then deduce that Blake had informed the Soviets and thus was a spy. Blake was valuable to the USSR. The tunnel operation would not harm them as much as the loss of Blake. As a consequence, the Soviets did not inform many of their own people of the tunnel, and some valuable intelligence information was passed on tunnel traffic and intercepted by the CIA and SIS.

2. Joe Skura experienced the close security of the tunnel: "When the tunnel ceased operations in 1956 there was no apparent change in our activity. We kept right on going. I did not even know that there was a tunnel. The information was so closely held, many of our people did not know of the tunnel nor did we know when it ceased operation. My wife worked for Bill Harvey as his secretary. She never breathed a word about it to me. She still doesn't. I ask her occasionally what she remembers about the tunnel. She says nothing. We both worked in the same building in different sections." Interview.

3. June describes working with George: "I had never met George until I arrived there in Berlin. For some reason, he took to calling me his *dushka*, which is Russian for 'little soul.' There was a special room, where only the two of us were allowed. This room was shielded such that no sounds or emissions of electrical impulses within it could emanate out. Here was total privacy. We worked in this room, almost around the clock, transcribing and copying from the Popov tapes as well as editing our take. George was completely absorbed in his work, so much so, that, at the end of the year, when we went to a staff Christmas party and he tried to introduce me to his friends, he couldn't remember my name. This, after being locked up together, just the two of us, since May. He could remember the first names, the patronymics, the last names, and the birthdays of all of the Soviet officers, but he couldn't remember my name." Interview by author, McLean, Va., 2 December 1997.

4. The fact that Popov was transferred to Schwerin in the GDR was actually intercepted in tunnel traffic, but the CIA did not recognize this until after Popov's January meeting with the British officer.

5. Skura, interview.

6. George himself had a reputation as having a propensity to talk. He liked to share his experiences with his buddies at the CIA. Such an action, though not particularly serious, nevertheless was frowned upon in the Agency. On at least one occasion, George's tendency was the subject of discussion by his superiors. In a conference with top management, it was suggested to Bill Harvey that George just had to be muzzled. Bill contemplated the suggestion, then asked the director, "What do you want? You cannot have it both ways. Do you want a case officer who can handle this man, Popov, or do you want somebody who will never talk about it?" They all agreed that George was unique and that they couldn't get everything rolled into one person. So they let things go as they were. Poling, interview.

7. During the Second World War, Heinz Paul Felfe, a Nazi in the SS, was in charge of a unit in Switzerland targeted against Allen Dulles and the O.S.S. After the war he was imprisoned in Canada until 1946. Upon his release, Hans Clemens, a friend and former SS captain, recruited Felfe to work for the KGB. Clemens got a job with the BND, the West German Intelligence organization, and then recommended that Felfe also be hired. In November of 1951 Felfe received a job with the BND and was assigned to the Pullach Headquarters. With leads supplied by the KGB, Felfe was able to "successfully deliver" a number of East German agents to the BND and thereby gain the confidence of Reinhard Gehlen, the BND chief, and others. He rose to the rank of Higher Government Counselor, was awarded a silver plaque for loyal service, and gained the position of head of the Counter-espionage Department vis-à-vis the USSR. He was discovered to be KGB in November of 1961 and given a fourteen-year jail sentence. He was released in 1969 in exchange for twenty-one incarcerated East Germans. See Cookridge, *Gehlen*, 321, and Harry Rositzke, The KGB: The Eyes of Russia (New York: Doubleday, 1981), 153.

8. Harold ("Kim") Philby was a notorious double agent who infiltrated the British SIS and rose to a powerful position within its ranks. Many believed that he would become the chief of the SIS. He was a Communist from his college days at Cambridge during the early 1930s and later became a Soviet agent. He did great harm to the Western nations and finally escaped to Moscow in 1963. See Cookridge, *The Third Man: The Truth About "Kim" Philby* (London: Arthur Barker Ltd., 1968).

Chapter 9

1. The foregoing was constructed from conversations with numerous people including George, Yuri Nosenko, Leonard McCoy, and others who wish not to be mentioned. It was further authenticated with documents provided to the author by the CIA. These included excerpts from declassified articles entitled, "The Popov Case," dated 22 September 1980, and "Popov: The Conformist Who Failed," undated. For additional descriptions of the steps in the ultimate apprehension of Popov, see *Battleground Berlin* (New Haven: Yale University Press, 1997), 279. The authors, David E. Murphy (former

chief of Berlin Base), Sergei A. Kondrashev (retired lieutenant general of the KGB and former head of its German Department), and George Bailey (reporter and former director of Radio Liberty), cite newly provided KGB source material.

Chapter 10

1. The Agency maintained a file of known or suspected espionage-connected individuals who could be threats to the U.S. In this file were all pertinent data. If anyone applied for a visa to enter the U.S., his name and photo on the application could be compared with the file data. Moreover, if one applied for a visa to an allied country, through a program of mutual cooperation, the CIA could also "do traces."

2. A prison town about 150 miles from Moscow.

3. See Sean Bourke, *The Springing of George Blake* (New York: Viking, 1970). In April 1961, the British also had in their custody Gordon Lonsdale, a.k.a. Konon T. Molody, the Soviet illegal who had been arrested earlier that year and was serving a twenty-five-year sentence for espionage. He had been working with the Americans Morris and Lorna Cohen as well as two British agents who had furnished Lonsdale with classified information they had stolen. The British asked George if he might assist in the interrogation of Molody. George did so but to no avail. He could not seem to make any headway with the agent, who insisted to George that everything had to be passed through his attorney.

Chapter 11

1. Many of the technical terms were not in a standard Russian dictionary. Since George's Russian education had been pre-Revolution, prior to the advent of common usage of these terms, there was a gap in the team's understanding of their true meanings. The most useful device found for interpreting some of the technical terms turned out to be a Dutch dictionary. This was because Peter the Great had traveled to Holland to learn about shipbuilding and brought back the roots of many of these words.

2. Later, the case officers had the dubious pleasure—with

tremendous trepidation, through a dentist in London—of having his false teeth replaced. Getting a cleared dentist and Penkovsky's fussiness about his teeth were stories in themselves. But since his teeth had been knocked out of his mouth by this combat action with the Nazis, the team felt justified in the action.

3. In 1943 there were 6.4 million men in arms in the Soviet Union. By 1958 this number had been reduced to 3.6 million. See Spahr, 220.

4. The Soviet Union, at that time, divided all of its offensive weapons into two designations: tactical and strategic. All artillery and missiles with ranges up to 1,000 kilometers were tactical; those whose ranges were in excess of that number were strategic.

5. Feliks Edmundovich Dzerzhinskiy was the founder of the Cheka, the first secret police of the Soviet Union and the predecessor of the KGB.

6. Since 1917, there has been a facility in Dayton, Ohio (once McCook Field, now Wright-Patterson, AFB) for the purpose of analyzing foreign aviation, scientific, and intelligence information. In 1951 the activities focusing on Soviet technology were incorporated as the Air Technical Intelligence Center (ATIC). In 1961, the air force added the National Air Intelligence Center (NAIC). Today's emphasis is on the evaluation of worldwide aerospace systems and the production of "tailored" customer-specific products.

7. A formal attestation, or testimonial to the pedigree of an individual, usually in the form of a certificate.

Chapter 12

1. Marshal Georgi Konstantinovich Zhukov was the quintessential Russian hero. He was associated with the successful defenses of Moscow and Leningrad as well as the victories at Stalingrad, Kharkov, and the Ukraine. He was also a dedicated Communist. His preeminence fostered great envy in Stalin, Khrushchev, and others, and he was therefore often subject to their vindictiveness. These tyrants denigrated him publicly only at the peril of enmity from the populace. To relegate Marshal Zhukov to the ranks of the retired, Khrushchev had to have great confidence in his own standing in the Party and with the people.

2. This information later appeared in various publications such

as *The Penkovsky Papers* (New York: Doubleday, 1965). It was principally the product of the meetings between Penkovsky and the case officers. Peter Deriabin is listed as the translator; but the translations were actually prepared by George and many other agency personnel. Leonard McCoy, interview by author, Great Falls, Va., 14 May 1999.

3. Gen. Charles P. Cabell, USAF, was the deputy to the director of Central Intelligence (DCI) during the 1950s and 1960s.

4. Crabbe was especially interested in the zinc anodes of the vessel. These attachments are special alloy metals placed along the bottom of the hulls and especially near propellers of high-speed cruisers, destroyers, etc., which chemically oxidize in order to reduce the tendency of the seawater near the hull and propellers to erode the metal of those components. Since seawater becomes ionized, it accelerates the deterioration of metals in those regions, and in particular, it tends to cause the propellers to become pitted. By having the zinc alloy in those regions, it, instead of the hull and propellers, becomes pitted. This is due to the higher preference of zinc over steel or bronze in the electrochemical reaction. Thus, with these attachments, one can have more durable naval vessels than otherwise.

Chapter 13

1. Etoile is the name given to the Arc de Triomphe and the place it stands because all of the streets go out from it like spokes of a wheel, or beams of light from a star (*étoile*).

2. This was the site of an old tile factory of Paris. When the Court assigned its ownership to the State, and it was made into the gardens, it became the Tuileries (the tile factories).

3. McCoy, interview.

Chapter 14

1. The Chisholms subsequently were replaced with Gervaise ("Gerry") Cowell and his wife, Pamela. Mike Stokes, letter to author, 2 February 2004.

2. Making him *persona non grata.*

3. Altogether ten American and British diplomats were declared *personae non gratae* and asked to leave the USSR at once. Interestingly, Paul Garbler, the CIA chief, was not one of those because his status was not detected, or at least not acknowledged, by the Soviets. This enabled him to remain on for a period of three years.

4. Capt. Nikolai Fedorovich Artamonov became invaluable to the West. He was murdered by the KGB in Vienna in 1975. See Henry Hurt, *SHADRIN: The Spy Who Never Came Back* (New York: Berkley Books, 1983).

Chapter 15

1. See Jerrold L. Schecter and Peter S. Deriabin, *The Spy Who Saved the World* (McLean, Va.: Brassey's, 1992), 290.

2. Harold Shergold, interview by author, Richmond, England, 7 November 1998.

3. Harold Shergold died on Christmas Day 2000. A somewhat reclusive man, and a widower without any close surviving members of his family who could be helpful, he died in the care of dear friends who had known him since his days with the SIS.

4. This course of action actually was suggested to George by the author. The logs, termed "waves," show the names of White House visitors and their times of entry and departure, along with who cleared them with the Secret Service.

5. Rupert Allason confirmed to the author the collapse of the lawsuit against him and his publishers in the face of evidence, including George's deposition, prior to Wynne's death.

Chapter 16

1. Circassia is in the northwestern Caucasus Mountains bordering the northeast coast of the Black Sea. Its population is concentrated in the quasi-independent Republic of Adygea. The history of its people, referred to as Circassians as well as Cherkess, extends back into the fifth to fourth century B.C. The Circassians were converted to Christianity in the thirteenth century but they became ardent Muslims in the seventeenth century. In the eighteenth century, the Russians, under Tsar Peter the Great and later Empress Catherine I,

engaged in military campaigns designed to control the Circassian clans. Intense fighting continued with these warlike people (also known for their beautiful women), who did not wish to compromise their Muslim persuasion. In 1829 Russia annexed the region, but because of the Circassians' stubborn resistance to the Russian occupation, it was 1864 before peace could be established. At that point large numbers of the population left for Turkey and other Middle Eastern countries.

2. Anatolia is the region of Turkey on the Asia Minor Peninsula.

3. Much of the Turkish historical background was suggested by Malia Natirbov in a personal interview on 16 June 1999 in McLean, Va. Malia Natirbov died in January 2002 at the age of ninety-two. He had been three months older than George.

Chapter 17

1. Pullach is about eight miles from Munich. It was built in 1938 as a housing facility for SS officers and their families. The entire community of houses, theaters, flower gardens, schools, and parks is hidden from view by severe topography augmented with tall walls. When the BND assumed occupation of the facility, it went under cover as a German corporation involved in scientific research. The story followed that the patents had to be protected from foreigners. The neighboring Bavarians responded patriotically for some time to this ruse. See Cookridge, *Gehlen*, 158.

2. By law, the director of the CIA is also the director of Central Intelligence (DCI) for the entire intelligence community. As such, he coordinates the flow of intelligence to the president. As deputy director for the intelligence community, General Wilson was serving as the chief of the staff that coordinates with all of the intelligence organizations for the DCI.

Chapter 18

1. Some of these comments were taken from an interview with Paul Garbler on 6 April 1998 in Tucson, Ariz., and some were provided by Yuri Nosenko. Various sources identify one substance as the chemical NPPD, nitrophenolpentadienal, luminol. The compound

is detected by "black light" devices. NPPD absorbs ultraviolet light waves and converts that energy into light in visible wavelengths. Therefore, shining an ultraviolet light on the substance makes it appear to "glow in the dark."

2. After protracted correspondence with the information and privacy coordinator of the CIA, taking place over a period in excess of five years, excerpts of the Cherepanov papers were found and provided to the author. An abstract of the relevant pages has been herein presented.

Chapter 19

1. See Anatoliy Golitsyn, *New Lies for Old* (New York: Dodd, Mead & Co., 1984).

2. Wise, *Molehunt,* 21. The book's principal subject matter is the hunt within the CIA for the mole "Sasha." George made numerous contributions to the work.

3. McCoy, interview.

4. See Edward Jay Epstein, *Legend: The Secret World of Lee Harvey Oswald* (New York: Readers Digest Press, 1978), 75.

5. Nosenko, interview.

6. See Martin, 111.

7. Partly as a consequence of Nosenko's 1962 revelation, Vassall was apprehended, tried, and convicted later that year. See Rositzke, 91. See also Martin, 149.

8. See Wise, *Molehunt,* 68.

9. In a 28 June 1999 letter to the author, Nosenko confirmed that Belitsky had been sent to the Brussels Fair in 1958 with the intent to deceive and indeed had been planted at that time. In addition, Nosenko knew about Belitsky's passing the polygraph test of 1961. Additionally, Len McCoy advises that when he was in London for the Penkovsky operation, he was assigned the added task of evaluating Belitsky's information. It was his conclusion at the time that Belitsky was under KGB control.

10. In telephone conversations with the author, on 29 May and 11 June, as well as a letter to the author on 5 June 1999, Goldberg conveyed that he always trusted George and that he had no reason ever to doubt him. "George was the senior man among all of the case officers; he was the oldest, the most experienced, the highest

ranking, the most scholarly. He was a wonderful man that all looked up to; he was our ideal." He consulted with George over the years, respecting his judgments, maturity, and honesty. He would not, however, confirm the author's version of the Belitsky episode.

11. Nosenko, interview.

12. See Wise, *Molehunt*, 78.

13. Nosenko also told George that Joseph Alsop, the noted American newspaper columnist, had been compromised in Moscow by homosexual activity. George later was asked by senior CIA personnel to delete that information from the tapes. It was of no general intelligence value and it might result in political harm to the Agency. It was information that people needed to know only if the FBI suspected Alsop of collaborating with the Soviets. He never was. In fact, his newspaper column was routinely highly critical of Soviet policy. See Wise, *Molehunt*, 77.

14. See John Barron, *KGB*: The Secret Work of Soviet Secret Agents (New York: Readers Digest Press, 1974), 13.

15. The KGB discovered this dead drop in late 1961 when an American diplomat was observed probing around one night (with matches in the dark) in a misguided effort to "check out" the location. After manning a lookout of the site for some six months, they gave up on its value. Ultimately, Penkovsky told his KGB captors of the site, who then baited it for his CIA handlers. Jacob, the CIA man, was apprehended in November of 1962 while attempting to retrieve a matchbox with a note inside presumed to be from Penkovsky. Other reports indicate that Nosenko did not provide the information about this dead drop at the 1964 Geneva meeting but at the 1962 meeting. George always insisted that Nosenko had told him of it in 1962 and that he had reported the information to those at the CIA who were actively working the Penkovsky case at the time. (By January of 1962 George had been removed from direct participation in the operational aspects of the Penkovsky case.) Nosenko reports that he provided the information in 1964 and that George must have been confused, otherwise, the Agency and SIS would have abandoned this location for another one. Nosenko, letter to author, 10 May 1999.

16. In September of 1963, Johnson had already been transferred to another area and no longer had access to the vault. Nosenko's information, however, did aid in Johnson's arrest and conviction. In May of 1964 Johnson was sent to the Pentagon. On 2 October, because of troubles with his wife, he went AWOL. On 25 November,

he turned himself in to police at Reno, Nevada, as a deserter. When interrogated about the illegal entries into the vault, he readily confessed to being a spy. On 30 July 1965, both Johnson and Mintkenbaugh received sentences of twenty-five years in prison. On 18 May 1972, Johnson's son visited him at the Lewisburg, West Virginia, Federal Penitentiary. There he stabbed his father with a knife, killing him. See Barron, 199.

17. See *The Warren Report: The Official Report on the Assassination of President John F. Kennedy* (Associated Press, 1964), 310.

18.Ibid., 322.

19. See H. Bradford Westerfield, *Inside CIA's Private World* (New Haven: Yale University Press, 1995), 395. See also Martin, 155.

20. See Barron, 335.

21. Nosenko, interview.

Chapter 20

1. Nosenko, interview.

2. See Epstein, 13.

3. See Martin, 158.

4. Ibid.

5. Ibid., 163.

6. See Wise, *Molehunt,* 145.

7. These flights probably were targeted over China. The U.S. had pledged not to fly over the USSR as a result of the May Day 1960 intercept of Gary Powers' U-2.

8. Martin, 155.

9. See Epstein, 45.

10. See Martin, 171.

11. Nosenko, telephone conversation, 2 July 1999. See also Wise, Molehunt, 146.

12. See Wise, *Molehunt,* 69.

13. See Martin, 171. See also Westerfield, 379, for a presumably authoritative opinion of the Nosenko case. J. Heuer, Jr.'s *Nosenko: Five Paths to Judgment,* is a reprint of a fall 1987 article (32, no. 3: 77-101) from *Studies in Intelligence,* an internal CIA publication, originally classified as secret.

Chapter 21

1. According to military personnel at the Russian Embassy, Washington, D.C., many military facilities called Poligon exist in Russia. Poligon (or Polygon) seems to be a generic term for artillery facilities. The Russian words "pole" and "ogon" translate into English as "field" and "fire," respectively. Combined, they could be "field of fire," an artillery term, or simply firing range. George's memory of Poligon is clouded. From correspondence with Kisevalters now living in St. Petersburg, unquestionably the location of which he speaks was a facility approximately twenty miles east of St. Petersburg. In George's childhood days, travel to Poligon required a train or carriage ride to the banks of the Ohta River, which runs around the city and empties into the Neva. A ferry ride across the Ohta at a particular wide section, where it forms a lake, then would be necessary to access Poligon.

2. In April of 1920, Jozef Klemens Pilsudski, Polish revolutionary, independence fighter, dictator, and national hero, with the help of White armies led by Baron Pyotr Nikolaievich Wrangel, led his Polish forces to a successful defense of Warsaw and the repulsion of the Red forces. In March of 1921, the Reds signed the Treaty of Riga (Latvia), agreeing to release parts of the Ukraine and Byelorussia to Poland.

3. David Guest started a Communist cell at Cambridge in April of 1931. Philby went up to Cambridge in October of 1929, Burgess in 1930, and Maclean in 1931. Many prominent intellectuals in Great Britain were Communists in those days. Burgess and Maclean eventually fled to Moscow in 1951, Philby in 1963. See Rositzke, 120.

4. Aldrich Ames was a CIA employee who, in February of 1994, was apprehended by the FBI, thus ending a decade of spy activities for the KGB. Ames sent ten Soviet defectors to their deaths and provided the KGB with information on numerous CIA operations. He was paid $4.6 million, purportedly the most paid to any spy in the history of the world. Former CIA director R. James Woolsey once expressed the view that Ames was more a traitor than Benedict Arnold. David Wise, *Nightmover* (New York: HarperCollins, 1995), 306.

Index